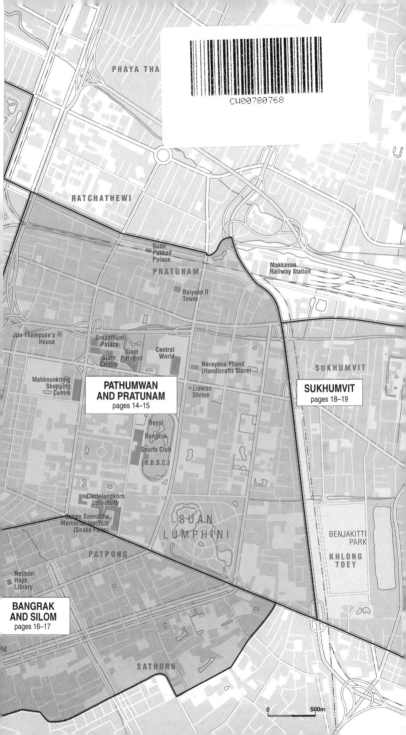

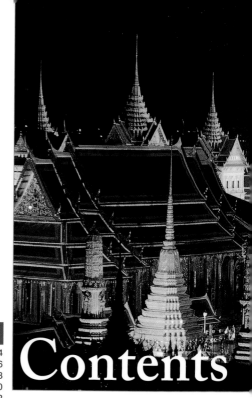

Contents

Areas

Below: Bangkok at dusk.

A–Z

Left: the Grand Palace complex all aglow at night.

Atlas

Below: a royal ceremonial emblem.

Bangkok

The metropolis of Bangkok is more than 30 times larger than any other city in the kingdom. Yet, just three centuries ago, it was little more than a sleepy riverside village with wild plum trees. Situated near the mouth of the Chao Phraya River, it is the country's capital, international gateway and seat of government, business and royalty.

Bangkok Facts and Figures

Area: 1,565sq km
Population: About 6 million (10–12 million in the greater metropolitan area)
Residents: Thai, Chinese, Malay and other minorities (Mon, Khmer, Indian, hilltribes)
Religions: Theravada and Mahayana Buddhism, Islam, Confucianism, Christianity
Monarch: King Bhumibol Adulyadej, who has reigned for 60 years
Visitors: More than 10 million per year
GDP: US$220 billlion, or 43 percent of Thailand's
Seasons: Hot season (Mar–mid June): 27–35°C; rainy season (June–Oct): 24–32°C; cool season (Nov–Feb): 18–32°C, with less humidity

City of Angels

Bangkok was established as the capital of Siam in 1732, when King Rama I moved his capital from Thonburi across the Chao Phraya River to the Bangkok side. Throughout the centuries, Thai kings have used the Chao Phraya River to define their royal cities. For strategic reasons, Rama I dug a canal between two of the river's bends and thus sliced off a parcel of land into an artificial island known as Rattanakosin. The king designated it the core of his new capital. Within its rim, he concentrated the principal components of his kingdom: religion, monarchy and administration.

A man of great ambition, Rama I decided that the name Bangkok, which means 'village of wild plums', was insufficiently noble for a royal city. So he renamed the capital city Krungthepmahanakhon Amonrattanakosin Mahintharayutthaya Mahadilokphop Nopphosin Ratchathaniburirom Udomrathani-wetmahasa Amonphiman Awatansathit Sakkathatiya Witsanukamprasit. In English,

this means 'City of Angels, Great City of Immortals, Magnificent City of the Nine Gems, Seat of the King, City of Royal Palaces, Home of the Gods Incarnate, Erected by Visvakarman at Indra's Behest'. The Thais call it Krung Thep, or 'City of Angels', for short.

Orientation

This low-lying capital began as a city of canals and elephant paths. But since World War II, Bangkok's population has grown nearly ten-fold. Its biggest growth spurt took place during the economic boom from the 1980s to the mid 1990s, when the Bangkok dream became a reality for many. Today, one out of every six Thais lives in Bangkok and its environs.

The city spreads out haphazardly. Roads in Bangkok run in all directions, and a street can change its name four times along its length. There are, however, some discernible sections. Rattanakosin holds most of the city's historic architecture. Chinatown lies between Charoen Krung and the river. The business

Above: the striking Phra Si Rattana *chedi* at Wat Phra Kaew. **Below:** friendly Bangkokians.

section occupies the areas of Sathorn, Silom and Ploenchit, and the major shopping areas are along Rama I, Ploenchit, Ratchadamri, Silom, Sukhumvit and Surawong roads. All this is built up to the east of the Chao Phraya River. On the other side of the river is Thonburi, where life is quieter. Canals still thread through colourful neighbourhoods with old wooden houses perched precariously by the water's edge.

Cool Hearts Having Fun

Thailand's culture and society have traditionally been centred on agriculture, an activity that nurtures a sense of community. It is a rare Thai who does not enjoy getting together with friends. Gatherings of friends always have high value of *sanuk*, a Thai word that means 'fun'. The quantity and quality of *sanuk*, whether in work or play, determines if something is worth pursuing.

The essential ingredient to surviving the stresses of daily life in Bangkok is the concept of *jai yen* (literally 'cool heart'), which is about taking obstacles in your stride. It ensures calmness exists inside every Bangkokian; fistfights are rare and misunderstandings are countered with a smile. The accompanying phrase that answers to all of life's vicissitudes is *mai pen rai*, or 'never mind'. Make use of both these concepts and Bangkok will seem a little less difficult.

Highlights

◀ **Jim Thompson's House** A showcase of Thailand's rich cultural heritage in its collection of artefacts, paintings and furniture.

▶ **Canal cruise** Hop aboard a longtail boat and visit a floating market, or glide along the canals to see Bangkok's riverside life.

◀ **Wat Pho** Bangkok's largest and oldest surviving temple houses the massive Reclining Buddha.

▲ **Wat Phra Kaew and Grand Palace** This complex dazzles with golden *chedis*, towering mythological statuary and fabulously ornate palace structures. It also houses the sacred Emerald Buddha.

▲ **Chatuchak Weekend Market** Chatuchak draws in nearly half a million people every weekend.

▶ **National Museum** Traces Thai history from the Sukhothai period to the present and includes a prehistoric gallery.

Rattanakosin

For more than a century after Bangkok was established as Siam's capital in 1782, the man-made island of Rattanakosin was the heart of the royal district of Phra Nakorn. Bounded by the Chao Phraya River to its west and a long *khlong* (canal) to its east, Rattanakosin, with the majestic Grand Palace as its epicentre, was where the seeds of a modern kingdom were planted. Today, the historic district brims with architectural grandeur and temples galore. It also hosts two of Thailand's most respected universities, in addition to being the nation's religious and cultural nucleus, where royal ceremonies, festivals and parades are held frequently.

See Atlas Pages 134, 138

0   500m

The Grand Palace and Surroundings

The southern side of Thanon Na Phra Lan is lined by the white walls of the complex of **Wat Phra Kaew** ① and the **Grand Palace** ②. The **Emerald Buddha** image housed here is credited with miraculous powers, and was shifted to many locations as a prize of war over the centuries.

South of the Grand Palace, on Thanon Thai Wang, is **Wat Pho** ③, Bangkok's largest and oldest temple, built in the 16th century. The sprawling

grounds of this historic place are home to 300 monks, the massive **Reclining Buddha** and the **Wat Pho Thai Traditional Massage School**.

Located across Thanon Sanam Chai from the eastern wall of the Grand Palace is **Lak Muang** ④, or the City Pillar. Similar to the Shiva lingam that represents potency, this is the capital's foundation stone, from where the city's power emanates. Across Thanon Lak Muang is the **Museum of Old Cannons**.

SEE ALSO MONUMENTS, P.78; MUSEUMS AND GALLERIES, P.82; PALACES, P.96; PAMPERING, P.98; TEMPLES, P.121–2

Around Saranrom Park

The Ministry of Foreign Affairs, formerly the **Saranrom Palace**, is on Thanon Sanam Chai, east of the Grand Palace. This entire area was once the site of palaces of members of the much extended royal family. Most were torn down during the Chulalongkorn era to make way for office buildings. Built in 1868, Saranrom is one of the few to survive. Once a royal mini-zoo, the front of the palace today is a monument-

studded public garden, **Saranrom Park**.

While not as grand as the other temples in this royal district, **Wat Ratchapradit**, located on Thanon Saranrom, next to Saranrom Park, offers a more intimate appreciation of royally connected divine edifices. Begun in 1864 on a reclaimed coffee plantation purchased by King Mongkut, this quaint grey marble-clad temple is yet another example of his, and later King Chulalongkorn's, preoccupation with infusing Thai architecture with pervasive Western traits. The interior murals depict Thai ceremonies such as Loy

Below: Phra Mondop scripture library at Wat Phra Kaew.

6

Left: the spectacular Reclining Buddha at Wat Pho.

Krathong, and King Mongkut, an avid astronomer, observing an eclipse.

Wat Ratchabophit ⑤ is located on the opposite bank of Khlong Lord canal. Started in 1869 by King Chulalongkorn, this complex on Thanon Fuang Nakhon was completed only after two decades. It is known for its characteristic amalgamation of local temple architecture and period European style, an unusual design fusion that places the main circular *chedi* and its circular cloister in the centre. The doors open into one of the most surprising temple interiors in Thailand, with a Gothic-inspired chapel of solid columns that looks more like a medieval cathedral than a Thai temple. The courtyard doors are carved in relief with soldiers wearing European-type uniforms.

SEE ALSO PARKS AND GARDENS, P.101

Sanam Luang and Surroundings

Directly north of the Grand Palace is the large oval-shaped lawn of **Sanam Luang** ⑥ (Royal Field), which was established as a cremation ground for royalty. In a city so short of green areas, it now provides space for soccer games, jogging and kite flying. Important ceremonies and festivals are also held here.

To the lower west of Sanam Luang is an **amulet market**, whose vendors' trail eventually leads to the entry to **Wat Mahathat**. One of two universities for monks, the Maha Chulalongkorn Rajavidyalaya University, is located here. The temple also houses the **International Buddhist Meditation Centre**, which conducts regular classes in English (tel: 0 2623 5881; www.mcu.ac.th/ibmc).

Just south are former royal office buildings that belong to the government's Fine Arts Department and the **Silpakorn University**, Thailand's first fine-arts school. Silpakorn sometimes holds art exhibitions of both Thai and foreign artists at its galleries.

North of Wat Mahathat, **Thammasat University** monopolises much of the western stretch of Sanam Luang. After Chulalongkorn University, it is the second-oldest university, founded in 1934 to educate people on the new political constitution introduced two years earlier. Its scholars have a reputation for being vocal about their strong political beliefs and have in the past been labelled as radicals. In October 1973 and 1976, students peacefully protesting for greater democracy were brutally suppressed by the military. Hundreds were killed.

The **National Museum** ⑦, a treasure house of both Thai and Southeast Asian riches, is to the upper west of the Sanam Luang. To its north is the **National Theatre**, and across the Saphan Phra Pin Klao bridge is the **National Gallery**, which occasionally hosts shows of foreign and Thai artists.

SEE ALSO DANCE AND THEATRE, P.36; MUSEUMS AND GALLERIES, P.82, 85; PARKS AND GARDENS, P.101

> In early May, Sanam Luang is the site of the Royal Ploughing Ceremony, which marks the official start of Thailand's rice-growing season. King Chulalongkorn, himself an avid kite flyer, sanctioned the use of the royal field as a kite-flying venue.

Thonburi

Established by King Taksin after the fall of Ayutthaya in 1767, Thonburi served as Siam's third capital for 15 years prior to Bangkok's establishment in 1782. It was not until 1971 that Thonburi was combined as a part of the Bangkok metropolis. The area has a more easy-going atmosphere than the frenetic city across the Chao Phraya River.

Life in this residential half of the capital revolves primarily around the river and its network of canals. From Bangkok city, Thonburi can be reached by boat and via numerous bridges, the oldest of which is Memorial Bridge (Phra Buddha Yodfa Bridge) at the southern tip of Rattanakosin.

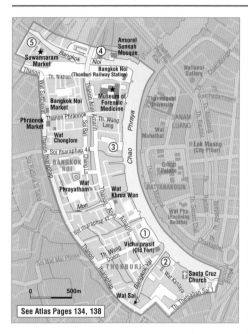

See Atlas Pages 134, 138

Above: the Santa Cruz Church.

Wat Arun and Surroundings

Across the Chao Phraya River opposite the Grand Palace is the spectacular **Wat Arun** ①, the Temple of Dawn. This is one of the river's oldest and most distinctive landmarks, dating back to the Ayutthayan period before King Taksin moved the capital south to Thonburi. The temple was originally attached to Taksin's palace, Wang Derm. Over the years, it grew in size and ornamentation, thanks to the attention of the first few monarchs.

South of Wat Arun, at the mouth of Khlong Bangkok Yai canal, are two sights worth visiting. The first is **Wat Kalayanamit** ②, a 19th-century temple with Chinese-style embellishments, built at the behest of King Rama III. Its tall main *viharn* (sermon hall) contains an impressive seated Buddha image. This image and the bronze bell in the grounds are the largest of their kind in Thailand.

The **Santa Cruz Church** is to the southeast of Wat Kalayanamit. The pastel-coloured church, topped by an octagonal dome, has been rebuilt twice since it was first constructed in the 18th century. The present edifice dates from 1913. The neighbourhood surrounding the church was once part of a flourishing Portuguese dis-

Left: a boat carries water urns
along a Thonburi canal.

waterways become. Rickety
teak houses, vendors on
boats, fishermen dangling
rods out of windows and kids
frolicking in the water are
some of the sights along the
canals, reminiscent of a more
peaceful bygone era.

Further on the northern
bank of the Khlong Bangkok
Noi is the **National Museum
of Royal Barges** ④, with a
collection of superb regal
river vessels dating back to
the reign of King Rama I.
From the museum pier, it's a
five-minute boat journey up
Khlong Bangkok Noi
canal to the historic **Wat
Suwannaram** ⑤. Built by
King Rama I on the site of an
earlier temple and extensively
renovated since, it features
magnificent, if slightly
deteriorated, murals from the
early 1800s that depict,
among other events and
scenes, the 10 lives of the
Buddha. The intricate artwork
that adorns every corner of
the interior was commis-
sioned by King Rama III and
is considered to be among
the finest examples of
19th-century painting.
SEE ALSO MUSEUMS AND GALLERIES,
P.83; WALKS AND VIEWS, P.131

trict that migrated here after
Ayutthaya was abandoned.
SEE ALSO TEMPLES, P.120

Wat Rakhang and Surroundings

North of Wat Arun is **Wat
Rakhang** ③, with a lovely
collection of bells that are
rung each morning. At the
temple's rear is the red-
painted *ho trai* (wooden
library), a three-part stilted
building that King Rama I
lived in as a monk before
becoming king. The superb
murals inside, dating from
1788, depict scenes from the
Ramakien epic.

Several museums are
located within the Sirirat
Hospital complex on Thanon
Phrannok. The most well
known is the **Museum of
Forensic Medicine**, which is
of particular interest to medical students and visitors with
a taste for the grotesque.
SEE ALSO MUSEUMS AND
GALLERIES, P.82

Khlong Bangkok Noi

The canals worth exploring
include **Khlong Bangkok
Noi**, which winds into
Khlong Bangkok Yai down-
stream, and connects to
Khlong Om upstream. Once
daily sources of fresh
produce, the floating markets
at **Wat Sai** and **Taling Chan**
have become little more than
tourist souvenir stops these
days. It might be better to
hire your own longtail boat
for a leisurely exploration
of the smaller canals.
The further down the canals,
the narrower and calmer the

Getting from pier to pier along
the Chao Phraya River is best
by Chao Phraya Express boats.
For shuttling from one side of
the river to the other, make use
of the cheap cross-river ferries;
these can be boarded at the
many jetties that also service
the Chao Phraya Express boats.
(See Transport, p.128–9)

Below: bells adorn
Wat Rakhang's towers.

The Old City and Dusit

Dominated by the wide boulevard of Thanon Ratchadamnoen, the Old City contains all the peripheral palace buildings and temples that lie outside Rattanakosin. At the turn of the 20th century, the area was occupied by traditional craftspeople and performing artisans, while devotional structures were the main protrusions on the skyline. Time has altered the area's visual appeal, yet there is still a strong sense of the past, making this a pleasant area to explore. Within the Old City as well is Banglamphu, with the backpackers' haven of Thanon Khao San. To the north is the Dusit area, the seat of the Thai government and where the monarch lives.

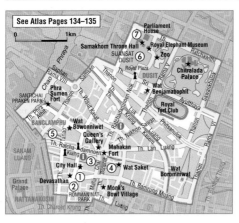

Thanon Bamrung Muang

This was one of the city's first paved tracks. The road intersects a large square with the City Hall at its northern end. Opposite are the **Giant Swing** ① and **Wat Suthat** ②, one of the country's six main temples. West of the Giant Swing are the Brahman shrines of **Devasathan**, while southeast of Wat Suthat, on Thanon Siri Phong, is the lively **Rommaninat Park**.
SEE ALSO MONUMENTS, P.78; PARKS AND GARDENS, P.100; TEMPLES, P.119, 123

Thanon Ratchadamnoen

Behind the City Hall, north om Thanon Dinso in the mid-

dle of a traffic circle, is the **Democracy Monument**. Just a short walk west from this landmark, on Thanon Ratchadamnoen Klang near the corner with Thanon Tanao, is the **14 October Monument**. Further north on Thanon Tanao is **Wat Bowonniwet**, where various kings have served their monkhoods.

Stretching all the way from the Grand Palace to the Dusit Park area, the wide **Thanon Ratchadamnoen** (Royal Passage) splits into three sections and is modelled after tree-lined Parisian boulevards. On royal birthdays, the area is turned into a

sea of decorative lights, flags and royal portraits.
SEE ALSO MONUMENTS, P.74, 77; TEMPLES, P.121

Loha Prasat and Wat Ratchanatda

At the point where Thanon Ratchadamnoen Klang crosses the Pan Fah bridge, veering left into Thanon Ratchadamnoen Nok, are several noticeable structures. Evocative of Burmese temple structures, the **Loha Prasat** (Metal Palace) shares the same grounds as **Wat Ratchanatda** ③. Originally meant to be the temple's *chedi*, Loha Prasat was built by King Rama III in 1846. Its 37 iron spires symbolise the virtues needed to attain enlightenment.

Across Thanon Maha Chai from the wat is the **Mahakan Fort** (closed to the public), one of the only two surviving

> The thriving amulet market behind Wat Ratchanatda is proof of Thais' superstitious belief in talismans. Most commonly worn as pendants on heavy neckchains and resembling modern-day bling bling, these amulets are thought to ward off evil and bring power and fortune to the wearers.

Left: the gilded *chedi* of the Golden Mount.

books. The area has undergone a significant upgrade recently with the arrival of boutique hotels and upscale bars.

SEE ALSO PARKS AND GARDENS, P.101

Dusit Park

At the head of Thanon Ratchadamnoen Nok is a large square known as the **Royal Plaza**, watched over by the bronze **Statue of King Chulalongkorn**. Directly north stands the Italian Renaissance-style **Ananta Samakhom Throne Hall** ⑥. Behind is **Vimanmek Mansion** ⑦, the world's largest golden teakwood mansion, and to the right is the **Abhisek Dusit Throne Hall**, now a museum. East of this hall is the **Royal Elephant Museum** and the **Dusit Zoo**. The **Chitralada Palace** (closed to the public), where the current king Bhumibol lives, is further east of the zoo. South of the Dusit area is **Wat Benjamabophit**, the Marble Temple.

SEE ALSO ARCHITECTURE, P.25; CHILDREN, P.31; MONUMENTS, P.79; MUSEUMS AND GALLERIES, P.85; PALACES, P.94, 95; TEMPLES, P.120

remnants of the 14 original watchtowers that once protected the old city wall. The other is the larger Phra Sumen Fort in Banglamphu *(see below)*. Opposite Mahakan Fort is the **Queen's Gallery**.

SEE ALSO MUSEUMS AND GALLERIES, P.84; WALKS AND VIEWS, P.133

Golden Mount

Located south of Mahakan Fort is the elevated spire of the **Golden Mount** ④ (Phu Khao Thong). At the bottom of the hill is one of Bangkok's oldest temples, **Wat Saket**. Skirting the western edge of the Golden Mount is **Thanon Boriphat**, a street lined with timber merchants and woodcarvers. Further along the same road are the narrow alleyways that run off Soi Ban Baat. Known as **Monk's Bowl Village** (Ban Baat), this is home to the only surviving community of traditional alms-bowl makers.

SEE ALSO WALKS AND VIEWS, P.132

Banglamphu

The Banglamphu (meaning 'village of the *lamphu* tree') district was originally settled by farmers from Ayutthaya, the old capital. The riverbank once held several mansions, a few of which survive on **Thanon Phra Athit** as offices of large companies and international agencies like UNICEF. The street is also filled with cosy 'art bars' frequented by budding artists from the Silpakorn University. In this area is the pleasant riverfront **Santichai Prakan Park**, which fringes the whitewashed **Phra Sumen Fort** (closed to the public).

In marked contrast is **Thanon Khao San** ⑤ (Khao San Road), just a stone's throw away. Since the early 1980s, Khao San has been a self-contained district for backpackers, offering requisites such as silver jewellery, hand-painted clothing and secondhand

Below: streetside hair-braiding service on Thanon Khao San.

11

Chinatown

Chinatown was settled in the 1780s by Chinese merchants, who were asked to relocate here from Rattanakosin so that the Grand Palace could be built. In 1863 King Mongkut built Thanon Charoen Krung (New Road), Bangkok's first paved street, and Chinatown soon began mushrooming outwards from the original dirt track of Sampeng (now Soi Wanit 1). Adjacent plots of land were given to the Indian and Muslim communities. Later, a third artery, Thanon Yaowarat, was built between Charoen Krung and Sampeng roads. Yaowarat soon became the main artery of Chinatown and the Thai name of the area.

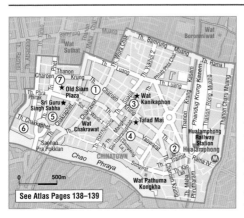

See Atlas Pages 138–139

Sampeng

The Sampeng area, the old pulse of Chinatown, has a rowdy history. What began as a mercantile zone quickly degenerated into a raunchy entertainment area. By 1900 it had a reputation as 'Sin Alley', with lanes leading to opium dens, gambling houses and brothels. Eventually, however, Sampeng lost its sleaze and became a bustling lane of

> Thailand's first Chinese immigrants were merchants in the 1500s. In the centuries since, the Chinese population has become strongly integrated into Thai society.

small shops selling goods from China. The stretch of **Sampeng Lane** (Soi Wanit 1) between Thanon Ratchawong and Thanon Mangkon is the place for bargains.
SEE ALSO MARKETS, P.73

Thanon Yaowarat

Parallel to Sampeng Lane is **Thanon Yaowarat**, which in places looks much like a Hong Kong street with its forest of neon signs. It is best known for its gold dealers. Between Thanon Yaowarat and **Thanon Charoen Krung**, at the corner with Thanon Chakrawat, is **Nakhon Kasem** ①, or Thieves' Market. A few

decades ago, this was where one searched after having been robbed, a likely place to recover stolen goods at very reasonable prices. It later became an antiques dealers' area, but now handles mainly household items.

Just east of where Thanon Yaowarat meets Thanon Charoen Krung, across from the Odeon Circle China Gate, is **Wat Traimit** ②. Although architecturally unremarkable, it houses the famous Golden Buddha, found by accident in the 1950s at a riverside temple. The 3-m-tall stucco figure was being transported to its present site when the crane lifting it snapped and sent the statue smashing to the ground, breaking one corner. A glint of yellow showed through the crack, revealing an image of solid gold weighing some 5½ tonnes. The gleaming image is said to date from 13th-century Sukhothai, and was probably encased in stucco during the Ayutthayan period to conceal its true worth from Burmese invaders, remaining undetected for centuries.

East of Wat Traimit is **Hualamphong Railway Station**, the city's main railway terminus.

Left: worshippers at a Chinatown temple.

On Thanon Pahurat and parts of Thanon Chakraphet, especially along the gravel track ATM Alley (named after the now-defunct ATM department store), are cheap curry eateries and tea and spice stalls.

Close to the Pahurat Market on Thanon Chakraphet is the golden-domed Sikh temple of **Sri Guru Singh Sabha**, a focal point for the Sikh community and said to be the second-largest Sikh temple outside India. Headscarves must be worn to enter the temple.

West of the Pahurat Market near the riverfront is **Pak Khlong Talad** ⑥ (Flower Market), and to the north of it, at the corner of Thanon Charoen Krung and Thanon Tri Phet, is the **Sala Chalerm Krung Theatre** ⑦, one of the oldest movie theatres in Thailand.

In the same vicinity is the three-floor **Old Siam Plaza**, a faux-nostalgic shopping arcade with architecture that takes its cue from Rattanakosin. The mall is a more sanitised alternative to the market lanes of Chinatown and Pahurat.

SEE ALSO DANCE AND THEATRE, P.37; MARKETS, P.72

Soi Itsaranuphap

Cutting across Thanon Yaowarat and Thanon Charoen Krung is **Soi Itsaranuphap** (Soi 16), the most interesting lane in Chinatown. It begins from Thanon Phlab Phla Chai and runs south, past a 19th-century Thai temple called **Wat Kanikaphon**. This is better known as Wat Mae Yai Fang, after the brothel madam who built it to atone for her sins. At the entrance to Soi Itsaranuphap are shops selling 'hell money' and miniature houses, cars and household items made of paper. Chinese burn these items to send to deceased relatives.

At the corner of Soi Itsaranuphap and Thanon Charoen Krung is Chinatown's biggest Buddhist temple, **Wat Mangkon Kamalawat** ③, or Leng Noi Yee (Dragon Flower Temple). Along Soi Itsaranuphap as well are the famous markets of **Talad Kao** ④ (Old Market) and **Talad Mai** (New Market).

SEE ALSO MARKETS, P.73; TEMPLES, P.121

Pahurat

West of Sampeng Lane is **Pahurat Market** ⑤, Bangkok's Little India. Bangkok's Indian community converged here in the late 19th century, and today their presence is still strongly felt.

Below: lotuses for sale at the Pak Khlong flower market.

Pathumwan and Pratunam

The man-made canal Khlong Saen Saep, cleaved in the early 19th century, enabled the capital to spread north to Pratunam and beyond. Pratunam is known for the bustling Pratunam Market and Thailand's tallest building, the Baiyoke II Tower. South of Pratunam is Pathumwan, the commercial heart of downtown Bangkok, a sprawl of glitzy shopping malls; yet, there are also plenty of sights reminiscent of an older and more traditional Bangkok. To the east is Thanon Withayu (Wireless Road) with a string of embassies, hotels and upmarket apartments. A patch of green to the south, Lumphini Park, offers a welcome breather amid the concrete jungle.

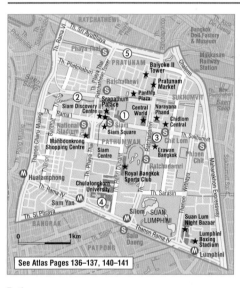

See Atlas Pages 136–137, 140–141

Above: Pratunam Market is a bargain hunter's playground.

Pathumwan

In the heart of Pathumwan is **Siam Square**, on Thanon Rama I, one of the city's few remaining streetside shopping enclaves. Across Thanon Phaya Thai is the bewildering mayhem of **Mahboonkrong Shopping Centre**, or MBK. Across Siam Square are the interconnected malls of **Siam Centre** and **Siam Discovery Centre**. The swanky retail haven of **Siam Paragon** ①, which also houses the child-friendly aquarium, **Siam**

Ocean World, is just next to Siam Centre. A short walk from the National Stadium BTS station, at the end of Soi Kasemsan 2 is **Jim Thompson's House** ②.

Few people know that hidden at the rear of Siam Centre is the **Srapathum Palace**, which still operates as a royal residence (not open to the public). The palace was given to King Bhumibol's late father, Prince Mahidol Adulyadej, in the early 20th century and became the

home of Bhumibol's late mother until she passed away in 1995.

Srapathum Palace's expansive grounds include **Wat Pathumwanaram**, between Siam Paragon and Central World. The temple holds the ashes of Prince Mahidol and his wife.

Next door is the **Central World** complex, Bangkok's largest mall. Opposite it is **Narayana Phand**, a large treasure trove of Thai arts and crafts.

At the end of Thanon Rama I is the chaotic junction where the street intersects with Thanon Ratchadamri and changes its name to Thanon Ploenchit. At the corner of Thanon Ratchadamri and Thanon Ploenchit stands the

Left: the dining room at Jim Thompson's House.

more sanitised and cooler alternative to Chatuchak Weekend Market. Also found here are the **Joe Louis Theatre** and a beer garden. At the **Lumphini Boxing Stadium**, east of the park, professional *muay thai* (Thai kickboxing) bouts are held. SEE ALSO DANCE AND THEATRE, P.36; MARKETS, P.73; PARKS AND GARDENS, P.100; SPORT, P.116

Pratunam

Across the Khlong Saen Saep canal lies **Pratunam Market**, a favourite with bargain hunters, standing in the shadow of Thailand's tallest building, the 88-storey **Baiyoke II Tower**.

Panthip Plaza, Bangkok's biggest mall devoted to IT products, is across Thanon Phetchaburi. Near Phaya Thai BTS station is **Suan Pakkad Palace** ⑤, the 'Cabbage Patch' palace. This splendid residence belonged to the late Princess Chumbhot, a gardener and art collector. The beautiful grounds contain plants from all over the world, as well as varieties found in Thailand's jungles. SEE ALSO ARCHITECTURE, P.23, 24; MARKETS, P.73; SHOPPING, P.115

The main shopping areas in downtown Bangkok are linked by the Skywalk – a covered elevated walkway beneath the Skytrain (BTS) tracks – connecting Chitlom, Siam Square and National Stadium BTS stations along Thanon Rama I.

---

famous **Erawan Shrine** ③ with an image of the four-headed Hindu god Brahma. In the area are more retail options, including **Erawan Bangkok** and **Gaysorn Plaza**, as well as **Chidlom Central**, a popular upmarket department store. SEE ALSO ARCHITECTURE, P.23; CHILDREN, P.33; SHOPPING, P.113–4; TEMPLES, P.119

Around Chulalongkorn University

South of Siam Square along Thanon Phaya Thai is **Chulalongkorn University**, the country's oldest and most prestigious institution of higher learning. Sporting both Thai and Western architectural styles, the university was named in honour of King Chulalongkorn. The campus hosts two contemporary galleries: **Jamjuree Gallery** and the **Art Centre**.

On Thanon Henri Dunant is the **Royal Bangkok Sports Club**. It has horse-racing on Sundays during all but the rainiest months. The **Queen Saovabha Memorial Institute** ④, commonly called the **Snake Farm**, is south of the university. SEE ALSO CHILDREN, P.33; MUSEUMS AND GALLERIES, P.80; SPORT, P.117

Lumphini Park

At the intersection of Thanon Rama IV and Thanon Ratchadamri is **Lumphini Park** (Suan Lumphini), a popular outdoor retreat. Across from Lumphini's Thanon Withayu (Wireless Road) gates, the **Suan Lum Night Bazaar** is a

Below: the Lacquer Pavilion at Suan Pakkad palace.

Bangrak and Silom

Extending eastwards from the Chao Phraya River, Thanon Silom is the principal route that intersects the business district, ending at Thanon Rama IV. Parallel to Silom are Sathorn, Surawong and Si Phraya roads; these thoroughfares, plus Thanon Silom, make up the district of Bangrak. Found in this area is the infamous den of Patpong, although despite the proliferation of girlie bars, the rattle of commerce rather than seduction resonates the strongest. Further east and running parallel to the river is Thanon Charoen Krung (New Road), which cuts across a waterside neighbourhood of upmarket developments and quiet sidestreets.

Thanon Silom

Taking its name from the irrigation windmills that used to occupy the area, **Thanon Silom** and its former canal transported life inland. Today, shopping and nightlife are the principal attractions.

Standing tall at the river-end junction of Thanon Silom and Thanon Charoen Krung is the **State Tower**, which houses a fashionable rooftop venue called **The Dome**. **Sirocco** on the 63rd floor claims to be the world's highest outdoor eatery.

About a quarter of the way up Thanon Silom, on the corner of Soi Pan, is the vibrantly coloured Hindu **Maha Uma Devi Temple** ①.

See Atlas Pages 139, 140–141

Named after Shiva's consort Uma Devi, the temple was established in the 1860s by the city's Tamil community. It has a prominent 6-m-high façade adorned with ornate religious statuary. SEE ALSO RESTAURANTS, P.108

Patpong

Come nightfall, the upper end of Thanon Silom transforms into a pleasure haven. With its trashy go-go bars and strip clubs, **Patpong** ② still deserves its sleazy image, although clampdowns over the years have reduced this slice of vice to little more than amusing eye candy. Today's Patpong offers a tamer experience with a blitz of neon, relentless techno beats and gyrating bikini-clad dancers on bar tops.

Developed on the site of a former banana plantation by the late millionaire Khun Patpongpanit, this playground first found favour among affluent locals and foreign airline crew before American GIs descended here from Vietnam in the late 1960s and 1970s.

Below: the stately Assumption Cathedral.

Left: the State Tower and The Oriental.

SEE ALSO ARCHITECTURE, P.24, 25; HOTELS, P.63, 64; MUSEUMS AND GALLERIES, P.84

Around The Oriental

The legendary **The Oriental** hotel, founded in the 1870s, sits off Thanon Charoen Krung. Turn right outside the hotel towards the river; a side road on the left leads to a small tree-lined square dominated by the red-brick **Assumption Cathedral** ⑤. Built in 1910, it has an ornate interior with a domed ceiling hovering over a large sacristy with gilded pillars.

To the left of the Oriental pier is the Venetian-inspired **East Asiatic Company**, erected in 1901. Next to The Oriental are two early 20th-century buildings, one of which houses the elegant **China House** restaurant run by the hotel. A side road to the left leads to the charming **OP Place**, dating from 1905. Today it is mostly filled with arts and crafts shops.

The restored **French Embassy** is nearby, hidden behind high walls. Further along, towards the riverside, is the crumbling but atmospheric 19th-century **Old Customs House**, currently used as a fire station.

SEE ALSO HOTELS, P.63; RESTAURANTS, P.106

A few lanes east from Patpong, Silom Soi 4 attracts revellers to its dance clubs and bars. The nearby Silom Soi 2 is similar in appeal, though designated for gay partiers. Further along, the hostess bars along Soi Thaniya cater to an almost exclusively Japanese clientele. There is also a **night market** along Thanon Silom from Soi 2 to 8.

SEE ALSO MARKETS, P.73

Thanon Sathorn and Surroundings

Many of Thanon Silom's even numbered lanes cut through to the parallel Thanon Surawong, which has seen little of the district's commercial development. The **Neilson Hays Library** on Thanon Surawong was an early 20th-century cultural haven for the city's foreign residents. It also houses the **Rotunda Gallery**, which showcases contemporary artworks.

Opposite Silom Soi 4 is **Thanon Convent**, a tree-shaded lane with a variety of streetside food stalls and restaurants. At the corner with Thanon Sathorn is the **Anglican Christ Church**. The Gothic-style building was built in 1905.

Thanon Sathorn was an affluent neighbourhood with colonial-style mansions for the city's elite. Modern Sathorn evokes little of this historic charm and is now home to a number of office towers and embassies. Noteworthy buildings include the slim **Thai Wah Tower II** ③, standing tall between two of the city's hippest boutique hotels, **The Sukhothai** and **The Metropolitan**. Halfway down Thanon Sathorn is the robot-like **UOB Building**, as well as **MR Kukrit Pramoj's Heritage Home** ④, a lovely wooden home that is now a museum, tucked away on Soi Phra Phinij.

> To soak in The Oriental's old-world ambience, have afternoon tea in its elegant Author's Lounge and muse over the literary greats who have passed through the doors, such as Somerset Maugham, Noel Coward and Graham Greene. Its Riverside Terrace is also a charming spot for a drink.

17

Sukhumvit

Anchored by Thanon Sukhumvit, Sukhumvit is a busy commercial and residential district. Although rather thin on tourist attractions, it is one of Bangkok's most cosmopolitan areas, where most of the expatriate community of Europeans, Americans and Asians nest. Africans and Arabs congregate in the hookah cafés, and there is also a sizeable contingent of Indian Thai residents who run many of the businesses in the vicinity. Found in the sidestreets (*sois*) are throbbing nightspots (some sleazier than others) and a tourist night market. Further east in the hip Thong Lor area, there are idiosyncratic shops and cafés, perfect for a leisurely afternoon.

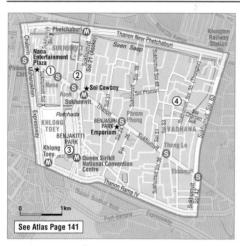

See Atlas Page 141

Once a dirt track surrounded by marshland, Thanon Sukhumvit was built in the 1930s and became Thailand's first proper road, transporting vehicles beyond the capital. Sukhumvit's odd and even sidestreets are not in sequence. For instance Soi 24 beside Emporium mall is opposite Soi 39 on the other side of the street.

Around Thanon Sukhumvit

Eastwards from Thanon Rama I and Thanon Ploenchit, beyond the British Embassy, the boulevard eventually turns into **Thanon Sukhumvit**. This traffic-clogged area is known simply as Sukhumvit, and stretches as far as the resort town of Pattaya and continues all the way to the Cambodian border. The efficient BTS provides the fastest means of transport between the upmarket shops, restaurants and entertainment venues that line Thanon Sukhumvit.

The BTS stations along this bustling artery include: Nana, Asok, Phrom Phong, Thong Lo and Ekkamai.

Starting at the trail of bars collectively nicknamed as 'Soi Zero' that huddle under the expressway, Sukhumvit's early blocks burst with a profusion of tailors, pool halls, beer bars and hotels. Proffering typical tourist souvenirs, fake goods and general tat, the **night market** ① crowds the pavements from Soi 5 to Soi 11. There are also a host of makeshift food and drink stalls with plastic stools and tables lining the

walkways, mostly offering noodles for breakfast or supper.

The area has a lascivious veneer, anchored by the three-storey clutch of raucous go-go bars at the **Nana Entertainment Plaza** on Soi 4. Working girls soliciting customers can be found along street corners from Soi 5 to Soi 19. Further along the road across the Soi 21 (Soi Asoke) intersection is Sukhumvit's other notorious neon strip devoted to pole dancing, **Soi Cowboy**. There are plenty of rowdy bars to choose from, though all of them will shut their doors by 1am.

Sukhumvit's overall appearance is in fact far from sleazy, with many of the city's best nightspots dotted within the side streets. The most glamorous is **Soi 11**,

Left: the Emporium mall attracts Bangkok's well-heeled.

shops, bakeries, coffee bars, galleries and restaurants.
SEE ALSO PARKS AND GARDENS, P.100; SHOPPING, P.113

Thong Lor

Further east, just off Thong Lo BTS station is **Soi Thonglor** (Soi 55), lined with hip restaurants, cafés and nightspots as well as boutique shopping enclaves such as the uber-stylish **H1** and **Playground**. This is where the new creative spirit that is making its way around Bangkok is most keenly felt. It also reflects a recent trend to build well-heeled shopping enclaves in the more residential neighbourhoods.

J Avenue ④, on the corner of Soi 15, has an intensely hip complex teeming with Japanese eateries, **Greyhound Café**, **iberry** and other chic outlets. It is a perfect spot for coffee, and is unquestionably less touristy than the main Sukhumvit stretch. J Avenue is especially lovely in the evenings with glittering fairy lights suspended on trees.
SEE ALSO FOOD AND DRINK, P.51; RESTAURANTS, P.110; SHOPPING, P.114

where the hip **Q Bar** and **Bed Supperclub** sit near each other.

One of Sukhumvit's oldest buildings is the headquarters of the **Siam Society** on Soi 21 (Soi Asoke), founded in 1904 to promote the study and preservation of Thai culture. On the same grounds is the **Kamthieng House** ②, a 150-year-old wooden home that once stood on the banks of Chiang Mai's Mae Ping River before being carefully reassembled here and opened as an ethnological museum.
SEE ALSO ARCHITECTURE, P.24; MARKETS, P.73; NIGHTLIFE, P.92

Sukhumvit's Parks

South of the Soi Asoke (Soi 21) intersection is the **Queen Sirikit National Convention Centre**, which hosts large-scale business, cultural and entertainment events. The centre looks out at the huge **Benjakitti Park** ③, dominated by a lake. Further east along Sukhumvit near Soi 24 is Sukhumvit's other green area, **Benjasiri Park**.

On the corner of Soi 24, where the Phrom Phong BTS station is found, is Sukhumvit's premier shopping magnet, **Emporium**. The side lanes around Emporium are cluttered with upmarket furniture and décor

Below: the futuristic façade of Bed Supperclub.

Bangkok's Suburbs and Surroundings

When the city seems too overwhelming, easy escapes within a three- to four-hour driving distance of Bangkok provide welcome relief. Choose from ancient ruins, sandy beaches dotted with sleepy villages, and picturesque national parks with waterfalls. Some excursions are strictly day trips but several, especially those to beach destinations, can be extended into week-long stays. Getting around is relatively easy; there is a good network of domestic flights, and train and bus services to many provincial centres.

Bangkok's Suburbs

Many of the sights in Bangkok's suburbs can be visited as stop-offs on longer journeys out of town or as half- to full-day trips. **Chatuchak Weekend Market**, located at the final stop on the BTS' northern line, Mo Chit, is a must for shopaholics. If you have kids in tow, head to attractions like **Dream World**, **Safari World** and **Siam Park**. Out in the eastern suburb of Huamak is the **Prasart Museum**, a little repository of Thai artefacts amassed by a private collector.

For a more relaxing trip, visit **Nonthaburi**, a provincial riverside town, about 10km north of Bangkok. The car-free island of **Ko Kret** is further upstream from Nonthaburi.
SEE ALSO CHILDREN, P.31, 32, 33; MARKETS, P.72; MUSEUMS AND GALLERIES, P.84

West of Bangkok

The flat, fertile Central Plains hold the remnants of former kingdoms and several expansive national parks. West of Bangkok are attractions like **Rose Garden Riverside Resort**, 32km from Bangkok, with its tourist-friendly cultural shows, and its neighbour **Samphran Elephant Ground**. Beyond the Rose Garden on Route 4 is the town of **Nakhon Pathom**, famous for the colossal **Phra Pathom Chedi**, reputedly the tallest Buddhist monument in the world.

From the province of **Samut Songkhram**, 74km southwest from Bangkok, you can hire a longtail boat for a trip up the Mae Khlong River to the **Damnoen Saduak Floating Market**.

Kanchanaburi ①, about 130km west of Bangkok, is an outdoor adventure playground with river rafting, trekking and waterfall scaling. It is also the site of the legendary **Bridge over the River Kwai**, built during World War II. Located near the bridge is the **World War II Museum**. In Kanchanaburi town are a few memorials to World War II, namely, the **JEATH War Museum**, the **Allied War Cemetery**, and the **Death Railway Museum** at the Thai-Burma Railway Centre.

Situated about 70km north of Kanchanaburi is **Erawan National Park**, home to a seven-tiered waterfall.
SEE ALSO CHILDREN, P.32;

Left: fruits for sale at the Damnoen Saduak market.

escapades. Everyone has heard of scandalous **Pattaya** ⑤, located 147km from Bangkok, but further afield is the island of **Ko Samet**, 200km from Bangkok, blessed with picturesque white-sand beaches.
SEE ALSO BEACHES AND ISLANDS, P.27, 28; CHILDREN, P.30. 31, 33; TRANSPORT, P.124

North of Bangkok

Ayutthaya ⑥, a grand repository of faded ruins dating to the 14th century when it was the capital, is 85km north of Bangkok. Ayutthaya was abandoned after the Burmese army sacked it in 1767.

Sixty kilometres north of Bangkok is **Bang Pa-In** ⑦, the summer palace for Thai kings since the late 19th century.

Korat province's **Khao Yai National Park** is about 200km northeast of Bangkok. This is a spot for great walks, views and waterfalls.
SEE ALSO MONUMENTS, P.74; PALACES, P.94; WALKS AND VIEWS, P.130

> Some say the best part about Ayutthaya is getting there – on a teakwood barge winding up the sinuous Chao Phraya River.

MARKETS, P.72; MONUMENTS, P.77, 78; MUSEUMS AND GALLERIES, P.80, 81, 85; WALKS AND VIEWS, P.130

South of Bangkok

Phetchaburi ②, some 120km south of Bangkok, is one of Thailand's oldest towns and has been an important trade and cultural centre since the 11th century. West of the town is the **Phra Nakhon Khiri Historical Park**, perched on a hilltop with fabulous sunset views. About 40km south of Phetchaburi is the peaceful weekend getaway of **Cha-am**.

Around **Hua Hin** ③, south of Cha-am and 203km from Bangkok, are a string of beaches where Thais first began taking their summer holidays a century ago. This is where Thai royalty and Bangkok's wealthy maintain their plush holiday homes.
SEE ALSO BEACHES AND ISLANDS, P.26; WALKS AND VIEWS, P.133

East of Bangkok

About 30 minutes' drive southeast of Bangkok is **Samut Prakan** ④, where the **Suvarnabhumi Airport** is located. Attractions here include **Ancient City** and the **Crocodile Farm & Zoo**. The coastal town of **Si Racha** is home to the **Sriracha Tiger Zoo**, said to be the largest of its kind.

The **Eastern Seaboard** provides ample beach

Below: the Bridge over the River Kwai.

Architecture

In this city increasingly dominated by Western architecture, traditional gems can still be found. As well as temples and palaces, there are noteworthy Thai-style residences, a number of which have been turned into museums. As is true for much of Thai artistic expression, these buildings show the influences of several cultures, including Indian, Khmer, Burmese, Chinese and even Western. Yet at the same time, all are identifiably Thai with their bright colours, gabled rooflines, ornate decorations and stunning murals. On the other end, contemporary architecture in Bangkok shows a commitment to depart from the past.

Architectural Styles

TRADITIONAL HOUSES

Like the temple, the Thai house has gone through centuries-old evolution. Some trace the style to southern China, the origin of much of today's Thai population. Steep roofs, sometimes multilayered like the temples that dominated village life, a few rooms or one large partitioned room, and elevation on pilings characterised the earliest homes. The structures were positioned to shed rain and take advantage of the prevailing winds, and many of the components were prefabricated, then fitted together with wooden pegs.

Over time, the houses were raised higher on stilts to protect the home from flooding and animals while creating a space beneath the house for keeping livestock or to be used for daily work such as weaving. Such homes are common in villages throughout Thailand, although in urban areas, nearly all houses are more Western in design and steadfastly anchored to the ground with brick and mortar. Most of the early homes were made of teak and bamboo.

In Thailand's warmer, wetter southern provinces, the houses feature shorter pillars, no exterior verandah, and windows with hinged shutters that closed from the top, more effectively shielding against rain during monsoons.

WESTERN INFLUENCES

With the arrival of Western traders and missionaries in Bangkok in the 18th century, Western architectural design started to make its impact. This was further bolstered by Thai monarchs' trips to Europe in the 19th century. By the mid 19th century, Western-style buildings were taking root alongside traditional Thai structures along both sides of the Chao Phraya River, the centre of government and commerce.

Even palatial buildings such as the Grand Palace *(see p.96)*, the Vimanmek Mansion *(see p.25)*, and the Italianate palace at Bang Pa-In *(see p.94)* sport Western styles.

SINO-PORTUGUESE STYLE

Another legacy are the shophouses built in the Sino-Portuguese style. These narrow and long two-storey linked buildings with ornate window and roof treatments can still be seen at the Tha Chang pier along the Chao Phraya River. As in the past, the ground floor serves as shops, while families live on the floors above.

CONTEMPORARY STYLES

Most contemporary architecture shows little regard for

Below: the graceful interior of Jim Thompson's House.

Left: Jim Thompson's House is set in a lush compound.

guided tour; BTS: National Stadium; map p.136 B1

Standing on the bank of the Khlong Saen Saep canal is Jim Thompson's well-preserved Thai house. An architect by training, Thompson arrived in Thailand at the end of World War II, serving as a military officer. After the war he returned to Bangkok, where he became interested in the almost-extinct art of Thai-silk weaving and was credited for reviving the silk industry.

The compound comprises six teak structures that were transported from Ayutthaya and elsewhere to the silk-weaving enclave of Ban Khrua, just across Khlong Saen Saep, before being reassembled at its current spot in 1959. The structures, making up the various rooms of the house, are painted the red-brown hue characteristic of Thai houses. They feature dramatic outward-sweeping roofs covered with rare tiles designed and fired in Ayutthaya. Curving gracefully in a *ngo* (peak), the wide roofs allow the airy rooms to remain open all year long, sheltered from the downpours of the rainy season. The entire structure, enveloped by lush tropical greenery, stands elevated a full storey above the ground as protection against flooding.

Thompson also made design choices that departed

the past, as hundreds of new high-rises go up each year in the cities while cardboard copy rows of townhouses are erected for the country's growing middle class in the suburbs and small towns. During the building boom of the 1980s and 1990s, many architects tried to outdo one another and some quirky designs evolved in Bangkok.

Baiyoke II Tower

Thanon Ratchaprarop; observation deck daily 10am–10pm; entrance charge; BTS: Phaya Thai; map p.136 C1

Hardly an aesthetic breakthrough but this is striking for its neck-craning 304-m height. Built with reinforced concrete, this 85-storey tower is the tallest building in Thailand. Its 84th floor observation deck offers eye-popping views of the city and beyond. Baiyoke Sky Hotel, the world's third-tallest hotel, occupies the 22nd to 74th floors.
SEE HOTELS, P.61

Elephant Tower

Soi Pahon Yothin 26;
BTS: Mo Chit; map p.20

Located in the North Bangkok Business District, this 32-floor landmark is made up of three towers, connected to form the shape of Thailand's national animal, complete with eyes, tusks and a trunk. The building functions as office space and condominium housing.

Jim Thompson's House

6 Soi Kasemsan 2, Thanon Rama 1; tel: 0 2216 7368; www.jimthompsonhouse.com; daily 9am–5pm; entrance charge includes compulsory

Below: the whimsical Elephant Tower.

On Easter day in 1967 Jim Thompson went for a walk in the jungles of the Cameron Highlands in Malaysia and never came back. Even after many years, the mystery of his disappearance is still unsolved.

Above: the Kamthieng House on the Siam Society grounds.

from the conventional Thai style. Instead of laying out the rooms in a cluster, he opted to have them in rows, adjoined to one another or linked by raised corridors.

The buildings are now a museum housing Thompson's collection of Thai artefacts. His assemblage includes precious Buddha images, porcelain, paintings, and finely carved furniture and panels collected from old homes and temples throughout Thailand.

Next to the old house is a wooden annex, housing a pond-side café with an elegant bar and restaurant, while opposite is the **Art Centre at Jim Thompson's House**, a contemporary gallery that holds regular exhibitions of local and international art and crafts. Before leaving, be sure to stop by and pick up some silk accessories from the branch of **Jim Thompson Thai Silk Company**.

Kamthieng House

Sukhumvit Soi 21; tel: 0 2661 6470–7; www.siam-society. org; Tue–Sat 9am–5pm; entrance charge; BTS: Asok or MRT: Sukhumvit; map p.18
On the grounds of the **Siam Society** is the Kamthieng House, a small pocket of northern Lanna culture transported to Bangkok. The 150-year-old wooden home, originally from the banks of Chiang Mai's Mae Ping River, was reassembled here and is now an ethnological museum presenting audio-visual displays on northern folk culture and daily life. The home is reputedly still inhabited by the ghosts of three former residents.

MR Kukrit Pramoj's Heritage Home

Soi Phra Phinj; tel: 0 2286 8185; Sat–Sun 10am–5pm; entrance fee; BTS: Chong Nonsi; map p.16
Born of royal descent (signified by the title Mom Ratchawong – MR), the late Kukrit Pramoj had a brief stint as prime minister during the disruptive 1970s, but is better remembered as a prolific author and cultural preservationist. His splendid traditional Thai home comprises five single-room stilt buildings that were brought over from separate locations in the Central Plains over a period of time, beginning from the 1960s. Three of the buildings are more than a century old and are linked by a raised verandah with an open living space beneath.

The buildings are now a museum, enlivened by antique pottery, memorabilia and photos of the famous statesman. The ornate garden adds a sense of serenity.

Suan Pakkad Palace

Thanon Sri Ayutthaya; tel: 0 2245 4934; www.suan pakkad.com; daily 9am–4pm; entrance charge includes a guided tour; BTS: Phaya Thai; map p.136 C2
The name Suan Pakkad, meaning 'Cabbage Patch', refers to the grounds' former use as farmland before the palace was constructed in 1952. The former residence of the late Prince and Princess Chumbhot, who were prolific gardeners and art collectors, Suan Pakkad comprises eight traditional teak houses sitting amid a lush garden with a lotus pond. Converted into a museum, the wooden houses display an eclectic collection of antiques and artefacts, including Buddha images, Khmer statues, paintings, porcelain, musical instruments and ancient pottery from Ban Chiang.

At the rear of the garden stands the **Lacquer Pavilion**, which dates to the mid 17th century. Prince Chumbhot discovered it in a temple near Ayutthaya and restored it as a birthday present for his wife

Above: Suan Pakkad's Lacquer Pavilion has an ornate interior.

in 1959. Depicting scenes from the Buddha's life, the *Ramakien* and the vernacular life of the period, the pavilion's black-and-gold-leaf panels are considered masterpieces.

Thai Wah Tower II

Thanon Sathorn Tai; BTS: Sala Daeng; map p.140 C1

Remarkable for its unusually slim profile, this building stands 60 storeys tall with its gaping arch between two boutique hotels, The Sukhothai and The Metropolitan. The **Banyan Tree hotel** occupies the 33rd through the 60th floors, with the open-air rooftop home to the **Vertigo Grill & Moon Bar**, from where the views are simply unforgettable.
SEE HOTELS, P.62; NIGHTLIFE, P.91

UOB Building

Corner of Thanon Sathorn and Soi Pikun; BTS: Chong Nonsi; map p.16

It's no surprise this building, formerly known as the Bank of Asia Building, is affection-ately dubbed the 'robot build-ing'. Looking more like a creation of a child's fantasy than a bank headquarters, the 20-storey UOB Building was built in 1985, designed by Dr Sumet Jumsai, the country's foremost modern architect who was inspired by his son's toy robot. Complete with eyes and antennae, the robotic appearance is sym-bolic of modernisation in Thai banking. Yet, the whimsicality belies the functionality and cleverness of its various elements. For instance, the oversized wheel and bolts function as sunshades.

Vimanmek Mansion

Dusit Park; tel: 0 2628 6300; www.thai.palaces.net; daily 9.30am–4pm; entrance charge, or free with Grand Palace ticket, with compulsory tours every 30 minutes; map p.135 D4

The Vimanmek (meaning 'Palace in the Clouds') Mansion is billed as the world's largest golden-teak building, originally built, without the use of a single nail, in 1868 as a summer house for King Chulalongkorn on the east-coast island of Ko Si Chang. The king ordered the three-storey, 72-room mansion dismantled and reassembled on the Dusit grounds in 1901. The ginger-bread fretwork and octagonal tower look more Victorian than period Thai. The king and his large family lived here for only five years, after which it was occupied on and off over the next two decades before being abandoned and later restored for the Bangkok Bicentennial in 1982.

Vimanmek offers an interesting glimpse into how the royal family of the day lived. Only 30 of the rooms are open to the public. A highlight is the king's bed-room, which has a European-style four-poster bed, and the bathroom, which has what was probably Thailand's first bathtub and flushing toilet. The plumbing, however, was a little primitive – the waste had to be carried out via a hidden spiral staircase beneath. Among the porcelain and hunting trophies are rare finds such as the first typewriter with Thai characters.

Below: the world's largest teak house, Vimanmek.

Beaches and Islands

If the frenetic city and crowds get too over-whelming, it's time to escape to the seaside. Pack your swimsuit and sunblock, and head south to the calming beach town of Hua Hin, a traditional getaway for the royal family and wealthy Bangkokians, or to Cha-am, the weekend beach paradise popular with younger Thais. Other seaside retreats, located southeast of Bangkok, include the touristy, anything-goes beach town of Pattaya and the unspoilt palm-fringed island of Ko Samet.

Cha-am

160km south of Bangkok; taxi from Bangkok, train from Hualamphong Station to Phet-chaburi, or bus from Southern Bus Terminal; map p.20

Cha-am is a long stretch of beach popular with young Bangkokians on weekends. Weekdays are a better time for a trip to Cha-am, as the resort sees fewer day trip-pers. There are plenty of good seafood restaurants to choose from.

PHRA RATCHANIWET MARUKHATHAYAWAN

Roughly 10km south of Cha-am, heading towards Hua Hin, is the seaside palace of

Phra Ratchaniwet Marukhathayawan (daily 8am–5pm; entrance charge). Built in 1923 from golden teakwood, the airy stilted structures are European in style and have been beauti-fully renovated. Intercon-nected by raised covered walkways, the palace build-ings were a retreat for King Vajiravudh (Rama VI) for the last two years before he died.

Hua Hin

203km south of Bangkok; taxi from Bangkok, train from Hualamphong Station, or bus from Southern Bus Terminal; map p.20

Prachuap Kiri Khan is Thai-land's narrowest province and its coast is fringed by mountains and quiet beaches, the most popular of which is the 5-km-long sandy beach at Hua Hin. This former fishing village has long had an air of exclusivity, thanks to the residences maintained by Thai royalty and Bangkok's wealthy elite,

Left: Phra Ratchaniwet Marukhathayawan palace.

who come here for the clean air. Partly because of this it retains more of a family ambi-ence than most other beach destinations in Thailand.

Hua Hin has the aura of a European spa town. Several exclusive spa retreats, such as the award-winning Chiva Som, cater to the holistic needs of international jetsetters. A string of brand-name resorts, like the Hilton, Hyatt and Marriott, have opened here, along with local and equally expensive concerns like Dusit and Anantara. The beaches south of Hua Hin (towards Pranburi) also have some stylishly designed boutique resorts like the Evason and Aleenta.

Today, Hua Hin beach is backed by opulent summer homes alongside a slew of condominium developments. Hua Hin is fast gaining an international reputation as a place to retire, and many con-dos and beach houses are being built to accommodate the upsurge in interest. The beaches south of town, Suan Son and Khao Tao, are rather nicer and more secluded.

Left: boats on Hua Hin beach.

Phnom Penh Hotel in the 1984 movie *Killing Fields* before being restored to its original wood-panelled glory as the Hotel Sofitel Central.

OUTSIDE HUA HIN

Located about 50km south of Hua Hin is **Khao Sam Roi Yot National Park**. It is named 'Three Hundred Mountain Peaks' after the limestone pinnacles that jut from the park's mangrove swamps to heights above 600m. Carved from the rugged coastline and a haven for kayakers, the park has superb beaches, marshes, forest walks and caves. Wildlife includes a multitude of birdlife, crab-eating macaques, and mountain goat-antelopes.

Tham Phraya Nakhon is the most famous attraction here; the huge cave has a large sinkhole that allows shafts of light to shine down and illuminate the grand Thai-style pavilion (*sala*) built in the 1890s for a visit by King Chulalongkorn.

Ko Samet

200km southeast of Bangkok; taxi from Bangkok or bus from Eastern Bus Terminal to Ban Phe pier in Rayong province, then

Nightlife has picked up as more beer bars have opened (but no go-go bars as yet). Along with the burgeoning nightlife, many new restaurants have appeared too. While Hua Hin is known for its fresh seafood, the diversity of culinary options has expanded beyond just Thai, and now features a spectrum of Continental and Asian cuisines. The restaurants and bars are clustered into a small area around **Thanon Naresdamri** and behind on the parallel **Thanon Phunsuk. Soi Bintabaht** has the highest concentration of beer bars, and the pier area along Naresdamri offers delicious grilled seafood.

> Weekend activities held in Hua Hin include the annual Hua Hin Jazz Festival in June and the popular King's Cup Elephant Polo Tournament in September.

ish-style villa is still regularly used by the royal family and is not open to the public.

Railway Hotel

Just across from the quaint Hua Hin Railway Station is another historic landmark, the colonial-style former Railway Hotel. Constructed in 1922, the Victorian-looking hotel masqueraded as the

HUA HIN SIGHTS
Klai Kangwon Palace

Hua Hin's royal connection can be seen at the seafront teakwood summer abode called Klai Kangwon Palace, whose name means 'far from worries'. Built in 1926 at the northern end of Hua Hin beach under the command of King Prajadhipok, the Span-

Below: the luxury hotel Hilton Hua Hin at dusk.

boat to Na Dan pier in Ko Samet; entrance charge; map p.20

The postcard-perfect island of Ko Samet is a popular weekend getaway for Bangkok residents. The island is famous among Thais as the place where Sunthorn Phu (1786–1855), a flamboyantly romantic court poet, retired to compose some of his works. Born in nearby Klaeng on the mainland, Sunthorn called the island Ko Kaew Phisadan, or 'island with sand like crushed crystal', and it was here that his best-known work *Phra Aphaimani*, a tale about a prince and a mermaid, was set. A weathered statue stands as tribute on the rocky point at the end of the main beach of **Hat Sai Kaew** (Diamond Sand).

The island is part of a national marine park, so, technically, most of the resort and bungalow operations are illegal. However, development along the coast has continued despite the law; thankfully it remains fairly unobtrusive with simple single-storey huts and bungalows. But as a sign of things to come, a couple of resorts have upgraded their facilities, and the west coast's only beach of

Ao Phrao has two upmarket resorts nestled into this small scenic bay.

Most activity here is relaxed – sunbathing, beach strolls, swimming and snorkelling – though jet skis do occasionally interrupt the peace. Almost all the island's sandy beaches run down the east coast, starting near the larger northern tip with Hat Sai Kaew, and gradually getting less isolated as the island narrows to the southern bay of **Ao Karang**.

The island is relatively small and can be walked from north to south in a few hours, though the coastal track traverses some rocky headlands. The single road turns to bumpy dirt track fairly quickly. Hat Sai Kaew is where Thais prefer to stay, having more air-conditioned rooms and seafood restaurants, whereas foreign visitors like to nest at the bays of **Ao Phai** and **Ao Hin Khok**.

Ko Samet is best avoided on public holidays, when visitors outnumber beds, and tents are pitched on any spare patch of land. Evenings are relatively low key, with restaurants setting up seafood barbecues on the beach. Restaurant-bars at small hotels like Naga (Ao Hin Khok) and Silver Sand (Ao

While the regular fishing boats are much cheaper, taking a speedboat across to Ko Samet (around B800) from the mainland is much faster. It drops you at the bay of your choice, and usually means you escape paying the National Park entry fee of B200 per foreigner, which is pretty steep compared to the B20 that Thais are charged.

Phai) are the only spots that offer music, late-night partying and the obligatory fire juggling.

Pattaya

147km southeast of Bangkok; taxi from Bangkok or bus from Eastern Bus Terminal; map p.20

Pattaya has a reputation that precedes itself, with most people having formed their opinion of this resort town even before they step foot here. Few areas in Asia have undergone such a precipitous rise to fame and subsequent plummet in popularity. This notoriety dates back to the Vietnam War when American GIs flocked to the then-quiet beaches and bars for R&R. Today occasional battalions of visiting US marines from the nearby port at Satthahip still descend on the resort.

This seaside town, dubbed the 'Riviera of the Eastern Seaboard', has long been popular with Thai youth, families and tourists. It is also a favourite spot for condos and beach homes for Bangkok expats, and for winter homes for European retirees.

While still retaining a provincial Thai character, Pattaya tries hard to invoke the ambience of a cosmopolitan playground, with glitzy malls and hotels, a pedestrianised shopping street and tree-lined beach paths.

Below: Hat Sai Kaew beach on Ko Samet.

Above: banana boats on Jomtien Beach.

BEACHES

Pattaya's beaches are nowhere near as pristine as those in the southern islands, but what Pattaya lacks, it more than compensates for in other areas. There is a plethora of good-value accommodation, international restaurants, a wide range of activities, and several cultural attractions. Beyond that, the magnitude of Pattaya's buzzing, if salacious, nightlife is something to be experienced, or avoided, depending on your sensibility.

On the beachfront, there is the crescent-shaped **Pattaya Bay**, the least attractive beach, followed by the nicer 6-km-long **Jomtien**, and, lastly, **Nakula**, with its fishing village ambience but no decent beach to speak of. Pattaya Bay and Jomtien are good locations for watersports, with equipment for windsurfing, sailing, snorkelling and diving available for rent, along with jet skis, water scooters and water-skiing equipment.

OTHER ATTRACTIONS

Besides land-based attractions such as golf courses, paintball parks, go-karting, bungy jumping and parachuting, there are several sights worth seeing.

At the Royal Garden Plaza is a branch of **Ripley's Believe It or Not!** with its collection of bizzare oddities (tel: 0 3871 0294; daily 11am–11pm; entrance charge). At Thanon Sukhumvit is the **Pattaya Elephant Village**, offering elephant shows and rides into the surrounding countryside (tel: 0 3824 9818; www.elephant-village-pattaya.com; daily 8.30am–7pm; entrance charge). At **Pattaya Park**, a large water amusement facility, the little ones will enjoy cable car rides as well as water slides and whirlpools (tel: 0 3825 1201; www.pattayapark.com; daily 9am–6pm; entrance charge). More entertainment for the kids is available at the **Underwater World** aquarium, where there are touch pools with small marine animals and a long viewing tunnel (tel: 0 3875 6879; daily 9am–6pm; entrance charge).

For a unique perspective on Thai temples, visit the **Sanctuary of Truth** on Nakula Soi 12, an elaborate woodcarved re-creation of a Khmer temple-palace (tel: 0 3822 5407; www.sanctuaryoftruth.com; daily 8am–6pm; entrance charge). Dramatically perched on the seafront and protected by fortification, the fantastical tower blends ancient religious iconography from Thailand and Cambodia.

Work began in 1981 and is still ongoing.

About 18km south of Pattaya is **Nong Nooch Tropical Garden** (tel: 0 3870 9360; www.nongnoochtropical garden.com; daily 8am–6pm; entrance charge), with elephant shows and a mini-zoo.

NIGHTLIFE

Pattaya's nightlife clusters along or off **Beach Road** and the so-called **Walking Street** in southern Pattaya. There are scores of bars, pubs and nightclubs, and an overwhelming number of go-go bars. The strip called **Boys' Town** (Pattayaland Soi 3) is where the gay crowd gathers. Pattaya also has at least three lip-synching cabaret shows, which feature a pageant of stunning *katoey* (transsexuals). **Tiffany's** (tel: 0 3842 1700) is especially good.

The multimedia cultural extravaganza, **Alangkarn Theatre**, on Thanon Sukhumvit, combines traditional Thai dancers and elephants with lasers and pyrotechnics (tel: 0 3825 6007; www.alangkarnthailand.com; Tue–Sun 6–10pm, shows 7pm and 8.45pm; entrance charge). It is kitschy but makes for a fun evening with dinner thrown in.

Below: a carving at the Sanctuary of Truth.

Children

Thailand is not the most ideal destination for children; the little ones may not take to the heat and humidity well, and few really enjoy visiting temples and taking in Thai architecture. That said, however, Bangkok and its surroundings do offer a number of family-friendly zoos, aquariums and theme parks. The city's larger shopping malls also often have designated kids' zones, with playgrounds for younger children and games arcades for teenagers. There are also special play areas in Bangkok's major parks such as Lumphini, Benjasiri, Benjakitti and Chatuchak.

Ancient City

Km 33, Old Thanon Sukhumvit, Bangpoo, Amphoe Muang, Samut Prakan; tel: 0 2323 9253; www.ancientcity.com; daily 8am–5pm; entrance charge; bus: 11, then minibus: 36; map p.20

One of Bangkok's best-value tourist, and surprisingly under-visited, attractions, Ancient City, or Muang Boran, is the brainchild of a Bangkok millionaire with a passion for Thai art and history. In what used to be 80 hectares of rice fields, designers sketched an area roughly the shape of Thailand and placed replicas of attractions in locations that parallel those of the real sights.

There are replicas – some full-size, most one-third the size of the originals – of famous monuments and temples from all parts of the kingdom. Some are recon-structions of buildings that no longer exist, such as the Grand Palace of Ayutthaya, others are copies of buildings such as the temple of Khao Phra Viharn on the Thai-Cam-bodian border, while a few are salvaged antiquities. Experts from the National Museum worked as consultants to ensure historical accuracy of the reproductions.

At present, there are over 100 monuments, covering 15 centuries of Thai history. The grounds are pleasantly land-scaped with small waterfalls, creeks, ponds, rock gardens and lush greenery, while deer graze freely among the inter-esting sculptures represent-ing figures from Thai literature and Hindu mythology. As the monuments are spread over such a large area, the best way to get around is on rented bicycles. Finish your tour at the Old Market Town, a street of shops disguised as traditional wooden houses, with local handicrafts and sculptures for sale.

Below: Ancient City features replicas of Thai monuments.

Left: bumper-car ride at Dream World.

Dream World

Km 7, Thanon Rangsit, Nakorn Nayok; tel: 0 2533 1152; www.dreamworld-th.com; Mon–Fri 10am–5pm, Sat–Sun 10am–7pm; entrance charge; bus: 523 or 538; map p.20

Those who have visited Disney World or other major theme parks aren't going to be rendered speechless by Dream World. Nevertheless, the park is worthwhile if you have children or teenagers with you. The park comprises Dream World Plaza, Dream Garden, Fantasy Land and Adventure Land. A sightseeing train circles Dream Garden, while a cable car and a monorail offer nice views of the park and surrounding rural areas. Thrillseekers should head for Adventure Land, the section with the most stomach-churning rides. In Snow Town, experience frosty weather with sled rides down a slope made of artificial snow.

Crocodile Farm & Zoo

555 M.7, Taiban District, Amphoe Muang, Samut Prakan; tel: 0 2387 0020; daily 7am–6pm; entrance charge; bus: 7, 8 or 11, then local *songthaew* (pick-up truck); map p.20

Located a short distance from the Ancient City on the old Sukhumvit Highway (Route 3) and 10km from Bangkok, this was started in the 1950s with a paltry initial investment. The owner now has three farms (two in the northeast) worth millions of dollars. The farm has over 60,000 freshwater and salt-water local crocodiles, making it the largest crocodile farm in the world, as well as some South American caimans and Nile River crocodiles. It also has the world's largest captive crocodile, the 6-m-long and 1,114-kg Chai Yai. The irony is that though the beasts are thriving in captivity, almost all wild Siamese and Asian species of crocodiles have been hunted to extinction.

A highlight of the farm are the eight daily shows (hourly 9am–4pm, reptile feeding 4–5pm) in which handlers enter a pond teeming with crocodiles to wrestle them and place their heads in the beasts' mouths. The farm's shops sell stewed crocodile meat as well as handbags, belts and shoes made from their skins. Used as an ingredient in traditional Chinese medicine, the meat is purportedly a tonic and aphrodisiac.

The farm also has a zoo featuring tigers, ostriches, camels and elephants, as well as a Dinosaur Museum and an amusement park.

Below: wrestling a crocodile at the Crocodile Farm & Zoo.

Dusit Zoo

71 Thanon Rama V, Bangkok; tel: 0 2281 2000; daily 8am–6pm; entrance charge; pier: Thewet; map p.135 E4

The grounds of Dusit Zoo were originally part of the Royal Dusit Garden Palace, where King Chulalongkorn

Bangkok's footpaths are not pedestrian friendly; they are often in disrepair or blocked: leave the baby stroller at home and bring back- or chest-mounted baby carriers. The tropical sun is intense, so use sunblock and hats. Make sure the kids keep their hands clean as well; kids who suck their fingers or thumbs can easily pick up stomach bugs.

31

Above: hippos at the Dusit Zoo.

had his private botanical garden. The 19-ha site became a public zoo in 1938. The zoo has around 300 different species of mammals, almost 1,000 bird species, and around 300 different kinds of reptiles, but conditions at some of the animal enclosures are less than adequate.

Rose Garden Riverside Resort

Km 32, Thanon Phetchkasem, Samphran, Nakhon Pathom; tel: 0 3432 2588; www.rose-garden. com; daily 8am–6pm; entrance charge; bus from Southern Bus Terminal; map p.20

Some 32km west of Bangkok on Route 4 towards Nakhon Pathom is the Rose Garden Riverside Resort, with well-landscaped rose and orchid gardens, a resort-style hotel, restaurants and sports facili-ties. The main attraction is the **Thai Village Cultural Show**, held daily in the garden. In a large arena, costumed actors perform folk dances to live traditional music and re-enact a traditional wedding ceremony and a Thai boxing match.

Outside, elephants put on their own show, moving huge teak logs as they would in the forests of the north. The elephants then carry tourists around the compound for a small fee. You can also spend time browsing at the Cultural Village, with gift shops and demonstrations by weavers creating thread from silkworm cocoons.

Safari World

99 Thanon Ramindra, 45km northeast of Bangkok city; tel: 0 2914 4100–19; www.safari world.com; daily 9am–5pm; entrance charge; bus: 26 to Minburi, then minibus; map p.20

The reputation of this destination, popular with Bangkok families, took a severe beating in 2003 when it was discovered to be harbouring some 50 orang-utans smuggled in from Indonesia. For a long time, the questionable orang-utan boxing shows were one of the park's most popular attractions. The wildlife park is open as usual, though the apes have been seized by the authorities.

Other animals on view at the 81-ha park include giraffes, zebras, ostriches, rhinos and camels. The adjoining Marine Park features acrobatics performed by sea lions and dolphins, as well as antics by parrots and cockatoos.

Samphran Elephant Ground

Km 30, Thanon Phetchkasem, Samphran, Nakhon Pathom; tel: 0 2284 1873; www.elephant show.com; daily 8am–5.30pm; entrance charge; bus from Southern Bus Terminal; map p.20

Just a stone's throw from the Rose Garden is the Samphran Elephant Ground & Zoo, another family-oriented attraction that provides a chance to ride an elephant, feed crocs and learn about the pachyderm's importance in Thai culture. Other fauna on view include gibbons, macaques, pythons and a diverse flock of local birds.

At the Crocodile Show, men wrestle with these scaly creatures, while the Elephant Show explains Thailand's historical relationship with its national symbol. The war re-enactments are exciting displays, but the elephants'

Below: a bamboo dance demonstration at Rose Garden.

majesty somewhat diminishes when they are made to do silly things like dancing and playing football in oversized shirts. After the show, you can feed the elephants or go on a 30-minute elephant trek.

Each 1 May, a travesty of a beauty contest takes place here as oversized women weighing over 80kg compete for the ignominious title of Jumbo Queen (www.jumboqueen.com). The contest seeks a 'well-padded lady who best exhibits the characteristics of the majestic pachyderm to persuade people to support the cause of elephant conservation in Thailand'. It's strange, but true.

Siam Ocean World

B1–2 Siam Paragon, 991 Thanon Rama I, Bangkok; tel: 0 2687 2000; www.siamoceanworld.com; daily 9am–10pm; BTS: Siam; entrance charge; map p.140 B4
The massive Siam Paragon mall houses the impressive Siam Ocean World. The aquarium is divided into seven zones and has a giant oceanarium filled with over 30,000 marine creatures. Visitors can also ride in a glass-bottomed boat and dive with the sharks.

Siam Park

99 Thanon Serithai, Bangkok; tel: 0 2919 7200; www.siamparkcity.com; daily 10am–6pm;

Above: resident at the Samphran Elephant Ground.

entrance charge; bus: 60, 71, 168 or 519; map p.20
Known locally as Suan Siam, this water park has water rides, a waterfall and a large artificial beach with rolling waves. There is also an amusement park with 10 adult rides in Fantasyland and 20 children rides in Small World, and a theme park where kids can learn about dinasours and the history of China, as well as experience a safari adventure.

Snake Farm (Queen Saovabha Memorial Institute)

1871 Thanon Rama IV, Bangkok; tel: 0 2252 0161–4; Mon–Fri 8.30am–4.30pm, Sat–Sun 8.30am–noon; entrance charge; MRT: Silom or Sam Yan; map p.140 B2
Travellers to the tropics often worry about encounters with dangerous beasties and a visit to the Queen Saovabha Memorial Institute, popularly called the Snake Farm, will either allay or enforce such trepidations. Located south of the Chulalongkorn University, it was founded in 1923 as the Pasteur Institute. Now operated by the Thai Red Cross, the institute's principal work lies in the research and treatment of

snakebites and the extraction of antivenins.

Venom-milking sessions (Mon–Fri 11am and 2.30pm, Sat–Sun 11am; slide show 30 minutes before) are the best times to visit, when various snakes are pulled from the pit and generally goaded for a squealing audience. Of Thailand's six species of venomous snakes, the King Cobra is the largest and most common. A single yield of its venom is deadly enough to kill some 50,000 mice; fortunately its basic diet is other snakes. Willing spectators can drape a snake around their necks for a one-of-a-kind photo memento.

Sriracha Tiger Zoo

341 Moo 3, Highway 7, Km 20, Nongkham, Si Racha; tel: 0 3829 6556–8; www.tigerzoo.com; daily 8am–6pm; bus from Eastern Bus Terminal; entrance charge; map p.20
Said to be the largest tiger zoo in the world, this has over 200 Bengal tigers in captivity, alongside other animals like crocodiles, elephants, ostriches and chimps. Visitors can visit the nursery to hold and feed the young cubs. There are also daily circus shows of crocodile wrestling and pig racing.

Below: a photo opportunity with a python.

33

Dance and Theatre

Many visitors to Thailand seek out some form of traditional artistry to enforce their perceptions of Thailand as an exotic land rich in cultural heritage. By all means, while in Bangkok, do experience a traditional puppetry performance or Thai dance-drama, recognised as among the world's most dazzling and stylistically challenging, with elaborate costumes and graceful movements. But don't miss out on the country's contemporary dance and theatre scenes, which are fast gaining recognition in international circles.

Thai Dance-Drama

The origins of traditional Thai theatrical arts are entwined with court ceremony and religious ritual. When discussing Thai theatre, one cannot use the word 'drama' without uttering the word 'dance' immediately before it. The two are inseparable, as the dancer's hands and body express the emotions that the silent lips do not, with the storyline and lyrics provided by a singer and chorus on the side of the stage. A *phipat* orchestra *(see p.86)* creates not only the atmosphere, but also an emotive force.

Above: musicians accompanying Thai dance-drama.

ORIGINS

It is thought that the movements of dance-drama originated in *nang yai* (shadow puppet) performances of the 16th and 17th centuries. Huge buffalo hides were cut into the shapes of characters from the *Ramakien*, which is the Thai version of the Hindu epic *Ramayana*.

The *Ramakien* is the vivid tale of the god-king Rama and his beautiful wife, Sita, the paragon of beauty and virtue. Sita is abducted by the nasty 10-headed, 20-armed demon king Totsakan, who imprisons her in his palace on the island of Longka (Sri Lanka), importuning her at every turn to divorce Rama and marry him. With his brother Phra Lak, Rama sets off in pursuit, stymied by mammoth obstacles that test his mettle. Along the way, he is joined by the magical white monkey-god Hanuman, a mischievous but talented general who is one of the Thais' favourite characters. Hanuman and his army of monkeys build a bridge to Longka. After a pitched battle, Totsakan is killed, Sita is rescued, and everyone lives happily ever after.

Against a torch-lit translucent screen, puppeteers manipulated puppets, using their silhouettes to tell complex tales of good and evil from the *Ramakien*. As they moved the figures across the screen, the puppeteers danced the emotions

Left: lakhon dancers in traditional costume.

The counterparts to classical Thai dance are the more traditional and less structured dances performed in rural villages by farm families. Each region has a special form unique to it. Harvest, fingernail, candle and fishing dances are performed by groups of women in village costumes. In flirtation dances, they are joined by male dancers attempting to weave romantic spells on unsmiling but appreciative partners.

they wanted the stiff figures to convey. These movements gradually evolved into an independent theatrical art.

KHON

The most identifiable form of dance-drama is the *khon*, historically performed by a large troupe of male dancers wearing beautifully crafted masks for the royal court. These days a condensed version of several episodes from the *Ramakien* is adapted into a short medley of palatable scenes for tourist dinner shows. The entire *Ramakien* would take 720 hours to perform. The colourful masks depict beasts and demons from the epic tale, with each performer trained to portray the particular character of each creature through gestures and actions.

LAKHON

The most graceful dance is the *lakhon*. There are two forms: the *lakhon nai* ('inside' *lakhon*), once performed only inside the palace walls by women, and the *lakhon nawk* ('outside' *lakhon*), performed

beyond the palace by both sexes. Garbed in elaborate costumes, the performers use slow, heavily stylised movements to convey the plot. Even during the most emotional moments, their faces are devoid of expression. *Lakhon*'s rich repertoire includes scenes from the *Ramakien* and tales like *Inao*, with their romantic storylines.

LIKAY

There have always been two cultures in Thailand: palace and village. The village arts are often parodies of the palace arts, but more burlesque, with pratfalls and bawdy humour. *Likay* is the village form of *lakhon*, played out against gaudy backdrops to an audience that walks in and out of the performance at will, eating and talking, regardless of what happens to the performers on stage.

Puppet Theatre

Visually mesmerising and based on *khon* masked dance-drama, the traditional Thai puppetry of *hun lakhon lek* requires three puppeteers to manipulate sticks attached to marionettes to bring them

Below: Joe Louis puppeteers.

Above: a scene from *Eclipse*, a Patravadi Theatre production.

to life. Once only performed for royalty, the endangered art was revived by Sakorn Yangkeawsot, who goes by the moniker Joe Louis.

Updating the *hun lakhon lek* theatre by allowing freer movements and more detailed costuming, and also by incorporating contemporary themes and modern speech, Joe Louis has been successful in reviving this art form without diluting its origins. You can see these elaborately costumed puppets twist and turn nightly at the **Joe Louis Theatre** at Suan Lum Night Bazaar.

Modern Performing Arts

This is one area where modern innovation has been stifled, compounded by a language barrier for international appreciation.

One venue that stages and produces quality modern productions is **Patravadi Theatre** in Thonburi. The open-air venue is run by Patravadi Mechudhon, whose adaptations of classic Thai tales meld traditional local dance and theatre with modern Western styling. Some of its works fuse elements of Asian dance forms like Japanese *butoh* and Indonesian *wayang kulit* (shadow puppetry). Patravadi Theatre stages its acclaimed shows, some of which have toured overseas, on Saturday and Sunday nights from June to February.

Its past shows include the landmark *Sahatsadecha* in 1997, which artfully blends *khon* with *nang yai*. The show was so successful that it went on to perform at the Biennale de la Danse, in Lyon, France. Other notable works include *Eclipse*, which presents a visual feast of Thai drummers and dancers based on a tale of Buddhist suffering during an eclipse of the moon. Patravadi Theatre also hosts the annual Bangkok Fringe Festival, which presents a varied programme of dance, drama and music.

Venues

Joe Louis Theatre
Suan Lum Night Bazaar, 1875 Thanon Rama IV; tel: 0 2252 9683; www.joelouis-theater.com; MRT: Lumphini; map p.141 D2
Sakorn Yangkeawsot, who goes by the name Joe Louis, is responsible for reviving the fading art of *hun lakhon lek*, a unique form of puppetry inspired by local folk tales and the *Ramakien*. Three puppeteers move visibly on stage, manipulating expressive marionettes. One show nightly at 7.30pm.

National Theatre
Thanon Ratchini; tel: 0 2224 1342; pier: Phra Athit; map p.134 B2
North of Sanam Luang, next to the traffic-clogged Saphan Phra Pin Klao bridge along Thanon Rachini, is the grand old National Theatre. Unfortunately, this large white modern edifice doesn't open its doors as frequently as it used to. It has weekly and monthly performances of folk and classical Thai music, dance and drama. Occasionally it showcases highbrow concerts and theatre from abroad. Call ahead for schedules.

Patravadi Theatre
69/1 Soi Wat Rakhang; Thanon Arun Amarin; tel: 0 2412 7287;

Above: Sala Rim Naam presents a nightly dance-drama show.

www.patravaditheatre.com; pier: Wat Rakhang; map p.134 A1

This is the nucleus of the Thai contemporary theatre scene, led by Patravadi Mechudhon, who artfully melds traditional and modern dance and drama. Dinner shows on Friday and Saturday nights at 7.30pm.

Sala Chalerm Krung Theatre

66 Thanon Charoen Krung; tel: 0 2222 1854; pier: Saphan Phut; map p.138 C4

North of the Pahurat Market, this theatre was presented as a gift to the Siamese people from King Rama VII in 1933 to mark the city's 150th anniversary. With a distinctive Western art deco façade and Thai-style interior, it was once hailed at the biggest and grandest theatre in Asia. Sala Chalerm Kung was also the first Thai movie theatre to screen talkies. In 1941, because of the scarcity of celluloid during World War II, the theatre was converted into a performance venue for traditional *khon* drama. In 1993, the theatre was renovated to its original splendour, and today, hosts special film screenings as well as traditional Thai dance-drama shows for tourists.

Dinner Dance & Drama

For free traditional *khon* performances, head to either **Erawan Shrine** *(see p.119)* in the Pathumwan area or **Lak Muang** *(see p.78)* near the Grand Palace, both of which have resident dance troupes who are paid by devotees to dance in thanksgiving for having prayers answered.

Astonishingly, Bangkok has almost nowhere else to view dance-drama spectacles except in condensed forms at a few restaurants. They present hour-long shows of bite-sized dance-drama performances after a Thai dinner.

Riverside Terrace

Bangkok Marriott Riverside Resort & Spa, 257/1–3 Thanon Charoen Nakhon; tel: 0 2476 0022; BTS: Saphan Taksin, then shuttle boat; map p.139 D1

Large stone pillars set alight with Olympic-style flames frame a stage fringed by a lily pond. It's a great riverside setting for the nightly 7.30–9pm dance performance.

Ruen Thep Room

Silom Village, 286 Thanon Silom; tel: 0 2234 4581; BTS: Chong Nonsi; map p.140 A1

A large hall of dark wood and Thai paintings and sculptures creates the right ambience for the nightly hour-long performance at 8.30pm.

Sala Rim Naam

The Oriental, 48 Oriental Avenue; tel: 0 2437 6211; pier: Oriental; map p.139 E1

The Oriental's riverside restaurant offers set dinner accompanied by an entertaining dance and drama performance at 8.30pm nightly.

Siam Niramit

19 Thanon Tiamruammit, Huaykwang; tel: 0 2649 9222; www.siamniramit.com; MRT: Thai Cultural Centre

A beautifully costumed extravaganza that traverses the country's history and diverse cultures in three acts. The nightly performance is at 8pm.

Supatra River House

266 Soi Wat Rakhang, Thanon Arun Amarin; tel: 0 2411 0305; www.supatrariverhouse.net; pier: Wat Rakhang; map p.134 A1

This atmospheric riverside restaurant housed in an old renovated Thai house hosts classic and contemporary dances by graduates from the nearby Patravadi Theatre on Saturdays from 8.30am to 9pm.

Below: dancers at the Erawan Shrine.

Environment

From a sleepy backwater a hundred years ago, Bangkok has transformed, beyond recognition, into the sprawling metropolis it is today. Leafy avenues lined with wooden houses have turned into Manhattan-style thoroughfares with towering skyscrapers, open-air markets have been replaced by air-conditioned shopping malls, and the city's once-famous canals, for which it was known as the 'Venice of the East', have fallen stagnant or been filled in to make roads. With little urban planning involved in the city's rapid expansion, it's no surprise Bangkok is now facing significant environmental challenges.

Air Pollution

With over 5.5 million cars on the streets, Bangkok's traffic is inevitably atrocious. Successive city governors have touted new solutions – ring roads, overpasses, the BTS (Skytrain) and underground MRT (metro), park-and-ride schemes – but none has managed to alleviate the capital's notorious bumper-to-bumper gridlock.

Above: masked motorcyclists caught in rush-hour traffic.

All this congestion causes air pollution that poses serious health risks to Bangkokians, particularly those who live or work near major roads. The major threat comes from particulate matter (known as PM10) emitted by the diesel engines of buses and trucks, which can cause chronic respiratory diseases after long-term exposure.

Unlikely as it may seem, however, Bangkok is considered a role model for other Asian capitals in its efforts to improve air quality. Thanks largely to stricter controls on vehicle emissions and two-stroke motorcycles, pollution levels have been cut in half over the past 10 years.

To prevent your own contribution to both pollution and traffic jams, take a tip from traffic authorities who urge Bangkokians to forgo private vehicles for public transport and take the BTS, MRT and buses.

Recycling

In this overcrowded and ever-expanding metropolis, the Bangkok Metropolitan Administration (BMA) has a multitude of woes to contend with. One of these is the extraordinary amount of rubbish that the city's residents throw away. In 2002, the city was tossing out almost 9,500 tons of solid waste (mostly food scraps, plastics, foam and paper) each day. By the year 2015, this mountain of daily garbage is expected to have doubled. The city's garbage disposal system is already overburdened and landfills on the city's edge are insufficient.

The BMA encourages residents to 'reuse, recycle and repair'. There is already an inbuilt grassroots system for recycling in the city's *saleng* men, who you can see combing the streets with pushcarts powered by bicycles or motorcycles.

Left: bumper-to-bumper gridlock in Bangkok.

Electricity

Bangkok also guzzles energy, and up to 50 per cent of the country's total energy usage is burned up in the capital. In May 2007, the BMA launched a 'lights off' energy-conservation campaign. At 7pm on the 9th of every month, all offices and households in Bangkok are called upon to switch off their electricity for 15 minutes. Other tips from the BMA include turning off any electrical appliance one is not using and setting the air conditioner at no colder than 25°C.

Climate

Heat is another big challenge in the city. Temperatures are rising annually and Bangkok is about 5°C hotter than rural areas. The on-going building boom means that green spaces have given way to concrete and tarmac, which trap heat during the day and expel it at night. The only temporary escape may be to head for one of the bars or restaurants on top of the city's skyscrapers, where you can enjoy the cool breeze and the spectacular neon-pink-and-orange sunsets, made possible by Bangkok's particular blend of heat haze and pollution.

They buy old newspapers, plastic, glass, cardboards and metals which they sell to recycling plants for a small profit. If you separate the rubbish you dispose of in your hotel or guesthouse, someone will probably make sure it gets to a *saleng* recycler.

Flooding

During the rainy season, which usually lasts from May until October, severe floods drown large parts of the city. The result of rainwater draining down from the mountainous north, rising water levels in the river and tidal surges of seawater, this annual deluge always causes havoc; traffic worsens as cars break down and traffic lights fail, and pedestrians are forced to wade knee-deep through sewage-laced waters.

The BMA cleans drains and sewers, lines up sand bags along the river, uses pumping stations to control water flows, and diverts floodwater to nearby provinces. But all these efforts to combat Mother

> Thailand's National Disaster Warning Centre has predicted that Bangkok will be submerged under one metre of water in less than 20 years if corrective measures are not taken now.

Nature's monsoon rages have proved largely futile.

The swampland on which the city is built is subsiding at 10cm per year due to excessive groundwater extraction, and sea levels are rising due to global warming. Unless a massive dyke is built to protect the city, Bangkok may have to revert to yesteryear's waterways for which it was once renowned.

Below: floods are common during the rainy season.

Essentials

Travelling in Bangkok is easy, especially if you have the right information about the sights, local culture and travel practicalities. A good first stop when you arrive is a Tourism Authority of Thailand information outlet or service kiosk, where you can obtain maps, promotional materials as well as advice on things to do and places to see. In addition, here is the practical information you need to understand Thai currency, customs regulations, entry regulations and etiquette. There are also details on embassies, healthcare, tipping and taxes, telecommunications, and on where to get help in emergencies.

Customs Regulations

The Thai government prohibits the import or export of drugs, dangerous chemicals, pornography, firearms and ammunition. Attempting to smuggle hard drugs in or out may be punishable by death.

Tourists may freely bring in foreign banknotes or other types of foreign exchange, and without tax 200 cigarettes and one litre of wine or spirits. The maximum amount permitted to be taken out in Thai currency without prior authorisation is B50,000. Buddha images, antiques and art objects cannot leave Thailand without a **Department of Fine Arts** (tel: 0 2226 1661) permit.

For more details, check with the **Thai Customs Department** (tel: 1164; www.customs.go.th).

Embassies

Australia
37 Thanon Sathorn Tai;
tel: 0 2287 2680
Canada
15/F, Abdulrahim Place, Thanon Rama IV; tel: 0 2636 0540
New Zealand
M Thai Tower, 14/F,

All Seasons Place, 87 Thanon Withayu; tel: 0 2254 2530
United Kingdom
14 Thanon Withayu;
tel: 0 2305 8333
United States
120–122 Thanon Withayu;
tel: 0 2205 4000

Emergency Numbers

Police
Tel: 191
Tourist Police
Tel: 1155 or 0 2281 5051, 2664 0222; Tourist Service Centre, TAT headquarters, 4 Thanon Ratchadamnoen Nok

Tourist police booths can also be found in Lumphini Park (near the intersection of Thanon Rama IV and Thanon Silom) and Patpong (at the Silom intersection).

Entry Requirements

Visa regulations vary for different nationalities. For updated information, check with a Thai embassy or consulate or on the Thai **Ministry of Foreign Affairs** website (www.mfa.go.th).

All foreign nationals entering Thailand must have valid passports with at least six-month validity. At the

airport, nationals from most countries will be granted a visa-on-arrival, valid for up to 30 days. This can be extended by 7–10 days for a fee of B1,900, or you can leave the country (even for half an hour) and return to receive another 30-day visa.

Sixty-day tourist visas can be obtained from the Thai embassy or consulate in your home country prior to arrival. This can be extended for another 30 days for B1,900.

Overstaying your visa can carry a fine of B200 daily, up to a maximum of B20,000.
Thai Immigration Bureau
507 Soi Puan Plu, Thanon Sathorn Tai; tel: 0 2287 3101–10; www.imm.police. go.th; Mon–Fri 8.30am–4.30pm

Etiquette

Thais are remarkably tolerant, but there are a few things that upset them.

Metric to Imperial Conversions	
Metres–Feet 1=3.28	
Kilometres–Miles 1=0.62	
Hectares–Acres 1=2.47	
Kilograms–Pounds 1=2.2	

Left: a Bangkok policeman directing traffic.

unclean. It is thus insulting to touch another person on the head (children are an exception), point one's feet at anything or step over another person. In formal situations, when wishing to pass someone who is seated on the floor, bow slightly while walking and point an arm down to indicate the path to be taken, and a path will be cleared.

PUBLIC BEHAVIOUR

As in many traditional societies, displaying open affection in public, such as kissing, is a sign of bad manners.

Health & Medical Care

Visitors entering Thailand are not required to show evidence of vaccination for smallpox or cholera. Check that your tetanus boosters are up-to-date. Immunisation against cholera is a good idea, as are hepatitis A and B innoculations. Malaria and dengue persist in rural areas but generally not in Bangkok.

It is important to drink plenty of water, and use sunblock as the sun is far more powerful at this latitude than in temperate regions. Tap water in Bangkok has been certified as potable, but bottled water is still safer and is available widely. Within Bangkok, ice is clean and presents no health problems.

HOSPITALS

The hospitals listed also have dental clinics.
Bangkok Christian Hospital
124 Thanon Silom;
tel: 0 2233 6981–9
A medium-sized hospital with high standards.
BNH Hospital
9/1 Thanon Convent;

THE ROYAL FAMILY

Thais have a great reverence for the monarchy, and any slight or disrespect directed towards members of the royal family will be taken very personally. Thailand's lese majeste law is strictly enforced, with jail terms meted out to anyone convicted of defaming, insulting or threatening royalty. At theatres the King's Anthem is played before the movie starts and it is bad manners not to stand up when the others do.

Below: the traditional Thai greeting, *wai*.

TERMS OF ADDRESS

Thais are addressed by their first rather than their last names. The name is usually preceded by the word *khun*, a term of honour, a bit like Mr or Ms. For example, Silpachai Krishnamra would be addressed as Khun Silpachai.

THAI GREETINGS

The common greeting and farewell in Thailand is *sawadee* (followed by *khrap* when spoken by men and *kha* by women). In more formal settings this is accompanied by a *wai* – raising the hands in a prayer-like gesture, the fingertips touching the nose, and bowing the head slightly. However, don't make the mistake of giving a *wai* to hotel staff, children or the people at the corner shop – it embarrasses them. In these cases, a nod is sufficient.

HEAD AND FEET

The Hindu religion, which has had a strong influence on Thai Buddhism, regards the head as the wellspring of wisdom and the feet as

tel: 0 2686 2700;
www.bnhhospital.com
Offers top-notch equipment
and a large team of special-
ists. English is widely spoken.
Bumrungrad Hospital
33 Sukhumvit Soi 3;
tel: 0 2667 1000; www.bum
rungrad.com
This offers a huge range of
specialised clinics, excellent
staff and a selection of rooms
from basic to luxury suites.

MEDICAL CLINICS
British Dispensary
109 Thanon Sukhumvit
(between Soi 3 and 5);
tel: 0 2252 8056
British doctors on its staff
can treat minor problems.
All the major hotels also have
an on-premises clinic or a
doctor on call.

DENTAL CLINICS
Dental Hospital
88/88 Soi 49 Thanon Sukhumvit;
tel: 0 2260 5000–15
With a long-standing good
reputation and has the latest
equipment.

PHARMACIES
Many drugs that would
require a prescription in the
West are available in
Bangkok without a prescription. Purchase them from an
air-conditioned pharmacy
such as Boots and Watson's.

Internet

Wireless surf zones (WiFi)
at the airport, in some hotels
and cafés are a growing
phenomenon. All major
hotels offer Internet services,
though generally more
expensive than Internet
cafés. The latter usually
charge only B30 per hour and
the connections are mostly
good. There are Internet
cafés in the Khao San, Silom
and Ploenchit areas.

Lost Property

Airport
Tel: 0 2535 1254
BMTA City Bus Service
Tel: 0 2246 0973
BTS
Tel: 0 2617 6000
MRT
Tel: 0 2690 8200
**Hualamphong Railway
Station**
Tel: 1690
Taxis
Taxi drivers frequently listen
to two radio stations with
lost-property hotlines: JS100
Radio 100FM, hotline: 1137;
Community Radio 96FM,
hotline: 1677

Money

ATMS
ATMs are available 24 hours
at banks, malls, major train
and bus stations, and the
airports. Many of them

accept credit cards and
MasterCard and Visa
Debit Cards.

CURRENCY
The *baht* is the principal Thai
monetary unit. Banknote
denominations include 1,000
(light brown), 500 (purple),
100 (red), 50 (blue) and 20
(green). There is a 10-baht
coin (brass centre with silver
rim), a 5-baht coin (silver with
copper edge), a 1-baht coin
(silver), and two small coins
of 50 and 25 *satang* (both
brass-coloured).

CHANGING MONEY
Banking hours are Mon–Fri
9.30am–3.30pm, but nearly
every bank maintains
money-changing kiosks in
tourist areas. Hotels generally
give poorer exchange rates
than banks.

CREDIT CARDS
Credit cards can be used to
draw emergency cash at
most banks. If you lose your
credit card, call:
American Express
Tel: 0 2273 5222
Diner's Club
Tel: 0 2238 3660
Visa
Tel: 0 2273 7449
MasterCard
Tel: 0 2260 8572

TRAVELLERS' CHEQUES
Travellers' cheques can be
cashed at all exchange
kiosks and banks. There is
nominal charge of B25 for
each cheque cashed.

Postal Services

General Post Office
Thanon Charoen Krung,
tel: 0 2233 1050; Mon–Fri
8am–8pm, and Sat, Sun and
holidays 8am–1pm
Post offices elsewhere in
Bangkok usually open
8am–4pm on weekdays.

Below: Internet cafés are widely found in the Khao San area.

Left: Thai currency.

Thailand is 8 hours ahead of GMT and does not observe daylight savings time.

Kiosks along some streets sell stamps and also ship small parcels.

COURIER SERVICES
DHL
Tel: 0 2345 5000; www.dhl.co.th
Fedex
Tel: 0 2229 8800;
www.fedex.com/th
UPS
Tel: 0 2712 3300;
www.ups.com/th

Taxes

Thailand has a Value-Added Tax (VAT) of 7 percent. This is added on to most goods and services (but not goods sold by street vendors and in markets). You can get the VAT refunded if you buy goods from stores displaying the 'VAT Refund for Tourists' sign. Refunds can only be claimed

Below: postal box.

on single purchases of B2,000 or more, with a minimum overall expenditure of B5,000, at the airport. See the **Revenue Department** website (www.rd.go.th) for more details.

All major hotels add a 10 percent tax plus an 8 percent service charge to the room rate. At top-class restaurants, a 10 percent service charge is added to the bill.

Telephones
PUBLIC PHONES
Public telephones accept B1, B5 and B10 coins. Phone cards for local calls in denominations of B50, B100 and B200 can be purchased at convenience shops.

LOCAL CALLS
The prefix 0 must be dialled for all calls made within Thailand, even when calling local numbers within Bangkok. For local directory assistance, dial 1133. Any local number that begins with the prefix 08 is a mobile number.

INTERNATIONAL CALLS
The country code for Thailand is 66. When calling Thailand from overseas, dial your local international access code, followed by 66 and the 8-digit number (without the preceding 0) in Thailand. To make an international call from Thailand, dial 001 or 009 before the country and area codes

followed by the telephone number. For international call assistance, dial 100.

Prepaid international phone cards (called Thaicard), with values of B300, B500 and B1,000, can be used to make international calls. These are available at post offices and shops that carry the Thaicard sign.

MOBILE PHONES
Only users of GSM 900 or GSM 1800 mobile phones with international roaming facility can hook up automatically to the local Thai networks. If you're planning to travel in Thailand for any length of time, it's more economical to buy a local SIM card, for which you get a local number.

Tipping
Tipping is not a custom in Thailand, but do leave a small tip when service charge has not been included. There's no need to tip taxi or tuk-tuk drivers unless the traffic has been particularly bad and they have been especially patient.

Tourist Information
Tourism Authority of Thailand (TAT) Call Centre
Tel: 1672; daily 8am–8pm
TAT Main Office
1600 Thanon Phetchaburi, Makkasan; tel: 0 2250 5500; www.tourismthailand.org; daily 8.30am–4.30pm
TAT Information Counters
Suvarnabhumi Airport Arrival Hall; tel: 0 2132 1888; daily 8am–10pm; 4 Thanon Ratchadamnoen Nok; tel: 0 2283 1500, ext. 1620; daily 8.30am–4.30pm

Fashion

Thai craftsmanship and creativity extend far beyond the realm of the traditional, and Bangkok is fast becoming a hub for cutting-edge design. Bargain clothing and fake merchandise aside, Bangkok has evolved into a serious fashion centre in the region. Some talented young designers have made headlines and proven they are here to stay, and have set up voguish boutiques to showcase their unique collections. And if you get bored of the city's seemingly limitless supply of department stores and malls, there are also eclectic boutiques with vintage designs and funky fashions, as well as tailors for bespoke creations.

Contemporary Fashion

Thais follow fashion trends closely and are quick to copy the latest collections from foreign design houses and flog them at a fraction of the cost. The only downside is they fit the Thai physique, which is small and slim. There aren't any international Thai fashion houses but labels such as Fly Now and Greyhound are making inroads.

Fly Now

2/F, Gaysorn Plaza, Thanon Ploenchit; tel: 0 2656 1359; BTS: Chit Lom; map p.141 C4

One of the country's few homegrown fashion labels to grace the world's catwalks. Fly Now creates classic but modern outfits for women alongside accessories like bags, belts and shoes.

Greyhound

2/F, Emporium, Sukhumit Soi 24; tel: 0 2664 8664; www.grey hound.co.th; BTS: Phrom Phong; map p.18

This trendy fashion label, self-described as 'chic and simple', has three sub-brands: Greyhound Original, Playhound and Grey. It has 15 branches and seven restaurants and café outlets around Bangkok, as well as outlets in other Asian cities such as Manila and Taipei.

Inspired by Inner Complexity

235/3 Sukhumvit Soi 31; tel: 0 2258 4488; BTS: Asok or MRT: Sukhumvit; map p.18

This place has a tearoom downstairs, and a boutique featuring hip streetwear and accessories upstairs. The brand is created by two graduates of New York's famous Parsons School of Design. Clients include local celebrities and the well-heeled.

It Happened to Be a Closet

266/3 Soi 3 Siam Square, Thanon Rama I; tel: 0 2658 4696; BTS: Siam; map p.140 B4

This boutique mainly stocks one-of-a-kind vintage women's clothes made with antique fabrics scoured from around Asia, plus accessories designed by Siriwan Tharananithikul, a graduate of Brooklyn's Pratt Institute.

Jaspal

2/F, Siam Centre, Thanon Rama I; tel: 0 2251 5918; www.jaspal.com; BTS: Siam; map p.140 B4

Below: a fine example of Thai fashion design.

Left: trendy retail shop in downtown Bangkok.

Mae Fah Luang Foundation

4/F, Siam Discovery Centre, Thanon Rama I; tel: 0 2658 0424–5; www.doitung.org; BTS: Siam; map p.140 B4

A royal initiative to promote the livelihood of Thai villagers through traditional means; it has been credited for its traditional weaves infused with a funky sense of the contemporary. Handwoven silks and cottons in lengths or ready made into cushion covers and clothes.

Tailors

Bangkok's excellent tailors can whip up perfectly fitting three-piece suits for men and elegant dresses with appliqué and beadwork for women. Some shops offer a 24-hour service, but it's always best to return for at least one fitting.

Embassy Fashion House

57/6–7 Thanon Withayu; tel: 0 2251 2620; BTS: Phloen Chit; map p.141 D4

This place stands out for its relaxed service and wide range of local and imported fabrics. Staff from nearby embassies patronise it, and many big-name hotels recommend it too.

Below: a display of silk fabrics.

The annual Bangkok International Fashion Week promotes local fashion designers and helps them carve a spot on the global stage. Catwalks are erected at Siam Paragon mall and the event features creations by local designers and international brands.

Stylish local fashion chain with branches in most shopping malls. Japal's designs are influenced by British and European style trends. Unlike most Thai labels, which can only fit small and slim physiques, Jaspal has sizes that go up to XL.

Textiles

The glamour of Thai silk was first recognised in the late 1940s by American entrepreneur Jim Thompson, who successfully promoted it abroad. Today, silk has become a major Thai industry.

Also worth buying is *mudmee*, a northeastern silk characterised by subtle zigzagging lines and in more sombre hues such as dark blue, maroon and deep yellow. Dazzling embroidery can be found in the modern-day versions of *teen chok* – a method with which women of the ancient Lanna kingdom in northern Thailand symbolically wove their family histories into their sarongs. The country's northern hilltribes each have its own distinctive patchwork and embroidery designs, mainly in bright blue, magenta and yellow.

Almeta Silk

20/3 Sukhumvit Soi 23; tel: 0 2258 4227; BTS: Asok or MRT: Sukhumvit; map p.18

Made-to-order handwoven silk designs in stunning colour combinations that can be turned into home furnishings.

Jim Thompson Thai Silk

9 Thanon Surawong; tel: 0 2632 8100–4; www.jimthompson.com; BTS: Sala Daeng; map p.140 B2; and Jim Thompson Factory Outlet; 153 Sukhumvit Soi 93; tel: 0 2332 6530

This renowned silk company has several branches offering clothing, accessories and home furnishings. The best prices are found at its factory outlet store.

Festivals and Events

If you are lucky (or plan carefully), your visit can coincide with one of Thailand's festivals. Thais celebrate their religious holidays with gusto and invite everyone to join in. In addition to traditional festivals, there are secular events of all sorts, ranging from highbrow arts (such as the International Festival of Music and Dance) to sports (the Bangkok International Motor Show). The dates for these festivals and events change from year to year, so check dates with the Tourism Authority of Thailand (www.tourismthailand.org).

Above: fireworks during King Bhumibol's birthday celebrations.

Public Holidays

1 Jan: New Year's Day
Feb/Mar: Magha Puja
6 Apr: Chakri Day
13–15 Apr: Songkran
1 May: Labour Day
5 May: Coronation Day
May: Visakha Puja
July: Asanha Puja and Khao Pansa
12 Aug: Queen's Birthday
23 Oct: Chulalongkorn Day
5 Dec: King's Birthday
10 Dec: Constitution Day

Festivals and Events

JANUARY/FEBRUARY
Chinese New Year
Chinatown comes alive as the large Thai Chinese community celebrates with firecrackers, lion and dragon dances, and feasting galore.

FEBRUARY/MARCH
Magha Puja
The full moon of the third lunar month marks the gathering of 1,250 disciples to hear the Buddha preach before he entered nirvana. Thais gather at temples for a candle-lit procession with incense and flowers.

APRIL
Chakri Day
Celebrates the founding of the Chakri dynasty (which presently rules Thailand) in 1782. The festivities are confined to the palace. Most Thais celebrate it as a day off from work.
Songkran
During Thailand's official New Year, people wear new clothes and visit temples to offer food to monks. On the afternoon of 13 April, Buddha images are bathed as part of the ceremony. Young people pour scented water into the hands of their elders and parents as a mark of respect and ask for their blessings. People sprinkle water on each other's heads, or get wet and wild on the streets

The Songkran custom of throwing water apparently derived from a rainmaking ceremony. According to myth, *nagas* (mythical serpents) brought rain by spouting water from the seas. The more seawater they spouted, the more rain there would be, which is why, besides good fun, Thai people throw water during this time of the year.

Left: royal guards at the Trooping of the Colours.

Thai monks begin a season of prayers and meditation. Khao Phansa is celebrated immediately after Asanha Puja and marks the start of the annual three-month Rains Retreat. This is when young Buddhist novices are ordained at the temples.

Queen's Birthday

Thais decorate their houses and public buildings with flags and pictures of the queen.

OCTOBER
Ok Phansa

October's full moon marks the end of the three-month Buddhist Lent, and the beginning of the *kathin* season when Buddhists visit temples to present monks with new robes.

Chulalongkorn Day

Honours King Chulalongkorn, who led Thailand into the modern era.

with water pistols, drenching everyone in sight. Sanam Luang is one of the best places to witness the festivities. Nearby Thanon Khao San is a relentless party zone where both Thais and foreigners dance and douse one another with water.

MAY/JUNE
Royal Ploughing Ceremony

Held at Sanam Luang in early May, this Brahman ritual presided over by King Bhumibol marks the official start of the rice-planting season.

Visakha Puja

The most important Buddhist day marking the birth, enlightenment and entry into nirvana of Lord Buddha. Thais visit temples to listen to sermons on Buddha. In the evenings candle-lit processions are held at temples.

JULY/AUGUST
Asanha Puja and Khao Phansa

Celebrated on the full moon night, this marks the day when the Buddha preached to his first five disciples and the beginning of the three-month Buddhist Lent when

NOVEMBER
Loy Krathong

On the full-moon night of November, Thais launch small floats, called *krathongs*, with candles, incense and flowers, into rivers, canals and ponds, asking for blessings from the water spirits. The most beautiful of Thai celebrations, it is best viewed on the banks of the Chao Phraya River.

DECEMBER
Trooping of the Colours (3 Dec)

Amid pomp and ceremony, the royal guards swear allegiance to the royal family outside the old Thai Parliament.

King's Birthday

King Bhumibol's birthday celebrations, with fireworks at night.

Below: revellers get soaking wet during Songkran.

Food and Drink

Thai cuisine is not all about tongue-searing dishes. Although its spiciness initially overwhelms, what's most impressive is the complex balance of flavours that lies underneath. In fact, Thai food is not just blatantly spicy; most meals will include a sampling of less aggressive dishes, some subtly flavoured with only herbs. The variations of food and cooking styles are immense as each of the country's four regions has distinct cuisines of its own. The northeast is influenced by Laos, the south by Malaysia and Indonesia, the central area by the royal kitchens, and the north by Burma and Yunnan.

Northern Cuisine

This is the mildest of Thai cuisine. Northerners generally eat *khao nio* (sticky rice), kneading it into a ball to dip into sauces and curries such as the Burmese *kaeng hanglay*, a sweet and tamarind-sour pork dish.

Other northern Thai specialities include sausages, such as the spicy pork *sai oua* (roasted over a coconut-husk fire to impart aroma and flavour) and *naem* (fermented raw pork and pork skin seasoned with garlic and chilli). *Laab* is a salad dish of minced pork, chicken, beef or fish served with mint leaves and raw vegetables.

Dipping sauces include *nam prik ong* (minced pork, mild chillies, tomatoes, garlic and shrimp paste) and the potent *nam prik noom* (grilled chillies, onions and garlic). Both are eaten with the popular snack called *khaep moo* (crispy pork rind).

Northeastern Cuisine

Northeastern (Isaan) food is simple, generally spicy and eaten with sticky rice kept in

Above: satay is a popular street snack.

bamboo baskets. Dishes include *som tam* (shredded green papaya, garlic, chillies, lime juice, and variations of tomatoes, dried shrimp, preserved crab and fermented fish) and a version of *laab* that is spicier and sourer than the northern version.

The most popular Isaan food is perhaps *gai yang*, chicken grilled in a marinade of peppercorns, garlic, fish sauce, coriander and palm sugar, and served with both hot and sweet dipping sauces.

Southern Cuisine

The south, notable for Thailand's hottest dishes, also

has gentler specialities such as *khao yam*, an innocuous salad of rice, vegetables, pounded dried fish and fish sauce. Slightly spicier are *phad sataw*, a stir-fry usually made with pork or shrimp, and *sataw*, a large lima bean look-alike with a strong flavour and aroma. *Khao moke gai* is roasted chicken with turmeric-seasoned yellow rice, often sprinkled with crispy fried onions.

Spicy dishes include *kaeng tai plaa*. Fishermen who needed food that would last for days at sea are said to have created it by blending the fermented stomachs of

Left: a lavish Thai meal at Sala Rim Naam restaurant.

shells, steamed in a clay pot with lime juice and aromatic herbs).

Meat – usually chicken, pork or beef – is cooked in all manner of styles, such as pork fried with garlic and black pepper (*muu thawd kratiam prik Thai*) or the sweet-and-sour *muu pad prio waan*, probably of Portuguese origin, brought to Thailand by Chinese immigrants. *Neua pad nam man hoi* is a mild, delicate dish of beef fried with oyster sauce, spring onions and mushrooms. The popular and very spicy *pat pet pat bai kaprao* dishes include meat stir-fried with chillies, garlic, onions and holy basil (*bai kaprao*).

Noodles and Rice

Bangkok's ubiquitous street-side noodle shops sell two types: *kuay tiaw*, made from rice flour, and *ba mee*, from wheat flour. Both can be ordered broad (*sen yai*), narrow (*sen lek*) or very narrow (*sen mee*), and with broth (*sai naam*) or without (*haeng*).

Below: Thai red curry.

fish with chillies, bamboo shoots and vegetables together with an intensely hot sauce. Even hotter is *kaeng leuang* (yellow curry), a variant of the central Thai *kaeng som*, with fish, green papaya and bamboo shoots or palm hearts in an explosive sauce.

Central Cuisine

Central cuisine, which has been influenced by the royal kitchens, includes many of the dishes made internationally famous at Thai restaurants abroad. It is notable for the use of coconut milk, which mellows the chilli heat. Trademark dishes include *tom kha gai*, a soup of chicken, coconut milk and galangal, the celebrated hot-and-sour shrimp soup *tom yum goong*, and *kaeng khio waan* (green curry), with chicken or beef, basil leaves and green aubergines. The intricate fruit and vegetable carvings seen at fine Thai restaurants are also a legacy of royal Thai cuisine. Stir-fries and noodle dishes are everywhere, due to the large Chinese presence in the central region.

Common Dishes

Kaeng is usually translated as curry, but it covers a broad range, from thin soups to near-dry dishes like the northern *kaeng ho*. Many *kaeng* are made with coconut cream, like the spicy red curry (*kaeng pet*) and *kaeng mussaman*, a rich, sweetish dish of Persian origin with meat, potatoes and onions.

Fish and seafood have largely featured in Thai cooking since ancient times. *Haw mok talay* is mixed seafood in a curried coconut custard and steamed in a banana-leaf cup or coconut shell. Other delicious choices to try are *poo pat pong karee* (steamed chunks of crab in an egg-thickened curry sauce with crunchy spring onion) and *hoi malaeng poo op maw din* (mussels in their

---

The small but very fiery Thai chillis (*prik*) come in red or green forms but both pack a potent punch. When sliced and served in fish sauce (*nam pla*) as a condiment, it's called *prik nam pla*.

Common dishes are *kuay tiaw raad naa* (rice noodles flash-fried and topped with sliced meat and greens in a thick, mild sauce) and *paad thai* (narrow pan-fried rice noodles with egg, dried and fresh shrimp, spring onions, tofu, crushed peanuts and bean sprouts). In *mee krawp*, the rice noodles are fried crispy, tossed in sweet-and-sour sauce and topped with sliced chillies, pickled garlic and slivers of orange rind.

Fusion Cuisine

There have been foreign influences in Thai food for centuries. Even chilli is a Portuguese import. Recent years have seen the growth of a dedicated style of Thai-fusion dishes. It often takes the form of Italian-Thai blends, such as Thai-style spaghetti with anchovies and chilli, served at modern cafés like Greyhound (several branches in the city).

Other modern Thai restaurants use non-traditional ingredients like lamb and salmon, and plate their essentially Thai dishes Western style. When the international Thai restaurant chain The Blue Elephant opened a Bangkok branch in 2002, it introduced several fusion items, including salmon *laab* and foie gras with tamarind. Many international restaurants – notably Jester's and Bed Supperclub – also incorporate Thai flavours like lemon grass and galangal into their East-West menus.

Thai-Chinese Cuisine

Many ethnic Chinese in Thailand still speak the Teochew dialect of their southern Chinese ancestry, and most Chinese restaurants serve Teochew fare,

Above: Thai desserts.

such as the famous goose feet cooked in soy sauce.

Desserts

In Bangkok, *khanom* (desserts) come in a bewildering variety, from light concoctions with crushed ice and syrup, to custards, ice creams and little cakes, and an entire category based on egg yolks cooked in flower-scented syrups.

Generally light and elegant popular treats include *kluay buat chee* (banana slices in sweetened and salted warm coconut cream) and *kluay kaek* (bananas sliced lengthwise, dipped in coconut cream and rice flour, and deep-fried until crisp). Another favourite is *taap tim krawp* (water chestnut pieces covered in red-dyed tapioca flour and served in coconut

cream and crushed ice), and *sangkhaya ma-praoawn*, a coconut cream custard steamed in a young coconut or a small pumpkin.

Look out for market vendors who sell 'rooftile cookies' (*khanom beuang*), crispy shells filled with strands of egg yolk cooked in syrup with shredded coconut, sweet and spicy dried shrimp, coriander and coconut cream. And don't miss the heavenly *khao niao ma-muand* (mango with sticky rice and coconut cream).

Refreshments

Thais drink locally brewed beers such as Singha, Kloster and the stronger Beer Chang. Foreign brands brewed on licence include Heineken. The middle-class obsession with French wines is waning, and there is now a decent selection available from the New World. Rice whisky brands Maekhong and Saeng Thip are popular, usually served as a set with ice, soda and lime. Note: fresh fruit and ice drinks often get a splash of syrup (and salt) unless you request otherwise.

> Thailand has its own special coffee made with a thick black melange of coffee, tamarind, and heaps of sweetened condensed milk. It is strong enough to set a dead person's heart palpitating. Thai ice tea is an orange-coloured concoction usually served with lashings of condensed milk.

Cookery Schools

Blue Elephant Cookery School

Blue Elephant Restaurant, 233 Thanon Sathorn; tel: 0 2673 9353; www.blueelephant.com/bangkok; BTS: Surasak; map p.16

Half-day hands-on sessions at the Blue Elephant Restaurant located in a restored mansion. The class begins with a trip to a local market in the morning. Thereafter, you will be taught four popular Thai dishes. This is followed by a lunch.

Oriental Thai Cooking School

The Oriental, 48 Oriental Avenue; tel: 0 2659 0000; www.mandarinoriental.com; pier: Oriental; map p.139 E1

Participants can choose to attend any of the hands-on classes held from Monday to Saturday. The menu (four dishes, including a dessert) for each day is different. The sessions are pricey, but they provide fascinating insights into Thai gastronomy.

Thai House

32/4 Moo 8, Tambol Bangmaung, Amphoe Bangyai, Nonthaburi; tel: 0 2903 9611, 2997 5161; www.thaihouse.co.th/thai_cuisine.html; map p.20

Combines Thai cookery lessons with a stay in a rustic Thai-style house in the suburb of Nonthaburi; one-, two- and three-day courses are available with meals and lodging included.

Wandee Thai Cooking School

294/16–17 Thanon Pradiphat, Samsean Nai, Phaya Thai; tel: 0 2279 9844–5, 0 2279 2204; www.wandeethaicooking.com; BTS: Saphan Kwai

Established in 1993 by Professor Wandee Na-songkhla, this is the first Thai cooking school accredited and approved by the Ministry of Education. Rustle up authentic Thai dishes and desserts and try your hand at fruit and vegetable carving.

Patisseries and Gourmet Food Shops

Gourmet Market

Siam Paragon, 991/1 Thanon Rama I; tel: 0 2610 9000; BTS: Siam; map p.140 B4; Emporium, 662 Thanon Sukhumvit; tel: 0 2269 1000; BTS: Phrom Phong; map p.18

There's a massive selection of local and imported products in this impressively laid-out supermarket.

The fresh-food section is especially appealing.

iberry

99/356 President Park, Sukhumvit Soi 24; tel: 0 2262 9473; www.iberryhomemade.com; BTS: Asok or MRT: Sukhumvit; map p.18

The first premium ice cream store in Thailand, established by two siblings. The home-made ice creams and sorbets come in about 100 flavours, including some featuring Japanese and Thai ingredients. (Other branches: Siam Square Soi 2, tel: 0 2658 3829; Sukhumvit Soi 55 (Soi Thonglor), J Avenue, tel: 0 2712 6054; and Central Chidlom, tel: 0 2655 0455)

Le Gourmet

Sukhumvit Soi 33/1; tel: 0 2258 5048; BTS: Phrom Phong; map p.18

Chocolates, pastries, French wines and a variety of lovely teas served in a charming setting. Le Gourmet also has another outlet in Siam Paragon and a counter at Emporium.

Lenôtre

61 Thanon Lang Suan; tel: 0 2250 7050–1; www.lenotre.fr; BTS: Chit Lom; map p.141 C3

This well-known Parisian patisserie is the ultimate place to tuck into beautifully crafted French-style cakes, éclairs, tarts and macarons. It also has counters in Emporium and Siam Paragon.

The Oriental Shop

The Oriental, 48 Oriental Avenue; tel: 0 2659 9000; pier: Oriental; map p.139 E1

This gourmet haven has a range of exquisite cakes, pastries, chocolates, ice creams and sorbets, as well as delicate Marriage Freres teas from France. Other branches are located in Central Chidlom, Central World and Siam Paragon.

Below: a cooking class at the Oriental Thai Cooking School.

Gay and Lesbian

The gay and lesbian nightlife scene in Bangkok is thriving. This is no wonder since Thailand is one of the most tolerant countries in the world. Thais are open-minded and understanding towards homosexuality and transvestism, and the country's gays and *katoeys* ('lady boys'), who are generally addressed as women, are largely accepted. The city even celebrates with the Bangkok Gay Pride Festival every November. However, as in many traditional societies, displaying open affection in public is considered bad manners, so it should be kept to a bare minimum.

Above: a Gay Pride parade participant makes a statement with a 'condom hat'.

Gay Neighbourhoods

Gay clubs and bars around Silom Soi 2 and Soi 4 cater to a variety of gay tastes. Soi 2 is exclusively gay, while Soi 4 is more of a free-for-all, its streetside tables hosting people of varying sexual inclinations blatantly ogling passers-by. Gay sex shows and sleazy gay pick-up joints with go-go boys are located around Thanon Surawong, particularly on Soi Tawan and Duangthawee Plaza. The lesbian scene is subtler; the action concentrates in only a few restaurants and pubs.

Gay Venues

@Richard's Pub & Restaurant
60/17 Silom Soi 2/1; tel: 0 2234 0459; www.richards-bangkok. com; daily 6pm–2am; BTS: Sala Daeng; map p.140 B2
A quiet, cosy pub dishing up 70s music as well as Thai and Western food, including steaks, pastas and sandwiches.

70's Bar
231 Thanon Sarasin; tel: 0 2253 4433; www.70sbar.com; BTS: Ratchadamri or MRT: Silom; map p.140 C3
Very busy men-only retro-chic venue packed wall-to-wall on most weekends with a young crowd moving to thumping rock and pop.

Babylon
34 Soi Nantha, Thanon Sathorn Soi 1; tel: 0 2679 7984–5; www.babylonbangkok.com; MRT: Lumphini; map p.141 C1
Not quite a nightlife spot but legendary as a gay meeting place. This all-in-one complex has accommodation (bed and breakfast), a gym, sauna, massage, hi-speed and WiFi Internet acess, a restaurant and café, as well as a swimming pool. It also has an ongoing schedule of themed entertainment and party nights. Live jazz every Friday and Saturday nights.

Balcony
86–88 Silom Soi 4; tel: 0 2235 5891; www.balconypub.com; daily 5.30pm–2am; BTS: Sala Daeng; map p.140 B2
Longstanding bar with a lively party crowd who spill out onto the street. Watch from the bar area upstairs or try your hand at karaoke. The regular cabaret nights are wildly popular. It's lesbian-friendly, too.

Boy's Bangkok
894/11–13 Soi Pratuchai, Duangthawee Plaza; tel: 0 2237

The city hosts the annual Bangkok Gay Pride Festival (www.bangkokpride.org) in November, a year-end climax of parades and celebration around the Silom-Patpong area. A similar one takes place in Pattaya in December (www.pattayagayfestival.com).

Left: drag queens get all dressed up for the Gay Pride parade.

Useful websites with listings and tips: www.utopia-asia.com; www.bangkoklesbian.com

Lesla, a lesbian community, at the Chit Chat Pub, a huge, cavernous beer hall out in the city's northern outskirts.
Shela
106 Soi Lang Suan; tel: 0 2254 6463; www.shela corner.com; daily 7pm–late; BTS: Ratchadamri or MRT: Silom; map p.141 C3
Located near Lumphini Park, this cosy all-girl restaurant and pub attracts sophisticated lesbians in their 30s, with great cocktails to go with some fabulous Thai food. Local bands perform and a pool table adds further interest.
Zeta
29/67–69 Soi Soonvijai, Thanon Rama IX; tel: 0 2203 0994; www.zetabangkok.com; daily 10pm–2pm; MRT: Phetchaburi
Younger, trendy 20-something lesbians are the main patrons of this chic girls-only outlet. A house band entertains with Thai and Western rock and pop.

Tours
Kinara Tours
SM Elite Co Ltd, 7/9 Thanon Yen Akat, Chong Nonsi; tel: 0 2671 3863; www.gaykinnara.com
There's a 'straight' Kinara Tours and a gay one. The latter offers packages that include tours of gay neighbourhoods in Bangkok.
Purple Dragon
Tarntawan Place Hotel, 119/5–10 Thanon Surawong; tel: 0 2634 3186; www.purpledrag.com
A Utopia-affliated travel agency that caters exclusively for gay travellers.

2006; daily 8pm–1am; BTS: Sala Daeng; map p.140 B2
One of the better gay go-go bars on a strip of several such places.
DJ Station
8/6–8 Silom Soi 2; tel: 0 2266 4029; www.dj-station.com; open till 2am; BTS: Sala Daeng; map p.140 B2
Bangkok's most popular gay club, packed throughout the night. The atmosphere is electric and patrons often dress outrageously, especially on theme nights. The age requirement to enter is 20 years old; bring your passport or ID.
Dick's Café
894/7–8 Soi Pratuchai, Duangthawee Plaza; tel: 0 2637 0078; www.dickscafe.com; daily 11am–2am; BTS: Sala Daeng; map p.140 B2
Taped jazz music and an exhibit of paintings by local artists create a mellow mood. At this great place to unwind. Thai and Western fare is offered from breakfast till supper.
Sphinx
100 Silom Soi 4; tel: 0 2234 7249; www.sphinxpub.com;

daily 6pm–1am; BTS: Sala Daeng; map p.140 B2
Friendly gay outfit with an extensive outside terrace area, indoor dining section and a large horse-shoe-shaped bar. The restaurant offers excellent regional Thai and international fare. Head upstairs for a karaoke session after your meal.
Telephone Pub
114/11-13 Silom Soi 4; tel: 0 2234 3279; www.telephone pub.com; daily 6pm–1am; BTS: Sala Daeng; map p.140 B2
Popular wth expats and locals, this is Bangkok's original gay pub and restaurant, established in 1987. Food and drink prices are affordable and the scene is lively. Chat (or flirt) with someone using the internal phones – simply dial an extension.

Lesbian Venues
Lesla
Chit Chat Pub, Choke Chai 4 Soi 85, Thanon Lad Prao; tel: 0 2618 7191–2; www.lesla.com; Sat 7pm–1am; MRT: Lat Phrao
The biggest lesbian party in Bangkok is organised by

History

3600–250 BC
The culture of Ban Chiang, a Bronze Age settlement known for its pottery, flourishes in northeastern Thailand.

250 BC
Trading with India begins.

4TH–8TH CENTURIES
Influence of Mon and Khmer empires spreads into Thailand.

9TH–13TH CENTURIES
The Khmer empire is founded in Angkor. Thai people migrate south from Yunnan province in China into northern Thailand. Lopburi becomes an important provincial capital in the Khmer empire and later tries to become independent.

1238
Khmer power wanes. King Intradit founds the kingdom of Sukhothai.

1277–1318
Reign of Ramkamhaeng in Sukhothai. Often called Thailand's 'Golden Age', the period saw the first attempts to unify the Thai people, the first use of Thai script, and the flourishing of the arts.

1281
The Chiang Saen kingdom is founded in the north.

1296
The Lanna kingdom is founded in Chiang Mai. King Mengrai controls much of northern Thailand and Laos.

1318–47
King Lo Thai reigns in Sukhothai. The slow decline of the Sukhothai kingdom begins.

1438
Sukhothai is now virtually deserted. The power shifts to Ayutthaya to the south and along the Chao Phraya River.

14TH CENTURY
The area around Ayutthaya is settled by representatives of the Chiang Saen kingdom.

1350
The city of Ayutthaya is founded by Phya U-Thong, who proclaims himself Ramathibodi I. Within a few years he controls the areas belonging to the Sukhothai kingdom and the Khmer empire.

1369
Ramesuen, son of Ramathibodi, becomes king.

1390
Ramesuen captures Chiang Mai.

1393
Ramesuen seizes Angkor, the base of the Khmer empire, in Cambodia.

1448–88
Reign of King Trailok, who finally unites the Lanna and Ayutthaya kingdoms.

1491–1529
Reign of King Ramathibodi II.

1549
First major war with the Mon kingdom of Bago.

1569

The Burmese seize and destroy Ayutthaya.

1584

Naresuen declares the independence of Siam.

1590

Naresuen becomes king and defeats the Burmese. Ayutthaya expands rapidly at the expense of the Burmese and Khmer empires and flourishes as a major city. Although the Thais are responsible for the decline and eventual collapse of the Angkor empire, the Ayutthayan kings adopt Khmer cultural and artistic influences from the very beginning.

1605–10

Ekatotsarot reigns and begins significant economic ties with Europeans.

1610–28

Reign of King Songtham. The British arrive and obtain land for a trading factory.

1628–55

Reign of King Prasat Thong. Trading concessions expand and regular trade with China and Europe is established.

1656–88

Reign of King Narai. British influence expands. The reputation of Ayutthaya as a magnificent city and a remarkable royal court spreads in Europe.

1678

Constantine Phaulkon arrives at King Narai's court and gains great influence; French presence expands.

1688

King Narai dies; Phaulkon is executed.

1733–58

Reign of King Boromakot. Ayutthaya enters a period of peace; the arts and literature flourish.

1767

Burmese King Alaungpaya captures and sacks Ayutthaya, destroying four centuries of Thai civilisation. Seven months later General Phya Taksin returns and expels the Burmese. He moves the capital from Ayutthaya to Thonburi, near Bangkok.

1767

Phya Taksin is crowned as King Taksin.

1779

Generals Chao Phya Chakri and his brother Chao Phya Surasi conquer Chiang Mai, expel the Burmese from what is now Thailand and take control of most of the Khmer and Lao kingdoms. The statue of the Emerald Buddha is brought from Vientiane, Laos, to Thonburi.

1782

The erratic Taksin is deposed and executed. Chao Phya Chakri ascends the throne, founding the Chakri dynasty and assuming the name Ramathibodi (later Rama I). The capital is moved to what is now known as Bangkok. Siam consolidates and expands its strength. King Rama I revives Thai art, religion and culture. Work begins on the Grand Palace and Wat Phra Kaew in Bangkok.

1809–24

Reign of King Rama II, who is best known for the construction of Wat Arun and many other temples. Rama II reopens relations with the West, suspended since the time of King Narai.

1824–51

Reign of King Rama III, who continues the open-door policy with foreigners. He encourages American missionaries to introduce Western medicine to Siam.

1851

King Mongkut (Rama IV) ascends the throne. Before becoming king, he spends 27 years as a monk, studying Western science. He is the first Thai king to understand Western culture and technology, and his reign has been described as the bridge spanning the new and the old.

55

1868

King Chulalongkorn (Rama V) ascends the throne, reigning for the next four decades, the second-longest reign of any Thai king.

He ends the custom of prostration in royal presence, abolishes slavery, and modernises schools, infrastructure, the military and the government. He also preserves the sovereignty of Siam, the only Southeast Asian country to escape colonisation.

1910–25

Reign of King Vajiravudh (Rama VI). The Oxford-educated and Westernised king makes Thais adopt surnames.

1925–35

Reign of King Prajadhipok (Rama VII). Economic pressures as a result of the Great Depression rouse discontent among Thais.

1932

A coup ends the absolute monarchy and ushers in a constitutional monarchy. King Prajadhipok accepts the provisional constitution by which he 'ceases to rule but continues to reign'.

1935

Dismayed by quarrels in the new government, King Prajadhipok abdicates. Ananda Mahidol (Rama VIII) succeeds as king.

1939

Siam's name is officially changed to Thailand, the 'Land of the Free'.

1941

Japan invades Thailand with the acquiescence of the military government, but a resistance movement thrives.

1946

King Ananda is killed by a gunman. King Bhumibol Adulyadej (Rama IX), his younger brother, ascends the throne.

1950–72

The 1950s is a time of turmoil, with many coups and a succession of military-backed governments. In the 1960s Thailand experiences an economic boom as a result of investments from the US.

1973–91

Bloody clashes between the army and students bring down the military government in 1973; political and economic blunders cause the subsequent civilian government to collapse three years later. Various military-backed and civilian governments come and go over the next 20 years.

1992

Another clash between military forces and civilian demonstrators results in the military leaving the government to civilian politicians. A new democratic government under Chuan Leekpai is elected. Thailand begins five years of unprecedented economic growth.

1996

King Bhumibol celebrates his Golden Jubilee of 50 years on the throne.

1997

Thailand's economy begins a free fall as the baht loses half of its value. This marks the start of the Asian economic crisis.

1998

Thailand follows guidelines established by the International Monetary Fund to resuscitate its economy. Chuan Leekpai returns as the prime minister.

1999

The government institutes legal and economic reforms. Thailand's economy returns to growth.

2000

Senators for the Upper House are democratically elected for the first time under a more liberal constitution issued in 1997. It is popularly called the 'people's constitution'.

2001

Populist leader Thaksin Shinawatra and his Thai Rak Thai (TRT) party win the national polls for the Lower House. Thaksin is elected as the prime minister.

2002

Unhappy with Thaksin's hardline policies in the south, Thai Muslim nationalists step up terrorist operations in Yala, Pattani and Narathiwat provinces.

2004

A tsunami generated by an earthquake in the Indian Ocean, measuring 9.0 on the Richter scale, causes widespread devastation and claims 8,000 lives along the Andaman coast.

2005

Thaksin's administration becomes the first Thai government in history to be re-elected to a consecutive second term in the February elections.

2006

King Bhumibol celebrates his 60th year of reign. He is the longest-reigning monarch in Thailand's history and in the world.

2006

Mass demonstrations rock Bangkok after Thaksin's family sells its shares of Shin Corp telecommunications firm to a Singapore investor for US$1.9 billion, tax free. Thaksin dissolves the National Assembly and holds elections, but a boycott by the opposition forces his demotion to caretaker premier. On 19 September the Royal Thai Army, led by General Sonthi Boonyaratglin, stages a bloodless coup, deposing Thaksin. Retired general Surayud Chulanont is appointed as the interim premier.

2007

Thais protest against the military's rule. Nine bombs explode in Bangkok on New Year's Eve and Day in apparent opposition. In August the majority of the Thai electorate vote in favour of a new constitution drafted by the military-led government in the nation's first-ever referendum. The junta sets 23 December as election day.

57

Hotels

Hotels in Bangkok, with their first-rate service and complete range of facilities, are among the best in the world. The Oriental has consistently been rated as one of the world's best, but nipping at its heels are the top-class Peninsula, Shangri-La and Sukhothai hotels. Many moderately priced hotels in Bangkok would be considered first class in Europe, and even budget hotels invariably have a swimming pool and at least one decent food outlet. Those on a tight budget will find numerous guesthouses offering decent accommodation, many with air conditioning and en-suite bathrooms.

Hotel Areas

Downtown Bangkok has the largest number of hotels and is the most convenient for getting around on the BTS (Skytrain) and underground MRT (metro) system. The prime shopping and entertainment area around Pathumwan and Pratunam is home to several mid- to upper-end hotels. The area around Chitlom and Ploenchit has some high-end chains, as do Silom and Sathorn, with the latter street featuring a cache of chic designer hotels. Heading east along the BTS line, Thanon Sukhumvit has numerous mid-range accommodation and is packed with dining, drinking and shopping options.

Further west to the Chao Phraya River, near Saphan Taksin BTS station (close to

Sathorn pier), is where many of city's most luxurious hotels are located on both sides of the river. The area north along the river towards Chinatown makes for an interesting cultural experience, though hotels tend to be faceless and traffic is horrendous.

Access to the Rattanakosin and the Old City areas is easiest from the backpacking enclave of Thanon Khao San and Banglamphu. Accommodation options here are principally budget guesthouses, once of primary interest only to backpackers because of their sparse facilities. In recent times, many have been upgraded to include air conditioning and en-suite bathrooms. New mid-range boutique inns and lodges have also opened for business in these areas.

Rattanakosin

Arun Residence

38 Soi Pratu Nok Yoong; tel: 0 2221 9158; www.arun residence.com; $$; BTS: Saphan Taksin; pier: Tha Tien; map p.138 B4

This tiny boutique hotel housed in an old Sino-Portuguese mansion along a residential street just off Thanon Maharat is a gem of a find. One side of it perches on the bank of the Chao Phraya River and offers views of Wat Arun. Its French-Thai restaurant, Deck, is the perfect place for cocktails and dinner.

Chakrabongse Villa

396 Thanon Maharat; tel: 0 2225 0139; www.thaivillas.com; $$$; BTS: Saphan Taksin; pier: Tha Tien; map p.138 B4

Only a short walk to the Grand Palace, this is a unique

Below: Bangkok Marriott overlooks the Chao Phraya River.

Price categories for a double room without breakfast and taxes:
$$$$ = over B8,000
$$$ = B4,000–8,000
$$ = B2,000–4,000
$ = under B2,000

Left: The Shangri-La's Riverside Lounge.

peninsula.com; $$$$; BTS: Saphan Taksin; map p.139 D1
This hotel – reputed to be one of the finest in the world – has the city's nicest river views. Stylishly contemporary but still Asian in character, it has some of the best dining options in the city, plus impeccable service. Free shuttle boat service to Sathorn Pier opposite and the Saphan Taksin BTS station.

The Old City and Dusit

Buddy Lodge
265 Thanon Khao San; tel: 0 2629 4477; www.buddylodge.com; $$; pier: Phra Athit; map p.134 C2
Khao San's best hotel has a rooftop swimming pool and even a well-run spa. The original Buddy Guesthouse was an institution in Khao San; its owner, whose business has taken off, now owns half of the entertainment in the area. From the outside, the brick building resembles a European municipal hall, though with a McDonald's downstairs.

D&D Inn
68–70 Thanon Khao San; tel: 0 2629 0526–8; www.khaosanby.com; $; pier: Phra Athit; map p.134 B2

Advanced hotel bookings are advised for the Christmas, New Year and Chinese New Year holidays, and for the Songkran festival in mid April.

---

early-20th-century residence. Book early, as there are only three villas, each designed in traditional Thai style: the Garden Suite, Riverview and Thai House. Beautiful gardens, a swimming pool and superb views of Wat Arun opposite add to its appeal.

Thonburi

Bangkok Marriott Resort & Spa
257 Thanon Charoen Nakhon; tel: 0 2476 0022; www.marriott hotels.com; $$$; BTS: Saphan Taksin; shuttle boat from Saphan Taksin pier; map p.139 D1
Lush grounds and a river-fronting pool make this resort a relaxing escape from the frenetic city. It is self-contained with six restaurants, three bars and the Mandara Spa. Its **Riverside Terrace** has nightly Thai dance-drama performances with dinner.
SEE ALSO DANCE AND THEATRE, P.37

Millennium Hilton Bangkok
123 Thanon Charoen Nakhon; tel: 0 2442 2000; www.bangkok. hilton.com; $$$; BTS: Saphan Taksin; pier: Hilton; map p.139 D2
The swish Hilton has a stylish modern Asian interior designed by Tony Chi. All rooms have expansive windows with river views and the pool has a resort feel. Spa, four restaurants and two bars, plus a complimentary shuttle boat service to the Bangkok side.

The Peninsula Bangkok
333 Thanon Charoen Nakhon; tel: 0 2861 2888; www.

Below: deluxe rooms at The Peninsula offer expansive city views.

59

Left: the glass-fronted InterContinental Bangkok.

swimming pool and three restaurants. It offers good value for the rates it charges.

Shanghai Inn
479–481 Thanon Yaowarat; tel: 0 2678 0101; www.shang hai-inn.com; $$; MRT: Hualamphong; map p.139 D4

A classy boutique hotel in a part of town often written off as lacking in any decent lodgings. The rooms have lovely over-the-top chinoiserie, four-poster beds and vibrant, saturated hues. Free Internet access and a spa on site.

Pathumwan and Pratunam

Amari Watergate
847 Thanon Phetchaburi; tel: 0 2653 9000–19; www. amari.com/watergate; $$$; BTS: Ratchathewi or Phaya Thai; map p.136 C1

This large tower doesn't look at all inspiring, but the hotel does have excellent facilities, including a great gym, the basement Americana bar and grill Henry J. Beans, and a Sivara Spa. Located just across the Pratunam Market and the shopping district around Central World.

A-One Inn
13–15 Soi Kasemsan 1, Thanon Rama I; tel: 0 2215 3029; www.aoneinn.com; $; BTS: National Stadium; map p.136 B1

The narrow lane on which this budget accommodation is located has become a downtown bargain-hotel area. Located beside Siam Square, this offers spacious rooms with all the mod cons and friendly service. With its many repeat visitors it can be difficult to get a room.

Asia
296 Thanon Phaya Thai; tel: 0 2215 0808;

Right in the middle of Khao San, this competent budget hotel offers a rooftop swimming pool, bar and an open pavilion for traditional massage. Rooms are well equipped with bathrooms, air conditioning, TV, fridge and IDD phone.

Khao San Palace
139 Thanon Khao San; tel: 0 2282 0578; $; pier: Phra Athit; map p.134 B2

Among the better guesthouses here, this is just off Khao San down a small alley. Stay in the newer annexe as the original section looks far tattier. Clean rooms, en-suite showers, air conditioning and TV.

My House
37 Soi Chanasongkram; tel: 0 2282 9263–4; $; pier: Phra Athit; map p.134 B3

The rooms are fairly basic but still comfortable. The main draw is its location on a quieter lane away from Khao San with Wat Chanasongkram right across. The restaurant-TV room-lounge area out front is a great place to perch and watch life pass by in backpacker land.

Peachy Guest House
10 Thanon Phra Athit; tel: 0 2281 6471; $; pier: Phra Athit; map p.134 B2

A real atmospheric find, this good-value guesthouse occupies a converted school with more old-world charm than most of Khao San's concrete box digs. The rooms are basic but comfortable with most rooms facing the pleasant garden. A short walk to Khao San, but still removed from all the mayhem.

Sawasdee Bangkok Inn
126/2 Thanon Khao San; tel: 0 2280 1251; www.sawas dee-hotels.com; $; pier: Phra Athit; map p.134 B2

Located on a quieter side street of Khao San, this is part of a growing chain of mid-range guesthouses run by the Sawasdee Group. The décor is an attempt on old Siam, and the rooms are clean, with most having air conditioning, hot shower and TV. Restaurant, bar, Internet access and travel agent on site.

Chinatown

Bangkok Centre
328 Thanon Rama IV; tel: 0 2238 4848; www.bangkokcentre hotel.com; $; MRT: Hualamphong; map p.139 E3

This budget place has a bit of an odd location, tucked just off busy Thanon Rama IV and on the outskirts of Chinatown, but within walking distance of the Hualamphong Railway Station. Smartly furnished air-conditioned rooms with TV, plus a

Many mid- and top-end hotels charge a standard 7 percent VAT and 10 percent service, so check ahead to see if the quoted rate includes these.

www.asiahotel.co.th; $$; BTS: Ratchathewi; map p.136 B1
This hotel is not particularly attractive from the outside but is well maintained within. Many facilities on site, which compensates for the noisy non-stop traffic at its doors.

Baiyoke Sky
Baiyoke II Tower, 222 Thanon Ratchaparop; tel: 0 2656 3000; www.baiyokehotel.com; $$; BTS: Phaya Thai; map p.136 C1
Located in Thailand's tallest building, the Sky Hotel has unparalleled views from well-priced, though unspectacular, rooms. A short distance from the downtown shopping district.

Conrad Bangkok
All Seasons Place, 87 Thanon Withayu; tel: 0 2690 9999; www.conradhotels.com; $$$$; BTS: Phloen Chit; map p.141 D3
Oozing class, this top-notch hotel is located near embassies and adjacent to the All Seasons Place shopping centre. Spacious and contemporary rooms are furnished with Thai silk and woods, with high-speed Internet access and large bathrooms with rainshowers. Excellent choice of eateries, as well as the **87+** nightclub and the **Diplomat** jazz bar. The serviced apartments are a better deal for longer stays.
SEE ALSO MUSIC, P.87; NIGHTLIFE, P.92

Four Seasons
155 Thanon Ratchadamri; tel: 0 2251 6127; www.fourseasons. com/bangkok; $$$$; BTS: Ratchadamri; map p.141 C3
From the magnificent lobby decorated with handpainted silk ceilings and Thai murals by renowned local artists to the city's best hotel swimming pool and the highest staff-to-guest ratio, the Four Seasons is consistently excellent. Only a few minutes' walk from the Ratchadamri BTS station. Some of the city's best dining outlets are here.

Grand Hyatt Erawan
494 Thanon Ratchadamri; tel: 0 2254 1234; www.bangkok. grand.hyatt.com; $$$$; BTS: Chit Lom; map p.141 C4
This Hyatt, smack in the middle of downtown shopping and beside the Erawan Shrine, sports a tasteful contemporary style. It has an excellent range of eateries, including its basement restaurant-nightclub **Spasso**, a favourite nightlife spot. Connected to the Erawan Bangkok mall.
SEE ALSO NIGHTLIFE, P.93

InterContinental Bangkok
973 Thanon Ploenchit; tel: 0 2656 0444; www.ichotels group.com; $$$$; BTS: Chit Lom; map p.141 C4
In the centre of downtown shopping and linked to Gaysorn Plaza, this glass-fronted tower has all the standard luxury and business facilities you'd expect from this hotel chain. Spacious

Above: the classy Four Seasons lobby has handpainted silk ceilings.

rooms come with Internet access and CD players. A rooftop swimming pool offers fine views of the cityscape.

Novotel Bangkok
Siam Square Soi 6; tel: 0 2255 6888; www.novotel.com; $$; BTS: Siam; map p.140 B4
Tucked among the maze of shopping alleys in Siam Square. Its massive basement entertainment complex, Concept CM2, is a frequently packed nightspot.

Pathumwan Princess
444 Thanon Phaya Thai; tel: 0 2216 3700; www.pprincess.com; $$; BTS: National Stadium; map p.140 B4
This centrally located hotel is joined to huge Mahboonkrong mall, making

Below: Conrad Bangkok offers pure luxury.

it ideal for shoppers. It's also a family-friendly place with a large saltwater pool, a gym, plus comfortable rooms. It offers good value for money.

Swissotel Nai Lert Park
2 Thanon Withayu; tel: 0 2253 0123; www.swissotel.com; $$$; BTS: Phloen Chit; map p.141 D4

Set within a beautiful garden estate with a landscaped pool and jogging track, this hotel is located in the central business and diplomatic district. Recently upgraded, it now sports a more contemporary edge; the hip lounge bar, **Syn**, affirms its new look. The curious should check out the mass of phallic totems at Nai Lert Shrine at the hotel rear beside the canal.
SEE ALSO NIGHTLIFE, P.91

Bangrak and Silom

Banyan Tree Bangkok
21/100 Thanon Sathorn Tai; tel: 0 2679 1200; www.banyan tree.com; $$$$; MRT: Lumphini; map p.140 C1

Located in the precariously narrow Thai Wah Tower II,

Below: Banyan Tree Bangkok is housed in the magnificently slim Thai Wah Tower II.

Bangkok's second-tallest hotel features large and stylishly appointed luxury suites with separate living and working areas, plus high-speed Internet access. The **Vertigo Grill & Moon Bar** on the rooftop and the pampering Banyan Tree Spa (the tallest in the city) offer spectacular views.
SEE ALSO NIGHTLIFE, P.91

Dusit Thani
946 Thanon Rama IV; tel: 0 2236 9999; www.dusit.com; $$$$; BTS: Sala Daeng or MRT: Silom; map p.140 C2

This classic example of fashionably retro 1950s architecture is located across Lumphini Park, near Patpong's nightlife. It has lost out a little to younger and more stylish hotels, but recent refurbishments have ensured its place among Bangkok's top digs. Enjoy a massage at the **Devarana Spa** and then float on to its top-floor **D'Sens** restaurant for impeccable French dining.
SEE ALSO PAMPERING, P.99; RESTAURANTS, P.106

Holiday Inn Silom
981 Thanon Silom; tel: 0 2238 4300; www.bangkok-silom. holiday-inn.com; $$; BTS: Surasak; map p.139 E1

Located right next to the Silom Galleria near the river end of Thanon Silom, this large, comfortable hotel is of much higher quality than its Holiday Inn brand suggests.

La Residence
173/8–9 Thanon Surawong; tel: 0 2266 5400; www.laresi dencebangkok.com; $; BTS: Chong Nonsi; map p.140 A2

A small boutique hotel a short distance away, yet far enough, from Patpong, with funky individually decorated rooms of different sizes. All the expected room amenities and a friendly vibe, though short on trimmings like a swimming pool.

Lebua at State Tower
State Tower; 1055/111 Thanon Silom; tel: 0 2624 9999; www.lebua.com; $$$; BTS: Saphan Taksin; map p.139 E1

These deluxe, contemporary Asian-style serviced apartments, with 1–3 bedrooms and kitchenettes, are located

Below: The Met exudes minimalist chic even on the outside.

Above: the stylish Sofitel Silom is known for its great service.

within the colossal 64-storey State Tower, which has established itself as a Bangkok landmark. The tower's opulent rooftop F&B outlets are collectively called The Dome, featuring the top restaurants **Sirocco**, **Mezzaluna** and **Breeze**, and the sophisticated **Distil Bar**.
SEE ALSO NIGHTLIFE, P.89; RESTAURANTS, P.108

Luxx
6/11 Thanon Decho; tel: 0 2635 8800; www.staywithluxx.com; $$; BTS: Chong Nonsi; map p.140 A1
The suites and studios are luxurious with large bathrooms, hi-tech entertainment systems and picture windows that look out to a tranquil pebble courtyard, while the standards and doubles are stylish and functional with comfy beds and the usual mod cons. Each of the 13 rooms comes with a quaint wooden barrel bathtub.

The Metropolitan
27 Thanon Sathorn Tai; tel: 0 2625 3333; www.

metropolitan.como.bz; $$$$; BTS: Sala Daeng or MRT: Lumphini; map p.141 C1
Sister to the famous Metropolitan in London, Bangkok's younger twin is cool and contemporary, blending East and West minimalist chic in equal measures. Its drinking and dining outlets, **Cy'an** and **Met Bar**, are among the city's top spots. **COMO Shambhala Spa** offers Asian-influenced treatments.
SEE ALSO NIGHTLIFE, P.91; PAMPERING, P.98; RESTAURANTS, P.107

The Oriental
48 Oriental Avenue; tel: 0 2659 9000; www.mandarinoriental.com; $$$$; BTS: Saphan Taksin; pier: Oriental; map p.139 E1
Even if you don't stay here, a visit is a must, if only to partake of the hotel's East-meets-West ambience. Established in 1876, it is well known for its grand setting on the Chao Phraya River and luminous guest list. The Authors' Wing, the only original structure surviving, is delightful for afternoon tea. **Le Normandie** French restaurant is the only place in town that requires a tie for dinner, while **The Oriental Spa** takes the East-meets-West theme further with inspired therapies.
SEE ALSO PAMPERING, P.99; RESTAURANTS, P.107

Royal Orchid Sheraton
2 Captain Bush Lane; tel: 0 2266 0123; www.starwoodhotels.com; $$$; MRT: Sam Yan; pier: Si Phraya; map p.139 E2
Located along the prime riverfront stretch, this hotel was once considered one of the best, though no longer the case. Most guests these days are package tourists. Still, the hotel does offer some great views of the Chao Phraya River.

The Shangri-La
89 Soi Wat Suan Plu; tel: 0 2236 7777; www.shangri-la.com; $$$; BTS: Saphan Taksin; map p.139 E1
The largest of the five-star hotels located along the river, with every one of its rooms facing the river. It consistently ranks among the top five hotels in Asia. Excellent amenities, including **Chi Spa** and the restaurants Angelini's and Maenam Terrace.
SEE ALSO PAMPERING, P.98

Sofitel Silom
188 Thanon Silom; tel: 0 2238 1991; www.sofitel.com; $$; BTS: Chong Nonsi; map p.140 A1
This 38-storey stylish hotel located in the quieter part of busy Thanon Silom is only a short walk to the Chong Nonsi BTS station. Its wine bar **V9** has stunning views

Below: the Somerset Maugham suite at The Oriental.

63

from its 37th-floor perch, while one floor above is the excellent Shanghai 38 Chinese restaurant.
SEE ALSO NIGHTLIFE, P.91

The Sukhothai
13/3 Thanon South Sathorn; tel: 0 2344 8888; www.sukhothai.com; $$$$; BTS: Sala Daeng or MRT: Lumphini; map p.141 C1
This stunning contemporary Asian hotel draws architectural inspiration from the ancient Siamese kingdom of the same name. One of the top hotels in Bangkok and indeed in the world, this class act has well-appointed rooms, the excellent La Scala Italian restaurant and the chic **Zuk Bar**, tropical gardens and a reflecting pool.
SEE ALSO NIGHTLIFE, P.92

Tarntawan Place
119/5–10 Thanon Surawong; tel: 0 2238 2620–39; www.tarn tawan.com; $$; map p.140 B2
While Thanon Silom received all the commercial action,

Surawong was left behind to some degree, making the area less hectic, but still in the middle of all the nightlife action. Located off a quiet *soi*, this small hotel has only one restaurant and bar, but who cares when in this neck of the woods? Excellent service and multilingual staff.

Sukhumvit

Amari Boulevard
Sukhumvit Soi 7; tel: 0 2255 2930; www.amari.com/ boulevard; $$$; BTS: Nana; map p.141 E4
Amenities include a 6th-floor swimming pool, fitness centre, restaurants and garden terraces attached to some of the deluxe rooms. This is an oasis in a raucous tourist area filled with markets, noodle shops and girlie bars.

Ambassador
171 Thanon Sukhumvit; tel: 0 2254 0444; www.amtel.co.th; $; BTS: Nana; map p.141 E4
A large hotel popular with tour

groups, tucked back slightly from the main road and only a 5-minute walk to the Nana BTS station. While not particularly attractive, it has a wide range of restaurants on site.

Atlanta
78 Thanon Sukhumvit Soi 2; tel: 0 2252 1650; www.the atlantahotel.bizland.com; $; BTS: Phloen Chit; map p.141 D3
This 1950s throwback is rich in character and a real treasure among faceless modern structures. The first hotel along Sukhumvit, it has a pool set in landscaped gardens and a great Thai restaurant. Quirky extras include Thai dancing on weekends and classic roll-top desks in the rooms.

Davis
88 Thanon Sukhumvit Soi 24; tel: 0 2260 8000; www.davis bangkok.net; $$$; BTS: Phrom Phong; map p.18
A boutique hotel with a melange of style influences. Different themed rooms all come with the latest mod cons, plus 10 villas with their own swimming pools. There is a rooftop pool with a bar, plus Club 88, a live-music joint.

Dream BKK
10 Sukhumvit Soi 15; tel: 0 2254 8500; www.dreambkk.com; $$$; BTS: Nana; map p.141 E3
This boutique property pampers with 100 rooms stylishly done up with clean lines and ambient lighting, plus a whole host of amenities, from plush Egyptian-cotton bedsheets to iPod players with preloaded music. Its restaurant serves both Thai and Western food, and the **Flava Lounge** is one of the top chill-out havens in town.
SEE ALSO NIGHTLIFE, P.90

Emporium Suites
622 Sukhumvit Soi 24; tel: 0 2664 9999; www.emporium suites.com; $$$; BTS: Phrom Phong; map p.18

Below: The Sukhothai's plush lobby.

Above: suite Dream: the living room of a suite in Dream BKK.

Conveniently located above the Emporium mall and connected to the Phrom Phong BTS station, this stylish serviced apartment complex offers a range of accommodation, from studio and 1-bedroom suites to 3-bedroom apartments. Full range of in-house facilities. Some rooms have nice views of Benjasiri Park.

The Eugenia
267 Sukhumvit Soi 31; tel: 0 2259 9011; www.theeugenia.com; $$$; BTS: Phrom Phong or MRT: Sukhumvit; map p.18
This 12-suite accommodation set in a 19th-century manor blends old-world colonial charm with warm Thai hospitality. Many of its rooms offer four-poster beds and all come with antique furniture and furnishings collected by the owner. For a ride in style, opt for a city tour or airport transfer in one of the Jaguars and Mercedes Benzes in the hotel's vintage fleet.

JW Marriott
4 Sukhumvit Soi 2; tel: 0 2656 7700; www.marriotthotels.com; $$$; BTS: Nana or Phloen Chit; map p.141 E4
This classy five-star hotel is just around the corner from

the risque Nana Entertainment Plaza, but don't let that deter you. All the usual amenities, plus Bangkok's largest fitness centre, efficient business facilities and spacious, well-appointed rooms make this one of the city's best hotels. Some of the city's best dining is at the **New York Steakhouse**.
SEE ALSO RESTAURANTS, P.109

Landmark
138 Thanon Sukhumvit; tel: 0 2254 0404; www.landmarkbangkok.com; $$; BTS: Nana; map p.141 E3
Good location, and geared toward the business traveller with a busy business centre. It is attached to a plaza with a few shops and eateries.

Novotel Lotus
1 Sukhumvit Soi 33; tel: 0 2261 0111; www.novotel.com; $$; BTS: Phrom Phong; map p.18
With its lotus pond the hotel lobby exudes a Zen atmosphere. It has a café plus two restaurants, and very tasteful rooms. While it has all the amenities expected of a business hotel and is also close to the Queen Sirikit Convention Centre, its location is also ideal for shoppers.

President Park
95 Sukhumvit Soi 24; tel: 0 2661 1000; www.presidentpark.com; $$; BTS: Phrom Phong; map p.18
Great for families or business executives, this large, modern apartment complex is tastefully designed. Its spacious studios come with kitchenettes. Three large pools and full leisure facilities in its Capitol Club. Daily, weekly and monthly rates available, with breakfast included.

Rembrandt
19 Sukhumvit Soi 18; tel: 0 2261 7100; www.rembrandtbkk.com; $$; BTS: Asok or MRT: Sukhumvit; map p.18
Decked out in European opulence, this good-value hotel is at the end of a lane with many shops, eateries and traditional massage services. There's a complimentary *tuk-tuk* shuttle to the end of the *soi* and then it's a short walk to the BTS or MRT station. The hotel claims to have the city's best Indian dining at Rang Mahal and the best Mexican at **Senor Pico**, which also features a Latin band.
SEE ALSO NIGHTLIFE, P.93

Sheraton Grande Sukhumvit
250 Thanon Sukhumvit; tel: 0 2653 0333; www.starwood.com/bangkok; $$$$; BTS: Asok or MRT: Sukhumvit; map p.141 E3

Below: a deluxe room at Landmark hotel.

Above: the Grande Spa at the Sheraton Grande Sukhumvit.

Above: the Aleenta resort in Pranburi, near Hua Hin.

This has a great location, not far from Benjakitti Park, and first-rate facilities and services, with extra large rooms containing all the bells and whistles you'd expect from a five-star property. Beautifully landscaped swimming pool and excellent spa, plus three good restaurants, nightclub and highly rated **Living Room** live-jazz bar.
SEE MUSIC, P.87

Sukhumvit 11
1/33 Sukhumvit Soi 11; tel: 0 2253 5927; www.suk11. com; $; BTS: Nana; map p.141 E4
Although the rooms are rather bare with no TV or fridge, this personable, family-run Thai-style guesthouse is still a gem of a find, and often booked out by budget travellers. It is housed in a row of airy Thai houses restored with lots of wood and rustic décor.

Westin Grande Sukhumvit
259 Sukhumvit Soi 19; tel: 0 2651 1000; www.westin. com/bangkok; $$$; BTS: Asok or MRT: Sukhumvit; map p.141 E3
This large, modern hotel has comfortable rooms and several dining outlets, and the upper-level Horizons Sky Lounge offers karaoke with a view. Other pluses include its outdoor pool with a swim-up bar, and the Vareena day spa with a hydrotherapy bath and aroma steam room.

Bangkok's Surroundings

KANCHANABURI

Comsaed River Kwai Resort
18/9 Moo 5 Ladya; tel: 0 3463 1443–9; www.comsaedriver kwai.com; map p.20
Many of the area's better hotels lie some way outside the main town in the rolling countryside, which is also true of the Comsaed. It has manicured lawns, wooden bridges and riverine views, and offers outdoor activities such as canoeing and biking.

River Kwai Jungle Rafts
Office: River Kwae Floatel Co., 133/14 Thanon Ratchaprarop, Bangkok; tel: 0 2642 6361–2; www.riverkwaifloatel.com; map p.20
For a unique Kanchanaburi experience, stay on a floating jungle raft. The lodgings are quaint, and you can eat and drink on the adjoining floating restaurant and bar. Activities include swiming and fishing in the river, elephant riding and excursions to tribal villages.

CHA-AM

Casa Papaya
810/4 Thanon Phetchkasem; tel: 0 3247 0678; www.casa papayathailand.com; $$; map p.20
A cute family-run boutique resort just south of the main Cha-am beach. Done in peachy pastel shades, it's evocative of the Mediterranean. Accommodation options are beachfront or sea-view bungalows, or rooms with garden views, but all with hammocks out front.

Veranda
737/12 Thanon Mung Talay; tel: 0 3270 9000; www.veranda resortandspa.com; $$$; map p.20
The large pool and pond elements are the central features of this boutique-style resort, and its trendy beachfront brasserie is unique in the area. The regular rooms are slightly cramped, but the sea-view villas are very spacious.

HUA HIN

Aleenta
Pranburi Beach; tel: 0 2519 2044; www.aleenta.com; $$$$; map p.20
This intimate resort along Pranburi Beach, about 30 minutes' drive from Hua Hin, plays host to Bangkok's smart set. Expect simple clean lines but luxury nonetheless, with a pool, restaurant, bar and spa.

Dinners can be arranged on the beach.

Anantara
43/1 Phetchkasem Beach; tel: 0 3252 0250; www.anantara.com; $$$$; map p.20
Luxurious hideaway tucked among verdant gardens and fronting the beach. Rooms have strong Thai accents with the more expensive ones facing the beach and the lagoon. Highly rated spa plus Italian and Thai restaurants.

Chiva Som
73/4 Thanon Phetchkasem; tel: 0 3253 6536; www.chivasom.com; $$$$; map p.20
This resort offers the best of traditional Thai style with a relaxing location beside Hua Hin's sandy beach. Superb range of spa facilities, including a unique flotation tank, Pilates room and gym, water therapy suites, pools and a tai chi pavilion. The spa cuisine is another bonus.

PATTAYA
Hard Rock Hotel
Pattaya Beach; tel: 0 3842 8755; www.hardrockhotelpattaya.com; $$$; map p.20
The rooms are fairly standard with colourful pop colours and music memorabilia typical of Hard Rock outlets. The vast hotel pool comes

complete with boulders and shady thatched pavilions.

Rabbit Resort
Dongtan Beach, Jomtien; tel: 0 3830 3303–4; www.rabbitresort.com; $$; map p.20
Slightly set back from the beach, this is a Thai-village-style resort set among pretty gardens. The cosy rooms are decorated with traditional furniture and fabrics. Two swimming pools, a restaurant and beachside grill.

Sheraton Pattaya
437 Thanon Phra Tamnak; tel: 0 3825 9888; www.sheraton.com/pattaya; $$$; map p.20
Located on the Phra Tamnak headland, this beautifully landscaped resort has calming water features and its own beach. Many of the rooms have their own ocean-facing pavilions, and the Amburaya Spa offers body tuning.

KO SAMET
Ao Phrao Resort
60 Moo 4, Ao Phrao Beach; tel: 0 3864 4101–7; www.samedresorts.com; $$$; map p.20
The island's most upmarket resort sits on the only beach on the sunset side. The comfortable bungalows come with cable TV. The resort also has the most expensive restaurant

Above: the rock 'n roll-themed Hard Rock Hotel.

on the island, though don't expect too much.

Samed Villa
89 Moo 4, Ao Phai Beach; tel: 0 3864 4094; www.samedvilla.com; $$; map p.20
Located on a headland with nice views of the sea, this popular family-run resort is full most weekends. The newer bungalows are good value.

AYUTTHAYA
Krungsri River Hotel
27/2 Moo 11, Thanon Rojchana; tel: 0 3524 4333; www.krungsririver.com; $; map p.20
A decent nine-storey hotel, though short on ambience, in a town with few options. The rooms have air conditioning and cable TV, and there's a pool, restaurant and bar.

Below: the Anantara Hua Hin is fronted by a pristine sea.

Language

Thai language's roots go back to the place Thais originated from – the hills of southern China, but it is also overlaid by Indian influences. From the original settlers come the five tones that seem to frustrate visitors and new learners of the language. These five tones each means a different thing. Therefore, when you mispronounce a word, you don't simply say a word incorrectly, you say another word entirely. It is not unusual to see a semi-fluent foreigner standing before a Thai and running through the scale of tones until suddenly a light of recognition dawns on the latter's face.

Phonology

The way Thai consonants are written in English often confuses foreigners. An 'h' following a letter like 'p' and 't' gives the letter a soft sound; without the 'h', the sound is more explosive. Thus, 'ph' is not pronounced 'f' but as a soft 'p'; without the 'h', the 'p' has the sound of a very hard 'b'. The word *thanon* (street) is pronounced 'tanon', in the same way 'Thailand' is not meant to sound like 'Thighland'. Similarly, final letters are often not pronounced as they look. A 'j' at the end of a word is pronounced 't'; 'l' is pronounced as an 'n'. To complicate matters further, many words end with 'se' or 'r', which are not pronounced.

Vowels are pronounced as follows: 'i' as in 'sip', 'ii' as in 'seep', 'e' as in 'bet', 'a' as in 'pun', 'aa' as in 'pal', 'u' as in 'pool', 'o' as in 'so', 'ai' as in 'pie', 'ow' as in 'cow', 'aw' as in 'paw', 'iw' as in 'you', 'oy' as in 'toy'.

In Thai, the pronouns 'I' and 'me' are the same word, but it is different for males and females. Men use the word *phom* when referring to themselves, while women say *chan* or *diichan*. Men use *khrap* at the end of a sentence when addressing either a male or a female to add politeness, or in a similar manner as 'please' (the word for 'please', *karuna*, is seldom used directly), eg. '*pai* (f) *nai, khrap* (h)' (where are you going, sir?) Women add the word *kha* to their statements, as in '*pai* (f) *nai, kha* (h)?'

To ask a question, add a high-tone *mai* to the end of the phrase, eg. *rao pai* (we go) or *rao pai mai* (h) (shall we go?) To negate a statement, insert a falling-tone *mai* between the subject and the verb, eg. *rao pai* (we go), *rao mai pai* (we don't go). 'Very' or 'much' and 'not' are indicated by adding *maak* to the end of a phrase, eg. *ron maak* (very hot), *phaeng maak* (very expensive).

Below: a sign at the Suan Pakkad palace.

Left: attempts to speak a little Thai are always welcome.

Do you have any in a smaller size? *Mii arai thii lek kwa mai (h)*
Hot (heat hot) *Ron (h)*
Hot (spicy) *Phet*
Cold *Yen*
Sweet *Waan (r)*
Sour *Prio (f)*
Delicious *Aroy*

DIRECTIONS AND TRAVEL
Go *Pai*
Come *Maa*
Where *Thii (f) nai (r)*
Right *Khwaa (r)*
Left *Sai (h)*
Turn *Leo*
Straight ahead *Trong pai*
Please slow down *Cha cha noi*
Stop here *Yood thii (f) nii (f)*
Fast *Raew*
Slow *Cha*
Hotel *Rong raem*
Street *Thanon*
Lane *Soi*
Bridge *Saphan*
Police station *Sathanii Dtam Ruat*
Ferry *Reua*
Longtail boat *Reua haang yao*
Train *Rot fai*
Bus *Rot may*
Skytrain *Rot fai faa*
Metro/subway *Rot fai tai din*
Pier *Tha Reua*
Bus stop *Pai rot may*
Station *Sathanii (rot may), (rot fai), (rot fai faa)*

THE FIVE TONES
Mid tone: voiced at the speaker's normal, even pitch.
High tone: pitched slightly higher than the mid tone.
Low tone: pitched slightly lower than the mid tone.
Rising tone: sounds like a questioning pitch, starting low and rising.
Falling tone: sounds like an English speaker suddenly understanding something: 'Oh, I see!'

Useful Words & Phrases

NUMBERS
0	*soon (m)*
1	*nung (m)*
2	*song (r)*
3	*sam (r)*
4	*sii (m)*
5	*haa (f)*
6	*hok (m)*
7	*jet (m)*
8	*bet (m)*
9	*kow (f)*
10	*sip (m)*
11	*sip et (m, m)*
12	*sip song (m, r)*
13	*sip sam (m, r) and so on*
20	*yii sip (m, m)*
30	*sam sip (f, m) and so on*
100	*nung roi (m, m)*
1,000	*nung phan (m, m)*

SHORT PHRASES
Hello, goodbye *Sawadee* (a man then says *khrap*; a woman says *kha*: thus *sawadee khrap* or *sawadee kha*)
How are you? *Khun sabai dii, mai (h)*
Well, thank you *Sabai dii, khopkhun*
Thank you very much *Khopkhun maak*
Never mind *Mai (f) pen rai*
I cannot speak Thai *Phuut Thai mai (f) dai (f)*
I can speak a little *Thai Phuut Thai dai (f) nit (h) diew*
Yes *Chai (f)*
No *Mai (f) chai (f)*
Do you have...? *Mii...mai (h)*
How much? *Thao (f) rai*
Expensive *Phaeng*
Can you lower the price a bit? *Kaw lot noi dai (f) mai (h)*
Do you have another colour? *Mii sii uhn mai (h)*
Too big *Yai kern pai*
Too small *Lek kern pai*
I don't want it *Mai ao*
I do not feel well *Mai (f) sabai*
Do you have any in a bigger size? *Mii arai thii yai kwa mai (h)*

There is no universal transliteration system from Thai into English. This is why names and street names can be spelled in different ways. For example, the surname Chumsai can also be written Jumsai or Xoomsai; Bangkok's thoroughfare of Ratchadamnoen is also spelled Ratchadamnern. If you ask Thais how they spell something, they may well reply 'How do you want to spell it?'

Literature

hen the Burmese sacked Ayutthaya in 1767, they destroyed most of Siam's classical written literature. The Thais have since then always placed a heavy emphasis on the oral tradition. Pivotal to Thai classical literature are the epics *Ramakien* and *Jataka Tales*, both of Indian origins and are mainly told through Thai dance-drama. Today, there are also numerous modern writings by authors ranging from local social critics to Western expatriates who give their perspective on life in the country. Look out for these books and other good reads in English-language bookstores in the city.

Classical Literature

At the heart of Thai literature is the *Ramakien*, the Thai version of the Indian *Ramayana*. The enduring story has found a home in the literature, dance and drama of many Asian countries. Familiarity with the *Ramakien* enables one to comprehend a variety of dramatic forms, its significance for the Thai monarchy, and its role as a model for exemplary behaviour.

The *Jataka* tales are also of Indian origin, telling of Buddha's reincarnations prior to enlightenment, though some are probably based on tales that existed before the Buddha lived. The first tales were translated from Pali script to Thai in the late 15th century. They have generated many other popular and classic stories, such as *Phra Aphaimani*, written by Sunthorn Phu, the 18th-century poet laureate.

Modern Literature

It wasn't until the 1920s that Thai novels were published, with themes mainly touching on social or political issues. In the 1950s, however, censorship became so heavy and writers so harshly persecuted that quality fiction practically disappeared for 20 years.

Thai writers since the 1980s have enjoyed a measure of political freedom. While they remain social critics, there are efforts to write fiction of literary merit. Many landmark Thai books were translated into English in the early 1990s. The late prime minister and cultural

Expatriate writers like Jake Needham and Christopher Moore bring a Western perspective to life in the kingdom, though the majority of such scribes tend to wallow in the seedier aspects of the capital's nightlife, with somewhat predictable storylines.

advocate Kukrit Pramoj's *Many Lives*, for instance, gives a good introduction to the Buddhist way of thinking. His *Four Reigns* is a fictional yet accurate account of court life in the 19th and 20th centuries.

Further Reading

GENERAL
Mai Pen Rai Means Never Mind by Carol Hollinger (Asia Books, 1995). A personal account of hilarious experiences in Thailand half a century ago. **Travellers' Tales Thailand** edited by James O'Reilly and Larry Habegger (Travelers' Tales Inc., 2002). A collection of stimulating observations and true stories from around 50 writers.

Left: a depiction of Buddha's third life in a Jataka tale.

Left: a performance of the epic *Ramakien*.

you've ever wondered why every compound in Thailand has a spirit house or why insect treats are such a hit, this book is for you.

Bookshops

Asia Books
4/F, Siam Discovery Centre Thanon Rama I; tel: 0 2658 0418–20; www.asiabooks.com; BTS: Siam; map p.140 B4; 2/F, Crystal Court Zone, Siam Paragon, 991 Thanon Rama I; tel: 0 2610 9609; BTS: Siam; map p.140 B4
Publisher and distributor with many outlets, including Emporium and at 221 Thanon Sukhumvit.

B2S
7/F, Central Chidlom, Thanon Ploenchit; tel: 0 2655 6178; BTS: Chit Lom; map p.141 D4; 4/1–2 Central World, Thanon Ratchadamri; tel: 0 2646 1270; BTS: Chit Lom; map p.140 C4
Major bookstore retail chain with several outlets.

Basheer Graphic Books
998 Sukhumvit Soi 55; tel: 0 2391 9815; www.basheergraphic.com; BTS: Thong Lo; map p.18
Wide range of art and design books.

Books Kinokuniya
3/F, Emporium, Sukhumvit Soi 24; tel: 0 2664 8554–6; BTS: Phrom Phong; map p.18; Unit 309–314 Siam Paragon, 991 Thanon Rama I; tel: 0 2610 9500; BTS: Siam; map p.140 B4
Japanese chain store with an well-organised and comprehensive selection of books.

Dasa Book Café
710/4 Thanon Sukhumvit (between Soi 24 and 26); tel: 0 2661 2993; www.dasa bookcafe.com; BTS: Phrom Phong; map p.18
Secondhand books in a cosy environment that offers drinks and desserts.

FICTION
Bangkok 8 by John Burdett (Vintage, 2004). About a half-Thai, half-American policeman who avenges his partner's death.
The Beach by Alex Garland. (Riverhead Trade, 1998). The beach read that inspired the movie starring Leonardo Dicaprio, about a group of backpackers trying to find their own paradise.
The Big Mango by Jake Needham (Asia Books, 1999). An action-adventure story about a search for millions of dollars that went missing during the fall of Saigon in 1975.

HISTORY/SOCIETY
The Balancing Act: A History of Modern Thailand by Joseph Wright (Pacific Rim Press, 1991). History of Thailand from 1932 to 1991.
A History of Buddhism in Siam by Prince Dhani Nivat (Siam Society, 1965). Written by one of Thailand's most respected scholars.
Jim Thompson: The Legendary American by William Warren (Asia Books, 1979). The intriguing story of the American Thai-silk magnate Jim Thompson.
The Revolutionary King: The True-Life Sequel to The King and I by William Stevenson (Robinson, 2001). An intimate portrait of the current King Bhumibol. As monarchy matters are taken very seriously, the book is unavailable in the kingdom.
Thaksin: the Business of Politics in Thailand by Dr Pasuk Phongpaichit and Chris Baker (Silkworm Books, 2004). A study of former prime minister Thaksin's impact on the nation.

ART AND CULTURE
The Grand Palace by Nng-noi Saksi, Naengnoi Suksri, and Michael Freeman (River Books, 1998). Beautifully illustrated and detailed account of Bangkok's Grand Palace and its surroundings.
Things Thai by Tanistha Dansilp and Michael Freeman (Periplus Editions, 2002). Quintessential Thai objects and artefacts.
Very Thai: Everyday Popular Culture by Philip Cornwel-Smith (River Books, 2005). If

Markets

Bangkok is one vast market. Shops spill out onto pavements, goods are hawked off tarpaulin sheets, and there are makeshift vendors' stalls on virtually every street. Indeed, a trip to the *talad*, or market, is an essential part of the Bangkok experience. The city's markets provide a tantalising assault on the wallet as well as on the senses, with smells, sights and sounds galore. At markets bargaining is *de rigueur* and considered part of the fun. Bangkok has a market for just about every hour of the day and night, and every neighbourhood has at least one of these memorable outdoor shopping emporiums.

Chatuchak Weekend Market

Corner of Thanon Phahon Yothin and Thanon Kamphaengphet; Sat–Sun 7am–6pm; BTS: Mo Chit or Saphan Khwai; map p.20
Reputed to be the world's biggest flea market with about 15,000 stalls, this is a must-see; even the least enthusiastic shopper cannot fail to be overawed by the sheer scale and variety of goods available. The market gets some 400,000 visitors every weekend, so it can get overwhelming; an early start (arrive by 9am) is essential to beat the heat and the ensuing claustrophobia. There are loosely partitioned sections selling clothing, accessories, shoes, antiques, handicrafts, plants and even pets. Numerous cafés, and snack and juice bars are dotted throughout the market.

Damnoen Saduak Floating Market

Ratchaburi, 105km west of Bangkok; daily 7am–1pm; bus from Southern Bus Terminal, then local bus, or bus from Southern Bus Terminal or train

Above: a stall at the Chatuchak Weekend Market.

from Wongwianyai Railway Station (in Thonburi) to Samut Songkhram, then longtail boat; map p.20
An early morning departure is necessary if you want to beat the tour buses from Bangkok, which flock to this famous floating market by 10am. While it is possible to walk along the bankside lined with souvenir stands, it's better to hire a longtail boat to get a better sense of the water-bound commercial bustle. This 100-year-old market is unfortunately little more than a sideshow today, with tourists clambering to snap pictures of the colourful fruit- and vegetable-laden wooden vessels, oared by smiling women wearing straw hats. If you've hired your own long-tail boat, it might be worth-while to go deeper into the canals to get a glimpse of the waterside communities.

Pahurat Market

Thanon Pahurat; daily 9am–6pm; MRT: Hualamphong; pier: Saphan Phut; map p.138 C4
Pahurat Market, Bangkok's Little India, is a two-level bazaar. Fabrics, saris, figurines of Hindu deities, wedding regalia, traditional Thai dance costumes and accessories as well as Indian tea and spices are sold here.

Pak Khlong Talad

Thanon Chakraphet; daily 24 hours; MRT: Hualamphong; pier: Saphan Phut; map p.138 B4
West of Pahurat Market, at the mouth of Khlong Lord, is Pak Khlong Talad (Flower Market), Bangkok's flower and vegetable garden. The vendors can arrange the bargain-priced blooms into bouquets and baskets.

Left: vendors at the Damnoen Saduak market.

Talad Kao and Talad Mai

Soi Itsaranuphap, Chinatown; MRT: Hualamphong; map p.139 D3, D4

The two-century-old Talad Kao (Old Market) wraps up by late morning and the newer Talad Mai (New Market), over a century old, keeps trading until sundown. These fresh-produce markets are reputed for high-quality ingredients and overflow with goods, especially during Chinese New Year.

Thanon Silom & Patpong Night Market

Thanon Silom; daily 6pm–midnight; BTS: Sala Daeng; map p.140 B2

The night market covers Silom Soi 1–8 and the Patpong area (Soi 1–2). Stalls offer mainly counterfeit watches, fake brand-name bags and clothes, CDs and DVDs.

Thanon Sukhumvit

Daily evening–midnight; BTS: Nana or Asok; map p.141 E3–4

Stalls along Sukhumvit Soi 5–11 hawk counterfeit goods and tourist souvenirs. The pavements are also lined with makeshift food and drink stalls later in the night.

Don't start bargaining unless you really want to buy. First, ask the price of the item. Then open the process with a request to lower the price. The seller will then lower the original price, thereby signalling he or she is open to offers. Thereafter, offer your first price, which is always too low. From there the volley of bargaining begins until the final price is agreed upon.

Pratunam Market

Thanon Ratchaprarop; daily 9am–midnight; BTS: Phaya Thai or Ratchathewi; map p.137 C1

This bustling warren of stalls is more a lure for residents than tourists, but with cheap piles of clothing, fabrics and shoes, it's of interest to any bargain hunter.

Sampeng Lane

Soi Wanit 1, Chinatown; MRT: Hualamphong; map p.139 D3

Stalls along Sampeng Lane (Soi Wanit 1), between Thanon Ratchawong and Thanon Mangkon, supply the basics for the average Thai Chinese household. Not a lot of quality here, but for fun kitsch and bargain hunting it's certainly worth a rummage.

Suan Lum Night Bazaar

Corner of Thanon Withayu and Thanon Rama IV; daily 3pm–midnight; MRT: Lumphini; map p.141 D2

The open-air Suan Lum has nearly 4,000 stalls selling handicrafts, souvenirs, clothing, jewellery, antiques and home décor. It is a smaller and cooler version of Chatuchak. There is also a large beer garden with live music and food.

Below: the bright and cheery Suan Lum Night Bazaar.

Monuments

Within the city are several monuments that commemorate momentous events and pay tribute to revered monarchs. These do not just appeal to history buffs but also inform those who are interested to know more about how the city was made. Religious ceremonies are held occasionally at some of these structures. Worth seeing outside of Bangkok include the Bridge over the River Kwai in Kanchanaburi, the Ayutthaya Historical Park with imposing remnants of Thailand's past, and the spectacular Phra Pathom Chedi, the world's tallest Buddhist monument, in Nakhon Pathom town west of the capital.

14 October Monument

Corner of Thanon Ratchadam-noen Klang and Thanon Tanao; free; pier: Phra Athit; map p.134 C2

Just a short walk west from the Democracy Monument, this chiselled edifice to the democratic struggle in Thailand is a sombre granite memorial to the victims of the 1973 mass demonstrations against authoritarian rule. Surrounded by a small amphitheatre, the central spire has the names of 73 of the victims inscribed in Thai. Beneath is an exhibition room, meeting rooms and a mini-theatre. Given the government's past denial of this traumatic event, it's somewhat remarkable that this pertinent 21st-century tribute (erected in 2002) stands at all.

Ayutthaya Historical Park

Ayutthaya, 85km north of Bangkok; daily 8am–5pm; entrance charge; train from Hualamphong, bus from Northern Bus Terminal, or boat (see box on p.75); map p.20

The old capital Ayutthaya is a UNESCO World Heritage Site. This beautiful city, founded in 1350, was built by 33 Ayutthayan kings over 400 years. Although it is in ruins, impressive remnants of its rich architectural and cultural achievements can still be seen today. As fast as it rose to greatness it collapsed, suffering destruction so complete that it was never rebuilt. Burmese armies had pounded on its doors for centuries before occupying it for a period in the 16th century. Siamese kings then expelled them and reasserted independence. In 1767, however, the Burmese triumphed again. They burned and looted, destroying most of the city's monuments and enslaving, killing and scattering the population.

The royal court resettled south near the mouth of the Chao Phraya River in what is today's Bangkok. Even after the Burmese were defeated, Ayutthaya was beyond repair, a fabled city left to crumble into dust. Today, the ruins, collectively known as the

Above: the 14 October Monument pays tribute to democracy in Thailand.

Ayutthaya Historical Park, stand on the western half of the island, with the modern city of Ayutthaya on the eastern side.

ALONG THE RIVER

Start close to the junction of the Nam Pa Sak and Chao Phraya rivers, passing by the imposing **Wat Phanan Choeng**, established 26 years prior to Ayutthaya's founding in 1350. The temple houses the statue of a giant seated bronze Buddha so

Left: Wat Phra Sri Sanphet at the Ayutthaya Historical Park.

complex in Cambodia, the dramatically placed temple is a photographer's favourite, especially at sunset. The temple was built by King Prasat Thong and has a large central Cambodian-style *prang* fringed by several smaller *chedis*. Perched high on a pedestal in front of the ruins, a Buddha statue keeps solitary watch. This extraordinary temple with rows of headless Buddha statues makes a fine contrast to the less impressive **Queen Suriyothai Chedi** on the city side. The shrine commemorates the sacrifice of the queen, who, dressed as a male soldier, rode into battle on an elephant and received a lethal lance blow from a Burmese prince that was intended for her husband King Maha Chakraphet.

Across a river bridge from the royal palace Wang Luang stands **Wat Na Phra Men**, which was used as a strategic attack post by the Burmese when they sacked the old city. Here, a large stone Buddha image is seated on a throne, a sharp contrast to the yoga position of most seated Buddhas. Found in the ruins of Wat Phra Mahathat *(see p.77)*, the statue is believed to be one of five that originally sat in the recently unearthed Dvaravati-period complex in Nakhon Pathom. The main hall or *bot* contains an Ayutthaya-style seated Buddha in regal attire, which is very unlike the more common monastic dress of Buddha representations.

PALACE AND SURROUNDINGS

The palace of **Wang Luang** (Royal Palace) was of

The Chao Phraya Express Boat (tel: 0 2623 6001; www.chao phrayaboat.co.th) operates a day trip to Ayutthaya every Sunday at 8am. The River Sun Cruise travels one way by coach and returns by boat (tel: 0 2266 9125; www.river suncruise.com). More expensive is the overnight trip on board a restored teakwood barge by Manohra Cruises (tel: 0 2477 0770; www.manohracruises.com)

tightly pressed against the roof that it appears to be holding the roof up. With an unmistakably Chinese atmosphere, Wat Phanan Choeng was a favourite with the Chinese traders of the time, who prayed there before setting out on long voyages. The temple also holds the **Mae Soi Dok Mak** shrine, a tribute to a Chinese princess who supposedly killed herself on this spot after an icy reception from her love interest, an Ayutthayan king.

One of the best-preserved sections is **Phom Phet**, across the river from Wat Phanan Choeng. Near Phom Phet is the restored **Wat Suwan Dararam**, built near the close of the Ayutthaya period. Destroyed by the Burmese in 1767, the temple was rebuilt by King Rama I. Most of its wall murals date from the reign of Rama III and includes an unconventional one that depicts King Narusuen's famous battle with the Burmese. Still used as a temple, the wat is magical in the early evening as the monks chant prayers.

Upstream from Wat Phanan Choeng by the river bank is the restored **Wat Phutthaisawan**. Seldom visited, it is quiet, and the landing is an excellent place to enjoy the river's tranquillity in the evenings. Further upstream, the **Cathedral of St Joseph** is a Catholic reminder of the large European population that lived in the city at its prime.

Where the river bends to the north is one of Ayutthaya's most romantic ruins, **Wat Chai Wattanaram**, erected in 1630. Modelled after the Angkor Wat

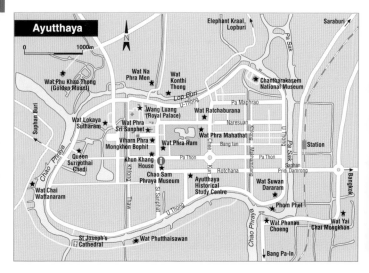

Ayutthaya

(Map legend: 0 — 1000m, N)

Locations shown on the map include: Elephant Kraal, Lopburi; Saraburi; Pa Sak; Wat Phu Khao Thong (Golden Mount); Wat Na Phra Men; Wat Konthi Thong; Chanthharakasem National Museum; Lop-Buri; U-Thong; Pa Maphrao; Suphan Buri; Wat Lokaya Sutharam; Wang Luang (Royal Palace); Wat Ratchaburana; Wat Phra Sri Sanphet; Naresuan; U Thong; Pa Sak; Viharn Phra Mongkhon Bophit; Wat Phra Mahathat; Bang Ian; Station; Chee; Wat Phra Ram; Chao Phraya; Queen Suriyothai Chedi; Khun Khang House; Pa Thon; Pa Thon; Chao Sam Phraya Museum; Rotchana; Saphan Pridi Damrong; Bangkok; Wat Chai Wattanaram; Ayutthaya Historical Study Centre; Khlong; Si Sanphet; Thaw; U Thong; Wat Suwan Dararam; Phom Phet; St Joseph's Cathedral; Wat Phutthaisawan; Wat Phanan Choeng; Wat Yai Chai Mongkhon; Bang Pa-In

substantial size, if the foundations for the stables of some 100 elephants are of any indication. Established by King Borom Matrailokanat in the 15th century, it was later razed by the Burmese. The bricks were moved to Bangkok to build the city's defensive walls, so only remnants of the foundations survive to mark the site.

Beside the palace stand the three Ceylonese-style *chedis* of **Wat Phra Sri Sanphet**, the royal temple. Two of the *chedis* were built in 1492 by King Borommatrailokanat's son, Ramathibodi II, to hold the ashes of his father and brother, while the third was added in 1540 by Ramathibodi II's son to hold the ashes of his late father. The three spires have become the archetypal image of Ayutthaya.

For two centuries after Ayutthaya's fall, a bronze Buddha dating back to the 15th century and over 12m tall sat unsheltered near Wat Phra Sri Sanphet. Its flame of knowledge (on the top of its head) and one of its arms had been broken when the roof, set on fire by the Burmese, collapsed. A new building based on the original, the **Viharn Phra Mongkhon Bophit**, was built in 1956 around the statue.

Across the road to the east, **Wat Phra Ram** is founded in 1369 by the son of Ayutthaya's founding king, Prince U-Thong. Elephant gates punctuate the old walls, and the central terrace is dominated by a crumbling *prang* to which clings a gallery of stucco *naga*, *garuda* and Buddha statues. The reflection of Wat Phra Ram's *prang* shimmers in the pool that surrounds the complex, making it one of Ayutthaya's most tranquil settings.

NOTABLE TEMPLES

Two of Ayutthaya's finest temples stand side by side across the lake from Wat Phra Ram. The first is **Wat Ratchaburana**, built in 1424 by the seventh king of Ayutthaya, King Borom Rachathirat II as a memorial to his brothers who died as a result of a duel for the throne. Excavations during its restoration in 1957 revealed a crypt below the towering central *prang*, containing a stash of gold jewellery, Buddha images and other art objects, among them a magnificent ceremonial sword and an intricately decorated elephant statue. The narrow, claustrophobic

Below: another view of Wat Phra Sri Sanphet.

One of the best ways of exploring the widely spread-out ruins of Ayutthaya is on bicycles. These can be rented for about B50 a day at many guesthouses in Ayutthaya. Otherwise, hire a motorised *tuk tuk* with a driver for about B180 an hour.

and dimly lit crypt can be accessed through a doorway in the *prang*, leading down steep stairs to some barely visible wall paintings.

The second temple, across the road, is **Wat Phra Mahathat**, Temple of the Great Relic, once one of the most beautiful temple complexes in Ayutthaya. Dating from the 1380s, the site was the focal point for religious ceremonies, and where King Ramesuen resided. Its glory was its huge laterite *prang*, which originally stood at 46m high. The *prang* later collapsed, but its foundations are still there circled by restored *chedis*. A much revered symbol here is a stone Buddha head that is embedded in the gnarled roots of an old banyan tree. Next door is a model of how the royal city may have once looked.

MUSEUMS

Looters quickly made off with many of Ayutthaya's glories, but the remaining treasures are now kept in the **Chao Sam Phraya Museum** just to the south (tel: 0 3524 1587; www.thailandmuseum.com; Wed–Sun 9am–4pm; entrance charge).

Nearby is another museum, the **Ayutthaya Historical Study Centre** (tel: 0 3524 5124; Mon–Fri 9am–4.30pm, Sat–Sun 9am–5pm; entrance charge). Funded by the Japanese government

and located on land that was once part of the Japanese quarter, the modern building houses hi-tech exhibits that guide visitors through 400 years of Ayutthaya's development, trade, administration and social changes.

To the east is the **Chantharakasem National Museum**, formerly the Chantharakasem Palace (tel: 0 3525 5124; www.thailandmuseum.com; Wed–Sun 9am–4pm; entrance charge). It was originally constructed outside the city walls. King Maha Thammaracha built it for his son Prince Naresuen (later king), and it became the residence for future heirs apparent. In 1767, the Burmese destroyed the palace, but King Mongkut resurrected it in the 19th century as a summer retreat. Today, it looks out on the noisiest part of modern Ayutthaya. The palace's collection isn't that impressive but still worth a look.

To its rear is the European-style **Pisai Sayalak** tower, built by King Mongkut for stargazing. Across the street from the palace is the boat pier for trips around the island, and the night market with food stalls set up beside the water. It is a good spot to unwind at the end of the day.

Bridge over the River Kwai

Kanchanaburi, 130km west of Bangkok; free; train from Bangkok Noi station (daily) or Hualamphong station (weekend only), or bus from Southern Bus Terminal; map p.20

Spanning the Kwae Yai River (also known as Kwai Yai), this latticed steel bridge, which takes its name from a 1957 film of the same name, has

Above: the Democracy Monument.

become a war memorial. It can be reached by boat or rickshaw from Kanchanaburi town.

The bridge was one of two bridges built side by side. The earlier wooden structure was completed in 1942, with the sturdier steel bridge erected by May 1943. Both bridges became constant targets for Allied bombers and were eventually bombed out of action in 1945. Only the eight curved segments on each side of the current structure are original; the rest were rebuilt after the war as part of Japan's war reparations.

Democracy Monument

Corner of Thanon Ratchadamnoen Klang and Thanon Dinso; free; pier: Phra Athit; map p.135 C2

Behind the City Hall is the Democracy Monument, designed by Italian sculptor Corrado Feroci (also known as Silpa Bhirasri), who is much honoured today as the founder of Silpakorn University and the father of Thailand's modern art movement.

Built in 1939, the monument is a celebration of Thailand's 1932 transition

77

Above: the Giant Swing was the site of a Brahman ceremony.

from absolute to constitutional monarchy. Marked by four elongated wings 24m tall, the central metal tray contains a copy of the constitution. Almost every detail and measurement of the monument has symbolic relevance. The 75 cannons are symbolic of the Buddhist year 2575, equivalent to AD1932. Plaster reliefs at the base represent the revolutionaries.

The monument is a potent symbol of democracy. The avenue between here and Sanam Luang is a natural site for public demonstration. It was in this vicinity that the massacres of 1973, 1976 and 1992 took place. A rallying point for civil discontent in May 1992, the monument became the scene of a bloodbath after the army violently suppressed peaceful demonstrations against the military dictatorship. More than 100 protesters were killed during the incident. The monument also serves as a memorial for those who died in those violent years.

Giant Swing

Thanon Bamrung Muang; free; pier: Tha Chang; map p.135 C1
In former days, the Giant Swing (Sao Ching Cha) was the venue for an annual Brahman ceremony dedicated to the god Shiva. As crowds gathered, four sturdy men would pump themselves back and forth to set the giant swing in motion, trying to grab bags of coins suspended on a 15-m-tall pole with their teeth. Not surprisingly, many plummeted to the ground, either injuring or killing themsleves, and the festival was halted in the 1930s during the reign of King Prajadhipok. With the swing itself now removed, the tall red-painted timber frame has become little more than a curious street marker.

Lak Muang

Thanon Sanam Chai; daily 5am–7pm; free; pier: Tha Chang; map p.134 B1
Every Thai city has a foundation stone, around which the city's guardian spirits gravitate, protecting and bringing good fortune to worshippers and the municipality. King Rama I erected the Lak Muang, or City Pillar, to mark the official centre of the Bangkok when the capital was officially established in 1782.

Located across the eastern wall of the Grand Palace, this gilded wooden pillar is sheltered by a Khmer-style *prang*. Resembling the Hindu Shiva lingam, which represents potency, it is accompanied by the taller city pillar of Thonburi, which was moved here when the former capital became part of Bangkok. The pillar is watched over by a pavilion containing several golden spirit-idols. Devotees thankful their prayers have been answered usually hire resident classical *lakhon* dancers to perform in an adjoining *sala* (pavilion).

Phra Pathom Chedi

Nakhon Pathom, 56km west of Bangkok; free; train from Hualamphong or bus from Southern Bus Terminal; map p.20
The town of Nakhon Pathom, west of the Rose Garden Riverside Resort on Route 4, is known for the colossal golden Phra Pathom Chedi.

Below: the Lak Muang is Bangkok's spiritual centre.

> Lak Muang and its attendant spirits are believed to have the power to grant fertility and other wishes. Floral offerings are piled high around the pillar, and the surrounding air is laden with incense. Devotees bow reverently before pressing a square of gold leaf to the monument.

Above: the the Statue of King Chulalongkorn.

This 130-m-tall landmark is claimed as the tallest Buddhist monument in the world, and possibly the oldest Buddhist site in the country, dating back to 3BC.

The original small Sri Lankan-style *chedi* was erected to commemorate the arrival of Indian Buddhist missionaries who supposedly brought Buddhism to Thailand via Burma in 3BC. Nakhon Pathom was settled in the 6th–11th centuries by the Dvaravati empire, a Mon civilisation whose culture flourished in Burma and Thailand. In the early 11th century the Khmers from Angkor invaded, overrunning the city and replacing the original *chedi* with a Brahman-style *prang*.

Then in 1057, the Burmese army besieged the town, leaving the religious edifice in ruins. When King Mongkut visited the old *chedi* in 1853, he was so impressed by its historical significance that he ordered the restoration of the temple. A new *chedi* was built, covering the older one; the present structure was completed by King Chulalongkorn.

Set in a huge square park, the massive *chedi* rests on a circular terrace and is accented with trees associated with the Buddha's life. Located in the compound is the **Phra Pathom Chedi National Museum** (tel: 0 4447 1167; www.thailandmuseum.com; Wed–Sun 9am–noon and 1–4pm; entrance charge), which is worth seeing for its collection of artefacts, which includes tools, carvings and statuary from the Dvaravati period.

Statue of King Chulalongkorn

Thanon Sri Ayutthaya, Dusit Park; free; pier: Thewet; map p.135 D4

The broad square in front of the old National Assembly building, along Thanon Sri Ayutthaya, is known as the **Royal Plaza**. The square is watched over by the bronze Statue of King Chulalongkorn on horseback. Chulalongkorn was responsible for the

construction of much of this part of Bangkok, which was once a rustic royal retreat from the city and the Grand Palace.

The king was the first Thai monarch to venture to Europe and his travels left a lasting impact on the architecture and layout of this district, which looks as much European as it is Thai. A great reformer and modern thinker, Chulalongkorn abolished slavery, put the country on the road to modernisation, and kept the colonialists from knocking at Thailand's door. He is revered as a god, and on the anniversary of his death each year on 23 October, people lay wreaths at the base of the statue in his honour. With the present king resident in the nearby Chitralada Palace and the day-to-day governance taking place in the Parliament House, this area is still the heartbeat of the nation.

Below: the Phra Pathom Chedi is the largest in the world.

Museums and Galleries

B angkok and its surroundings are home to scores of museums catering to various interests, including the history-filled National Museum, modest but sombre war memorials, and the charming, architecturally rich Jim Thompson's House Museum located in a cluster of traditional Thai houses *(see Architecture, p.23)*. Most contemporary art, by both local and international artists, is on view in commercial and non-profit art galleries as well as in alternative spaces in university campuses.

100 Tonson Gallery

100 Soi Tonson, off Thanon Ploenchit; tel: 0 2684 1527; www.100tonsongallery.com; Thur–Sun 11am–7pm; free; BTS: Ploen Chit; map p.141 D4
Housed within a private residence, this gallery attracts some of the country's best artists and holds high-profile exhibitions that create a lot of media buzz.

Ayutthaya Historical Park

Ayutthaya, 85km north of Bangkok; daily 8am–5pm; entrance charge; train from Hualamphong, bus from Northern Bus Terminal, or boat *(see box on p.75)*; map p.20
Within Ayutthaya Historical Park are a few museums worth visiting: the **Chao Sam Phraya Museum**, the **Ayutthaya Historical Study Centre** and the **Chantharakasem National Museum**.
SEE ALSO MONUMENTS, P.77

Bangkok University Gallery

Bangkok University City Campus, 3/F, Building 9, 40/4 Thanon Rama IV, Kluaynamtai;

Above: a work shown at the 100 Tonson Gallery, *Gaga Society*, by Chatchai Puipia.

tel: 0 2350 3635; Tue–Sat 9.30am–7pm; free; BTS: Ekkamai; map p.18
There is little mainstream art at this lofty space. It is one of the best places in Bangkok to view edgy conceptual installations from Thai artists.

Chulalongkorn Art Centre

7/F, Centre of Academic Resources, Chulalongkorn University, Thanon Phaya Thai; tel: 0 2218 2964; Mon–Fri 9am–7pm, Sat 9–8pm; free; BTS: Siam; map p.140 B3
One of the city's most progressive contemporary art

galleries, this attracts some of the country's most prolific artists, as well as influential foreign ones.

Death Railway Museum

73 Thanon Jaokannun, Kanchanaburi, 130km west of Bangkok; tel: 0 3451 2721; www.tbrconline.com; daily 9am–5pm; entrance charge; train from Bangkok Noi station (daily) or Hualamphong station (weekend only), or bus from Southern Bus Terminal; map p.20
Opened in 2003 and founded by Australian Rod Beattie, the local supervisor of the

Left: the Samranmukhamat pavilion at the National Museum.

H Gallery

201 Soi 12, Thanon Sathorn; mobile tel: 081 310 4428; www.hgallerybkk.com; Thur–Sat noon–6pm, Sun–Wed by appointment; free; BTS: Surasak; map p.16

Run by an American, this gallery is located in a late-19th-century wooden colonial building. It promotes a young and eclectic stable of commercially viable artists.

JEATH War Museum

Wat Chaichumpol, Thanon Pak Phraek, Kanchanaburi town, 130km west of Bangkok; daily 8.30am–6pm; entrance charge; train from Bangkok Noi station (daily) or Hualamphong station (weekend only), or bus from Southern Bus Terminal; map p.20

The acronym JEATH comes from the first letter of some of the principal countries that were involved in the regional conflict during World War II, namely Japan, England, America, Thailand and Holland. This small but informative museum is split into two buildings, the larger of which is a long bamboo hut similar to those that

Check the monthly free cultural map *Art Connection*, as well as the *Bangkok Post*, *The Nation* and local magazines for listings of exhibitions and cultural events.

Commonwealth War Graves Commission, the Death Railway Museum at the Thailand–Burma Railway Centre has eight galleries that trace the history and recount the sufferings of the people involved without making biased judgement. It even has a full-scale replica of the original wooden bridge.

The Japanese began work on a railway between Thailand and Burma in 1942. For most of its 400-km length, the railway followed the river valley because this allowed its construction to take place simultaneously in different areas. The Japanese forced some 250,000 Asian labourers and 61,000 Allied POWs to construct 260km of rail on the Thai side, leading to the Three Pagodas Pass on the

Thai-Burmese border. An estimated 100,000 Asian labourers and 16,000 Allied POWs lost their lives in 1942–5 from beatings, starvation and disease.

Adjacent to the museum is the **Allied War Cemetery** (daily 7am–6pm; free). Lined up row upon row are the graves of some 7,000 Allied soldiers from Britain, America, Australia, Holland and other countries, representing less than half of the 16,000 soliders who lost their lives.

Below: bomb display at the JEATH War Museum.

housed the POWs during their construction of the Thailand-Burma railway. Inside is a collection of poignant photographs, sketches, paintings, newspaper clippings and other war memorabilia, giving you an idea of the harsh conditions the POWs endured.

The museum is tucked away in the grounds of Wat Chaichumpol in the southern end of Kanchanaburi town. Its peaceful locale on the banks of the Mae Khlong River provides for a quiet moment of reflection.

Museum of Forensic Medicine

2/F, Adulaydejvigrom Building, Sirirat Hospital, 2 Thanon Phrannok; tel: 0 2419 7000; Mon–Fri 8.30am–4.30pm; free; pier: Sirirat; map p.134 A2

Within the Sirirat Hospital complex is the Museum of Forensic Medicine, frequented by medical students. Green arrows point the way from the hospital grounds to the museum, located on the second floor of the Forensic Department. The stomach-churning exhibits are definitely not for the queasy. Mummified corpses of Thailand's most notorious criminals, deformed foetuses in formaldehyde and a

Left: the National Gallery grounds are dotted with sculptures.

gallery of disturbing post-mortem photographs are among the exhibits here.

Museum of Old Cannons

Opposite Lak Muang, Thanon Sanam Chai; daily 24 hours; free; pier: Tha Chang; map p.134 B1

Across the street from the Lak Muang is this remotely interesting battalion of antique armoury belonging to the Museum of Old Cannons. In front of the 19th-century European-style former barracks are displays of battle-worn and bulky cast-iron cannons.

National Gallery

4 Thanon Chao Fah, opposite National Theatre; tel: 0 2281 2224; Wed–Sun 9am–4pm; entrance charge; pier: Phra Athit; map p.134 B2

The National Gallery has seen better days as an exhi-

bition space, with little renovation since the 1970s. Situated within a fine old colonial-style building that used to function as the Royal Mint, the gallery and its permanent collection of traditional and contemporary Thai art are not particularly outstanding. However, the annex on both sides of the gallery holds interesting monthly exhibitions, mainly by local groups, veteran Thai artists, the odd cutting-edge young artist and occasional international expositions.

National Museum

4 Thanon Na Phra That; tel: 0 2224 1333; www.thailandmuseum.com; Wed–Sun 9am–4pm; entrance charge; guided tours Wed and Thur 9.30am; pier: Phra Athit; map p.134 B2

To learn about Thai history and culture, the National Museum, located between Thammasat University and the National Theatre, is a good place to start.

Below: statue of King Chulalongkorn at the National Museum.

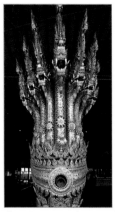

Above: barges at the Museum of Royal Barges: the Anantanaganaj barge *(left)* with a seven-headed *naga*; the Suphannahong and Narai Song Suban barges *(right)*.

Besides housing a vast collection of antiquities from all over Southeast Asia, the museum has an interesting history of its own. Its grounds and some of the principal rooms were part of the former Wang Na (Front Palace) of the king's second-in-line, the Prince Successor, a feature of the Thai monarchy until 1870.

The oldest buildings in the compound date from 1782. These include the splendid **Buddhaisawan Chapel**, built by the Prince Successor as his private place of worship within the palace. It contains some of Thailand's most beautiful and best-preserved murals, depicting 28 scenes from the Buddha's life and dating from the 1790s. Above the

The Sala Samranmukhamat pavilion was originally located in Dusit Palace, and was moved to the National Museum during the reign of King Rama VII (1925–35). Such open-sided pavilions, commonly found in temples and palaces, are used as meeting or resting places.

windows, five bands of angels kneel in silent respect to Thailand's second-most sacred Buddha image, the famous Phra Buddha Sihing. According to legend, the bronze image came from Ceylon (now Sri Lanka), but art historians attribute it to 13th-century Sukhothai. The image is paraded through the streets of Bangkok each year on the day before the Songkran festival.

To the left of the entrance is the **Sivamokhaphiman Hall**, originally an open-sided audience hall. The front of this building is devoted to the **Thai History Gallery**, covering Thai history from the Sukhothai period to the present Rattanakosin period.

Behind the Sivamokhaphi-man Hall is the **Prehistoric Gallery**, with 5,000-year-old exhibits excavated from the Ban Chiang archaeological site in Northeast Thailand.

Also on site is the **Red House** (Tamnak Daeng), an old golden-teak dwelling that once belonged to King Rama I's elder sister. Built in Ayutthayan style, the house has an ornate wood finish

and elegant early Bangkok-style furnishings.

The central audience hall of the **Wang Na** (Front Palace) is divided into rooms containing various ethnological exhibits of elephant howdahs, woodcarvings, ceramics, palanquins, *khon* masks, musical instruments and other treasures. Temporary exhibits are displayed in the **Throne Hall**.

Most of the exhibits are weak on contextual information, so buy a copy of the museum guidebook or join the excellent guided tour.

National Museum of Royal Barges

Khlong Bangkok Noi, off Chao Phraya River, Thanon Arun Amarin; tel: 0 2424 0004; daily 9am–5pm; entrance charge; boat; map p.134 A3
On the northern bank of the Khlong Bangkok Noi canal is the National Museum of Royal Barges. Its dry-dock warehouse displays eight vessels from a fleet of over 50 that are rarely put to sail except on auspicious occasions, such as the anniversary of King Bhumibol's 60th year

on the throne in 2006. During the royal barge procession, barges sweep down the Chao Phraya River in a formation that stretched nearly 1,200m wide. The 52 gilded barges were manned by 2,200 oarsmen while the king watched and entertained visiting royals from 25 nations from the old palace of King Taksin. The current fleet was built during the reign of King Rama I and originally numbered over 100. Half of these were destroyed in World War II.

The first royal barges preceding the present fleet date back to 14th-century Ayutthaya. In the old days, the royal family, like everyone else, would travel by boat. The king would sit in the largest of the barges, the magnificent Suphannahong, which was made from a single trunk of teak stretching over 46m. The model on display was built in 1911, based on the design of its 18th-century predecessor.

Other barges at the museum include the Anantanaganaj, second in rank and built in 1914; its prow features a *naga*, the seven-headed king of the serpents. The Narai Song Suban, its prow adorned by the god Vishnu riding a *garuda*, was built in 1996 to commemorate King Bhumibol's Golden Jubilee.

Prasart Museum

9 Soi 4A Krungthep Kreetha, Thanon Krungthep Kreetha, Huamak; tel: 0 2379 3601; Thur–Sun 10am–3pm only by appointment; entrance charge; map p.20

Although little visited, partly because of its rather remote location in the Bangkok suburb of Huamak, this museum makes for a worth-while excursion. Set within a garden, it displays a Thai antique arts and crafts collection that belongs to the private collector Prasart Vongsakul. The artefacts are contained in several magnificent buildings, all of which are replicas inspired by the region's architectural classics. These elegant structures include a European-style mansion, a Khmer shrine, and teak houses from Thailand's northern and central regions.

Queen's Gallery

101 Thanon Ratchadamnoen Klang; tel: 02281 5360–1; www.queengallery.org; daily Thur–Tue 10am–7pm; entrance charge; pier: Wat Sam Praya; map p.135 C2

This five-floor gallery, whose patron is Queen Sirikit, has exhibitions of local modern and contemporary paintings and sculptures.

Rotunda Gallery

Neilson Hays Library, 195 Thanon Surawong; tel: 0 2233 1731; www.neilsonhayslibrary. com; Tue–Sun 9.30am–5pm; free; BTS: Chong Nonsi; map p.140 A1

The circular Rotunda Gallery in the elegant **Neilsen Hays Library** building hosts monthly shows of mainly conventional art. Another art space in the building, the **Garden Gallery**, overlooking the peaceful garden, also hosts art exhibitions.

The nostalgic Neilsen Hays Library, founded in 1869, was and still is a cultural haven for the city's foreign residents. It takes its name from Jennie Neilson Hays, a founder of the Bangkok Ladies' Library Association. Today, it has a collection of over 20,000 English-language books.

Below: a Buddha image at the National Museum.

Above: inside the historical Neilson Hays Library.

Royal Elephant Museum

Thanon U-Thong Nai, Dusit Park; tel: 0 2282 3336; daily 9.30am–4pm; entrance charge, or free with Grand Palace ticket; map p.135 E4

This museum was formerly a stable with three very rare white elephants. It now displays a large model of one of the present king's prized living pachyderms, tusks and other paraphernalia. The white elephant is regarded as Thailand's national symbol, and every white elephant found in Thailand rightfully belongs to the king. White elephants look nearly the same as common grey ones. It is only by a complicated process of examining skin colour, hair, eyes and genitalia that an elephant's albino traits can be determined.

Silpakorn University Gallery

31 Thanon Na Phra Lan, opposite the Grand Palace; tel: 0 623 6120 ext. 1418; Mon–Fri 9am–7pm, Sat 9am–4pm; free; pier: Tha Chang; map p.134 B1

Thailand's oldest and most prestigious arts university has three galleries displaying works by students, teachers and visiting artists. Its **Hall of Sculpture** (Mon–Fri 8.30am– 4.30pm; free) features plaster casts of monuments honouring royalty and dignitaries, the originals of which are found throughout the country.

Thavibu Gallery

Suite 308, Silom Galleria, Thanon Silom; tel: 0 2266 5454; www.thavibu.com; Tue–Sat 11am–7pm, Sun noon–6pm; free; BTS: Surasak; map p.139 E1

This is a good gallery to see Thai, Vietnamese and Burmese art, usually by up-and-coming artists. It is located in Silom Galleria, an arts and crafts mall devoted to jewellers, galleries and antiques dealers. It is a great place to see and purchase works by Thai artists.

VER Gallery

2/F, 71/31–35 Klongsarn Plaza, Thanon Charoen Nakhon; tel: 0 2861 0933; www.ver.info; free; pier: Klong San; map p.139 D2

> Silpakorn University was the brainchild of Italian sculptor Corrado Feroci, known to Thais as Silpa Bhirasri. He was invited to Bangkok in the 1920s to work on public commissions, such as the Democracy Monument (see Monuments, p.77).

An eclectic range of works is found at this offbeat and funky art space founded by Thai superstar artist Rirkrit Vejjajiva.

Wat Phra Kaew Museum and Coins and Decorations Museum

Grand Palace and Wat Phra Kaew, entrance along Thanon Na Phra Lan; tel: 0 2623 5500; www.palaces.thai.net; daily 8.30am–3.30pm; entrance charge for Grand Palace; pier: Tha Chang; map p.134 B1

The Wat Phra Kaew Museum, located in the Grand Palace complex, showcases seasonal costumes of the Emerald Buddha (see p.123) and a superb collection of small Buddha images made of silver, ivory, crystal and other materials. Next to the ticket office is the Coins and Decorations Museum, which has a collection of coins dating from the 11th century and also royal regalia, decorations and medals made of gold and precious stones.

World War II Museum

Kanchanaburi, 130km west of Bangkok; daily 9am–6pm; entrance charge; train from Bangkok Noi station (daily) or Hualamphong station (weekend only), or bus from Southern Bus Terminal; map p.20

Located near the Bridge over the River Kwai, this is also known as the Art Gallery & War Museum. It contains an odd mix of exhibits, including war-related articles such as photographs and weapons. But many exhibits have nothing to do with the war at all. If you are into kitsch, there's plenty to interest you, such as life-sized statues of war figures like Hitler, Hirohito, and Churchill, and murals of past winners of the Miss Thailand pageant.

85

Music

Thai classical music eludes many finely tuned
Western ears. To novices, it sounds like a
melange of contrasting tones without any
pattern. To aficionados, it has a very distinct
rhythm and plan. Visitors normally get the
chance to hear repertoires of Thai classical music
during traditional drama-dance sequences or at
muay thai matches. Meanwhile, the classical
music and opera scenes in Bangkok continue
to thrive, supported by the Bangkok Opera and
the Bangkok Symphony Orchestra. Live-jazz
venues have also mushroomed in Bangkok,
particularly in five-star hotels.

Thai Classical Music

To the uninitiated, Thai
classical music sounds like
a jarring and ear-piercing
mishmash of tones. The
key is to listen to it as one
would jazz, picking out one
instrument and following it,
switching to another as the
mood moves one. Thai music
is set to a scale of seven full
steps, with a lilting and
steady rhythm. Each
instrument plays the same
melody, but in its own way
and seemingly without regard
to how others are playing it.
Seldom does an instrument
rise in solo; it is always
being challenged and cajoled
by the other instruments of
the orchestra.

A classical *phipat*
orchestra comprises a single-
reed instrument, the oboe-
like *phinai*, and a variety of
percussion instruments. The
pitch favours the treble, with
the pace set by the *ching*, a
tiny cymbal, aided by the
drums beaten with fingers.
The melody is played by two
types of *ranad*, a bamboo-
bar xylophone, and two sets
of *gong wong*, tuned gongs

Above: a *phipat* ensemble.

arranged in a semi-circle
around the player.

Another type of orchestra
employs two violins, the
saw-oo and the *saw-duang*.
It is usually heard accompanying a Thai dance-drama.
The *ja-khe*, a stringed instrument similar to a Japanese
koto, sits flush with the floor
and is often played as a solo
instrument in the lobbies of
some of Bangkok's larger
hotels and restaurants.

A separate type of
orchestra performs at Thai
boxing matches to spur
combatants to action.
It is composed of four
instruments: the *ching*, two

double-reed oboe-like
flutes, and a drum. It plays
a repertoire that is entirely
its own.

Opera and Western Classical Music

Multitalented Somtow
Sucharitkul set up the
Bangkok Opera
(www.bangkokopera.com) in
2002. Among its three or
four yearly productions are
classics like *The Magic Flute*
and Somtow's own works,
written in English, such as
Mae Naak, which is based on
a Thai ghost story. His works
are mainly staged at the
Thailand Cultural Centre.

Left: live jazz at the Saxophone Pub.

sugarbangkok.com; daily 11am–2pm and 5pm–1am; BTS: Ratchadamri or MRT: Silom; map p.140 C3
Long-established and intimate two-floor bar with modern jazz.

Diplomat Bar
Conrad Hotel, All Seasons Place; 87 Thanon Withayu; tel: 0 2690 9999; www.conradhotels.com; Sun–Thur 10am–1am, Fri–Sat 10am–2am; BTS: Phloen Chit; map p.141 D3
Seductive jazz singers and a chic décor featuring dark woods make this jazz bar one of the city's best. Sit at the circular bar.

Living Room
Sheraton Grande Sukhumvit; 250 Thanon Sukhumvit; tel: 0 2653 0333; www.starwood.com/bangkok; daily 9am–midnight; BTS: Asok or MRT: Sukhumvit; map p.141 E3
Top-notch jazz at this open-plan circular bar featuring respected jazz musicians from overseas.

Saxophone Pub
3/8 Thanon Phaya Thai; tel: 0 2246 5472; www.saxophonepub.com; daily 7.30pm–1am; BTS: Victory Monument; map p.136 C3
This lively two-floor venue, almost two decades old, features at least two resident bands each night that get the crowd jiving to excellent jazz, R&B, soul and funk.

Other Live Music
SEE NIGHTLIFE, P.93.

Bangkok's International Festival of Dance & Music from September to October every year brings in several hundred international opera, classical music, contemporary dance and ballet acts.

The **Bangkok Symphony Orchestra** (BSO) (www.bangkoksymphony.org) plays concerts throughout the year, often at the Thai Cultural Centre, and on Sundays in Lumphini Park during the cool season. The BSO has been actively preserving the country's musical heritage by releasing CD recordings of Thai classics.

Venues

Thailand Cultural Centre
Thanon Ratchada Phisek; tel: 0 2247 0028; www.thaiculturalcenter.com; MRT: Thailand Cultural Centre
This centre stages everything from pop concerts to performances by the Bangkok Opera and the Bangkok Symphony Orchestra. It is a venue for the International Festival of Dance & Music.

National Theatre
Thanon Ratchini; tel: 0 2224 1342; pier: Phra Athit; map p.134 B2
The Fine Arts Department periodically stages performances of traditional Thai music and dance-drama at the National Theatre. This venue also occasionally presents big-name foreign groups like the New York Philharmonic.

Live Jazz

Bamboo Bar
The Oriental, 48 Oriental Avenue; tel: 0 2236 0400; Sun–Thur 11am–1am, Fri–Sat 11am–2am; BTS: Saphan Taksin; pier: Oriental; map p.139 E1
This cosy bar with wicker furnishings evokes a bygone era. The band plays laid-back jazz classics and accompany distinguished guest singers.

Brown Sugar
231/20 Thanon Sarasin; tel: 0 2250 0103; www.brown

Below: Brown Sugar.

Nightlife

Bangkok's nightlife scene is among the very best in the world. Many visitors' expectations of Bangkok nightlife extend no further than the much-hyped Patpong go-go bar scene, but this cosmopolitan city has plenty of other options for entertainment. The Thai affinity for *sanuk* (fun) has seen a recent boom in microbreweries, bars offering everything from Cuban cigars and art on the walls, and clubs specialising in music as diverse as jazz, Latin, hip hop, house and techno, often all on the same street. Luxury hotels have also entered the scene with classy lobby bars and lounges with international sensibilities.

Nightlife Zones

The only damper in Bangkok's nightlife scene is the Social Order Campaign introduced in 2001, which forces nightlife spots to close early. Bent on clamping rampant drug abuse and underage drinking, the government has designated three nightlife zones: **Thanon Silom**, **Thanon Ratchadaphisek** and **Royal City Avenue** (RCA), in which venues with valid dance licences can stay open until 2am. The rest must close at 1am. Be prepared for the occasional police raid when revellers are urine-tested for drugs. During such raids, the police may ask foreigners to show their passports – or face a fine. Many clubs, including Bed Supperclub and Q Bar, won't let you in without one. To get around the miserably early closing time, do as what most Thais are forced to do: start your evening early, say, by 10.30pm.

The Silom zone includes the Patpong red-light district as well as numerous pubs and restaurants, but few dance clubs outside Soi 2 and Soi 4. Thanon Ratchadaphisek has been the traditional stomping ground of huge clubs and even larger massage parlours, visited mainly by Thais and Asian tourists, but recently, a clutch of smaller new bars are attracting young Thais. Of the three zones, RCA has developed into the most focused club scene, with a stretch of hip bars and clubs.

Venues

Entry fees for clubs were almost unheard of a decade ago, but in order to keep out the riff-raff (particularly working girls) and keep the crowd chic, several spots now impose a cover charge.

Dance music in clubs has evolved from techno to include hip hop, deep house, jungle, Indian vibes, and countless variations led by cutting-edge dance clubs like Bed Supperclub, Q Bar and Club Culture, all of which draw multinational crowds. All these spots regularly import international DJs like Felix da Housecat, Nick Zinner (from the rock band Yeah, Yeah, Yeahs) and Dimitri, in addition to hosting an increasingly confident posse of local DJs who go

Below: Q Bar is stylishly dark.

Left: Calypso cabaret at the Asia Hotel.

This two-floor bar with a stylish DJ booth draws in both backpackers and locals seeking great music. The DJs are mainly homegrown talent. Cocktails and Thai and Western fare are served.

Bar Baska

82/38 Soi Sukhumvit Soi 63; tel: 0 2711 4748–9; Tue–Sun 5pm–1am; BTS: Ekkamai; map p.18

Balinese-inspired bar and eatery set among lush tropical gardens and placid pools. Inside, the decor is just as atmospheric, with comfy sofas and chairs to sit on and soak up the chilled dance beats spun by local DJs.

Bull's Head

Soi Sukhumvit 33/1; tel: 0 2259 4444; www.greatbritishpub. com; daily 11.30am–1am; BTS: Phrom Phong; map p.18

Tucked away on a street dominated by Japanese eateries, this is as English and authentic as a pub can be. Attracts a loyal group of expats who enjoy the monthly visits by international comedians at the hugely popular Punchline Comedy Club. It offers a fine English bitter on draught.

Café Democ

78 Thanon Ratchadamnoen, next to Democracy Monument; tel: 0 2622 2571; Tue–Sun 11.30am–1am; map p.134 C2

Progressive drum 'n bass, hip hop and trip hop are the music choices here, mixed by local celebrity DJs. International guest DJs occasionally spin.

Distil

State Tower, 1055 Thanon Silom; tel: 0 2624 9555; www.thedome bkk.com; daily 6pm–1am; BTS: Saphan Taksin; map p.139 E1

Rising taller than any of the

by names like Dragon, Tay and Tui.

More local-oriented venues range from small trendy nightspots, such as Escudo on Sukhumvit Soi 55 (Soi Thonglor). A small Thai scene also flourishes in the backpacker quarter of Thanon Khao San, with hot venues like Café Democ and Susie Pub.

These days you can also sip fine champagne and cocktails at fashionable rooftop bars with scintillating views of the city and at plush hotel lobby bars frequented by sophisticated clientele. For good beers and hearty pub grub, head to an English or Irish pub around Thanon Silom or Thanon Sukhumvit.

Bars

Aqua

Four Seasons Hotel, 155 Thanon Ratchadamri; tel: 0 2251 6127; www.fourseasons.com/ bangkok; daily 6am–midnight; BTS: Ratchadamri; map p.141 C3

Sip martinis, cocktails or draught beers while enjoying the sophisticated ambience of this courtyard bar. It is set within a palm-lined tropical garden with a fish pond, bridges and fountains.

Bacchus

20/6–7 Soi Ruam Rudi; tel: 0 2650 8986; www. bacchus.tv; daily 5pm–1am; BTS: Phloen Chit; map p.141 D3

Located in the pleasant restaurant enclave of Ruam Rudi Village, this elegant four-storey wine bar sees a steady flow of creative and media types. Select from a list of 250 wines and 200 liquors.

Bangkok Bar

149 Soi Rambuttri; tel: 0 2629 4443; daily 7pm–1am; pier: Phra Athit; map p.134 B2

Touts on Patpong offer live sex shows. In some of these places, once inside you are handed an exorbitant bill and threatened if you protest. Pay, take the receipt and go immediately to the Tourist Police, who will usually take you back and demand a refund. Do keep track of the number of drinks you order and check your bill carefully before leaving.

Above: New York chic comes to Bangkok with the Flava Lounge.

city's other nightspots, Distil is part of the opulent Dome complex on the 64th floor of the State Tower building. Choose a fine champagne or single-malt scotch from the 2,000-bottle wine cellar, lie back on the outdoor balcony sofa cushions and enjoy the spectacular panorama of the Chao Phraya River.

Dubliner
440 Thanon Sukhumvit, corner with Washington Square (Soi 22); tel: 0 2204 1841–2; www.dublinerbangkok.com; daily 11am–1am; BTS: Phrom Phong; map p.18
Arguably the best of Bangkok's Irish pubs, this friendly place is decorated with Gaelic bric-a-brac. Pool tables, a big TV screen showing major sporting events, plus live music at weekends.

Afternoon and early-evening drinking isn't part of the Bangkok scene, so to draw customers, many bars offer excellent happy-hour deals like cheap drinks from noon till 9pm or two-drinks-for-one specials. Most bars close at 1am.

Face Bar
29 Sukhumvit Soi 38; tel: 0 2713 6048–9; www.facebars.com; daily 5pm–2am; BTS: Thong Lo; map p.18
A member of a small exclusive chain of restaurants and bars (branches in Shanghai and Jakarta), Face Bar is part of a Thai villa complex housing Indian and Thai restaurants. There's a mellow vibe in this beautiful, antique-filled lounge bar.

Flava Lounge
Dream BKK, 10 Sukhumvit Soi 15; tel: 0 2254 8500; www.dreambkk.com; BTS: Nana; map p.141 E3
One of Bangkok's newest boutique hotel, Dream, has jumped on the bandwagon with its own ultra-chic bar-cum-lounge located adjacent to Flava restaurant.

Gulliver's Traveller's Tavern
2 Thanon Khao San; tel: 0 2629 1988–9; www.gulliverbangkok.com; daily 11pm–1.30am; map p.134 B2
Perched at the end of the strip, this large alehouse is marked by a *tuk-tuk* above its door and usually teems with bleary-eyed tourists. This

American-style sports bar serves typical pub grub. (Also at 6 Sukhumvit Soi 5; tel: 0 2655 5340–2.)

Hu'u
The Ascott, 187 Thanon Sathorn Tai; tel: 0 2676 6677; www. huuinasia.com; daily 11am–2pm and 5pm–1am; BTS: Surasak; map p.16
This is a class act, combining a sophisticated cocktail lounge, restaurant and an art gallery. One of the highlights in this well-known outfit is the extensive cocktail list devised by its mixologist.

Indus
71 Sukhumvit Soi 26; tel: 0 2258 4900; www.indusbangkok.com; daily 6pm–midnight (bar), 11am–2.30pm and 6–11pm (restaurant); BTS: Phrom Phong; map p.18
This bar and restaurant sits in a 1960s art deco house nestled in a chichi neighborhood. A unique Indian-style bar that is great for cocktails and conversation. Unwind with an exotic drink and take drags on a *shisha* pipe.

Below: Distil boasts a huge cellar of 2,000 bottles.

Above: the exclusive Met Bar welcomes members and hotel guests only.

Londoner Brew Pub
Sukhumvit Soi 33; tel: 0 2261
0238–40; www.the-londoner.
com; daily 11am–1am;
BTS: Phrom Phong; map p.18
The main draw at this
cavernous basement pub is
the microbrewed beer, which
comes in several varieties,
including a slightly dark
English-style creamy bitter.
Shows major sports
competitions on TV.

The Met Bar
The Metropolitan, 27 Thanon
Sathorn Tai; tel: 0 2625 3399;
www.metropolitan.como.bz/
bangkok; BTS: Sala Daeng;
map p.141 C1
With the same panache of
London's trendy Met Bar, this
is one of Bangkok's most
exclusive yet friendly
nightspots. The dark, intimate guests- and members-
only bar features resident and
visiting international DJs.

Sunset Street
Thanon Khao San; tel: 0 2282
5823; map p.134 B2
Halfway up Khao San is this
complex, with a couple of
adjoining bars under the
same ownership. Fronting the
main street is **Sabai Bar** (daily
8am–1am), tucked behind is
Sanook Bar (daily 5pm–2am),
and right at the end of
the alley is a beautifully
renovated old house that
functions as the Kraichitti
Museum & Gallery.

Susie Pub
108/5–9 Soi Rambuttri, off
Thanon Khao San; tel: 0 2282
4459; daily 5pm–1am;
map p.134 C2
Hidden just off the strip, this
bar packs them in, no matter
what time of the night. The
draw seems to be the posse
of good-looking locals, and
enthusiastic backpackers try
to get into the action. A great
range of music, from reggae
to alternative, is played.

Syn Bar
Swissotel Nai Lert Park,
2 Thanon Withayu; tel: 0 2253
0123; www.swissotel.com;
BTS: Phloen Chit; map p.141 D4
This former lobby bar
has been dramatically
transformed into a retro-
chic cocktail lounge by
a New York designer.
The stunning all-female

bartenders mix up some
devilishly tasty cocktails and
flavoured martinis.

Vertigo Grill & Moon Bar
Banyan Tree Bangkok, 21/100
Thanon Sathorn Tai; tel: 0 2679
1200; www.banyantree.com;
daily 5pm–1am (bar),
6.30pm–11pm (restaurant);
MRT: Lumphini; map p.140 C1
Weather permitting, this
open-air rooftop lounge bar
is tops for panoramic views
of the city from 61 floors up.
Most come for the ravishing
vistas, though they are
sufficiently matched by
good barbecued dishes
and cocktails.

V9
Sofitel Silom, 188 Thanon
Silom; tel: 0 2238 1991;
www.sofitel.com; daily 5pm–
1am; BTS: Chong Nonsi;
map p.140 A1

Below: a quiet night out in Bangkok.

Above: 87+ at the Conrad is all sophistication and luxury.

Above: the Mexican-themed Senor Pico at the Rembrandt.

With awesome views from the 37th floor, this stylish wine bar and restaurant is a fine spot to sip great-value wines and enjoy fusion cuisine.

Zuk Bar

The Sukhothai, 13/3 Thanon Sathorn Tai; tel: 0 2344 8888; www.sukhothai.com; daily 4.30pm–1am; BTS: Sala Daeng or MRT: Lumphini; map p.141 C1

The chic lobby lounge bar, embellished with Asian antiques, overlooks tranquil ponds and offers instant relaxation on its plush sofas. DJ-mixed chill-out grooves play nightly from 9pm.

Clubs

87+

Conrad Hotel, All Seasons Place; 87 Thanon Withayu; tel: 0 2690 9999; www.conradhotels.com; Sun–Thur 9.30pm–2am, Fri–Sat 9.30pm–2am; BTS: Phloen Chit; map p.141 D3

This sexy upscale club appeals to a posh crowd comprising locals and hotel guests. Sink into one of the plush sofas, sip Cosmopolitans and enjoy music by international bands.

Bed Supperclub

26 Sukhumvit Soi 11; tel: 0 2651 3537; www.bedsupperclub.com; daily 7.30pm–1am; BTS: Nana; map p.141 E4

This striking, elliptically shaped eatery and lounge bar has diners literally eating on beds. Laid-back vibes are spun by resident DJs as diners mull over their meals. The other half of the venue operates as a bar-club.

SEE ALSO RESTAURANTS, P.110

Club Culture

Thanon Sri Ayutthaya; tel: 0 2653 7216; www.club-culture-bkk.com; daily 8pm–2am; BTS: Phaya Thai; map p.136 B2

This refurbished old theatre venue attracts international DJs. The eclectic music ranges from electro, garage and drum 'n bass to hip hop, house and disco.

Escudo

4–5/F, Dutchess Plaza, Sukhumvit Soi 55 (Soi Thonglor); tel: 0 2381 0865; daily 9pm–1am; BTS: Thong Lo; map p.18

This features a sleek interior that is packed on weekends with Bangkok's fashionable set. The club also hosts one of Bangkok's most popular models' nights, which brings in the crowds for obvious reasons.

Narcissus

112 Sukhumvit Soi 23; tel: 0 2258 4805; www.narcissusclubbangkok.com; daily 8pm–2am; BTS: Asok or MRT: Sukhumvit; map p.18

One of the city's biggest with fancy lights, sound system and décor. Clubbers are mainly dressy, cash-rich locals who come for the frenetic Euro-trance and techno beats.

Q Bar

34 Sukhumvit Soi 11; tel: 0 2252 3274; www.qbar bangkok.com; daily 8pm–2am; BTS: Nana; map p.141 E4

Modelled after a New York lounge bar, this stylishly dark and seductive two-floor venue plays the city's coolest dance music. The nightly line-up of mix maestros is legendary and the drinks list is impressive, with 50 brands of vodka.

Route 66

Royal City Avenue (between Thanon Phetchaburi and Rama IX); tel: 0 1916 2989; daily 8.30pm–2am; map p.18

Crammed with young Thais, this large club is divided into four directional themes – North, South, East and West. East features hip hop, while West plays more groovy fare. The décor is mostly white and minimalist.

Tapas Café & Tapas Room

Silom Soi 4; tel: 0 2632 0920–1;

daily 8pm–2am; BTS: Sala Daeng; map p.140 B2

A true survivor in the city's party scene, this compact, stylish two-floor dance bar is packed with beautiful twentysomething locals and expats downing margaritas. Choice of two music genres with different DJs on the decks downstairs and upstairs.

Zantika

Sukhumvit Soi 63 (Ekkamai); tel: 0 2711 5886–7; daily 9pm–2am; BTS: Ekkamai; map p.18

This spacious bar-club is a huge hit with trendy locals who nest either at the live music stage or at the separate dance club at the rear.

Live Music

Ad Makers

51/51 Soi Lang Suan, off Thanon Ploenchit; tel: 0 2652 0168; daily 5pm–1am; BTS: Chit Lom; map p.141 C4

The faux rustic charm and Thai menu obviously appeal but the two acts playing pop and rock covers are the main draws. This is one of the city's liveliest nightspots.

Mojos

10/20 Sukhumvit Soi 33; tel: 0 2260 8429; www.mojos

bangkok.com; daily 8pm–1am; BTS: Phrom Phong or MRT: Sukhumvit; map p.18

This is split into three areas: the Main Bar features live music from resident bands; the Sports Room offers telecasts of sports programmes on wide-screen TVs, and the Mezzanine Lounge is good for taking it easy.

Senor Pico

Rembrandt Hotel, Sukhumvit Soi 18; tel: 0 2261 7100; daily 5pm–1am; BTS: Asok or MRT: Sukhumvit; map p.18

This colourful open-plan cantina dishes up some wicked Latin treats, complemented nightly by an energetic Latin band.

Spasso

Grand Hyatt Erawan, Thanon Ratchadamri; tel: 0 2254 1234; www.bangkok.grand.hyatt.com; daily noon–2pm and 6.30pm–1.30am; BTS: Chit Lom; map p.141 C4

Throbbing with revellers every night, this basement club and Italian eatery is one of the capital's most consistently popular hotel nightspots. International bands play mainly pop, soul and R&B covers from 10pm to 2am. Working girls cruise the dance floor, though.

Kathoey Cabaret

The famous transsexual or *katoey* cabaret shows, whose artistes are making a name for themselves on the international circuit, have become a Bangkok staple. The shows feature saucy lip-synching song-and-dance routines performed by a revue of sequinned and feather boa-ed artistes who have gone through various stages of sex-change surgery.

Calypso

Asia Hotel, 296 Thanon Phaya Thai; tel: 0 2216 8937–8; www.calypsocabaret.com; BTS: Ratchathewi; map p.136 B1

One of the city's best cabaret shows is staged twice nightly at 8.15pm and 9.45pm. Each show is divided into bite-sized segments featuring anything from Marilyn Monroe impersonators to Thai classical dancers. A ticket costs B1,000 and includes one drink.

Mambo

Washington Square, Sukhumvit Soi 22–24; tel: 0 2259 5715; BTS: Phrom Phong; map p.18

Mambo's cabaret shows are glitzy, entertaining and professional. Daily shows at 8.30pm and 10pm; a ticket costs B800.

Below: Calypso's cabaret; a visit to Bangkok is incomplete without catching a cabaret show.

Palaces

The city's historic anchors of Rattanakosin and Dusit brim with stunning, extravagant palaces that were indicators of ancient Siam's prowess. Today, these palaces, with their mix of eclectic architectural styles, ornate interiors and grand halls, evoke romantic notions of an exotic Thailand, but are at the same time are windows onto Thai culture and history. Of the palaces in Bangkok, the must-see is the arresting Grand Palace complex, a collection of some of the country's most revered edifices. Worth visiting outside the city, best by cruise, is Bang Pa-In, a summer retreat for Thai kings.

Abhisek Dusit Throne Hall

Dusit Park; daily 9.30am–4pm; entrance charge, or free with Grand Palace ticket; pier: Thewet; map p.135 D4

Constructed in 1903 for King Chulalongkorn as an accompanying throne hall to Vimanmek, this ornate building is another sumptuous melding of Victorian and Moorish styles, but still retains its distinctly Thai sheen. The main hall is now used as a showroom-cum-museum for the SUPPORT Foundation, a charitable organisation headed by Queen Sirikit that helps preserve traditional arts and crafts. On view are examples of jewellery, woodcarving, nielloware, silk and wicker products. Next to the museum is a shop selling the handiwork of village artisans.

Above: the Abhisek Dusit Throne Hall.

Ananta Samakhom

Dusit Park; daily 8.30am–4.30pm; entrance charge or free with Grand Palace ticket; pier: Thewet; map p.135 D4

The Ananta Samakhom (Royal Throne Hall), an Italian Renaissance-style hall of grey marble crowned by a huge dome, is the tallest building within the manicured gardens of Dusit Park.

Built in 1907 by King Chulalongkorn as a grandiose hall for receiving visiting dignitaries and hosting state ceremonies, it was used for the first official meeting of the new parliament after Thailand became a constitutional monarchy in 1932. A parliament house has since been built behind the Abhisek Dusit Throne Hall. The Ananta Samakhom is now used for state occasions. The highlight of the rich interior are the dome ceiling frescoes depicting the Chakri monarchs from Rama I to Rama VI.

Bang Pa-In

61km north of Bangkok; daily 8.30am–4.30pm; entrance charge; tel: 0 3526 1673–82; www.palaces.thai.net; train from Hualamphong, bus from Northern Bus Terminal, or boat (*see box on p.95*); map p.20

About 24km south of Ayutthaya is Bang Pa-In, an eclectic collection of palaces and pavilions once used as a royal summer retreat. The palace buildings one sees

Left: the Chakri Maha Prasat (Grand Palace Hall) at the Grand Palace.

nearby islet with the **Withun Thatsana** observation tower, as well as the Italianate **Warophat Phiman Hall**. The 1876 Thai-style pavilion called the **Aisawan Thipphaya-at**, in the middle of the adjacent lake, is regarded as one of the finest examples of Thai architecture.

WAT NIWET THAMMAPRAWAT

Across the river and slightly south of Bang Pa-In, this temple looks more like a Gothic Christian church than a Buddhist temple, and is topped by a spire. There are canals, ponds, fountains, bridges and a topiary of large elephant-shaped hedges in its pleasant gardens. Coach tours to Ayutthaya stop off here in the morning, so to avoid the crowds, visit in the afternoon.

Chitralada Palace

Dusit Park; not open to the public; pier: Thewet; map p.135 E4

East of the Dusit Zoo, a thick tree-shaded fenced moat and sentry guards protect the grounds of the Chitralada Palace, the permanent home of the present monarchy. Once a rural retreat known as Sompoy Field, where King Vajiravudh sought solitude away from court life at the Grand Palace, it was built in 1913. Keen observers might spot some agricultural equipment along the fence perimeter, where King Bhumibol himself conducts experiments in agricultural sustainability for the benefit of his people.

today at Bang Pa-In date from the late 19th- and early-20th-century reigns of King Chulalongkorn and King Vajiravudh, who came here to escape the mid-year rains in Bangkok. Under the instruction of Chulalongkorn, the manicured grounds contain several buildings that feature Italian baroque, European gothic, Victorian and Chinese architectural styles. Only part of the royal quarters is open to public view, providing a glimpse into Chulalongkorn's penchant for European furniture and décor.

The noteworthy palace buildings include the two-storey Chinese-style **Wehat Chamrun Palace** and the

> Many cruises to Ayutthaya also stop over at Bang Pa-In. Contact River Sun Cruise (tel: 0 2266 9125; www.river suncruise.com) or the more exclusive Manohra Cruises (tel: 0 2477 0770; www. manohracruises.com). Chao Phraya Express Boat (tel: 0 2623 6001; www.chao phrayaboat.co.th) also has a trip to Bang Pa-In on Sundays.

Below: Bang Pa-In, with the Aisawan Thipphaya-at pavilion.

...ce along Thanon Na Phra Lan; daily 8.30am–3.30pm; entrance charge includes entry to Vimanmek and several other sights in Dusit; tel: 0 2623 5500; www.palaces.thai.net; pier: Tha Chang; map p.134 B1

Two of Bangkok's principal attractions are the breathtaking Wat Phra Kaew and the

Below: a *yaksha* protector guards the entrance to Wat Phra Kaew.

Grand Palace. The buildings in this complex are arresting spectacles of form and colour, from glistening golden *chedis* and glass mosaic-studded pillars to towering mythological gods and fabulously ornate temple and palace structures.

The site originally spread over 160ha by the banks of the Chao Phraya River. Its construction began in 1782, when King Rama I ordered a new residence to house the Emerald Buddha, the country's most revered religious image, and a palace befitting the newly installed capital of Bangkok. The entire compound is surrounded by high crenellated walls, securing a self-sufficient city within a city.

The complex is loosely divided into two sections, with the **Wat Phra Kaew** *(see p.122)* encountered first to the left (signs guide you to this sight first) and the Grand Palace and its peripheral

buildings to the right. Most of the Grand Palace's interiors are inaccessible to public view, but the exteriors are still awesome to witness. An early-morning visit is recommended, preferably when bright sunlight illuminates the buildings to their dazzling best.

It's worthwhile hiring the informative audio guide (B100, with passport/credit card deposit). Official guides (B300) are also available near the ticket office.
SEE ALSO MUSEUMS AND GALLERIES, P.85; TEMPLES, P.122

PALACE BUILDINGS

The Grand Palace has been added to or modified by every Thai king, such that today the complex is a melange of architectural styles, from traditional Thai, Khmer and Chinese to British, French and Italian Renaissance. In the early 20th century, the royal abode shifted to the more private

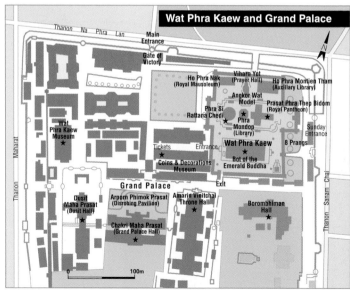

Wat Phra Kaew and Grand Palace

Thanon Na Phra Lan

Main Entrance

Gate of Victory

Ho Phra Nak (Royal Mausoleum)

Viharn Yot (Prayer Hall)

Ho Phra Montien Tham (Auxiliary Library)

Angkor Wat Model

Prasat Phra Thep Bidom (Royal Pantheon)

Phra Si Rattana Chedi

Phra Mondop (Library)

Wat Phra Kaew Museum

Thanon Maharat

Tickets   Entrance

Coins & Decorations Museum

Wat Phra Kaew

8 Prangs

Sunday Entrance

Bot of the Emerald Buddha

Exit

Grand Palace

Dusit Maha Prasat (Dusit Hall)

Arporn Phimok Prasat (Disrobing Pavilion)

Amarin Vinitchai Throne Hall

Borombhiman Hall

Chakri Maha Prasat (Grand Palace Hall)

Thanon Sanam Chai

0   100m

Above: the Chakri Throne Room.

Above: a Chinese-style statue outside the Dusit Maha Prasat.

Chitralada Palace in Dusit district. The Grand Palace is now reserved for special ceremonies and state visits.

As you exit from Wat Phra Kaew, you will see on your left, tucked behind a closed gate guarded by sentry, the French-inspired **Borombhiman Hall**. It was built in 1903 as a residence for King Vajiravudh, but is now reserved as a state guesthouse for dignitaries.

To its right lies the **Amarin Vinitchai Throne Hall**. Originally a royal residence, it contained the bedchamber of King Rama I, with the main audience hall beyond. Today the audience hall is used for coronations and special ceremonies. Traditionally each new king also spends the first night after his coronation here.

Next to it stands the triple-spired royal residence – and

the grandest building in the complex – the **Chakri Maha Prasat** (Grand Palace Hall). This two-storey hall set on an elevated base was constructed during King Chulalongkorn's reign to commemorate the 100th anniversary of the Chakri dynasty in 1882. Designed by British architects, the hall sports an impressive mix of Thai and Western architecture. The Thai spires, however, were added at the last moment, following protests that it was improper for a hallowed Thai site to be dominated by a European-style building.

The top floor contains golden urns with ashes of the Chakri kings; the first floor still functions as an audience chamber for royal banquets and state visits, while the ground floor is now a **Weapons Museum**. The central hall contains the magnificent **Chakri Throne Room**, where the king receives foreign ambassadors on a niello throne under a nine-tiered white umbrella, originally made for King Chulalongkorn. Outside, the courtyard is dotted with ornamental ebony trees

pruned in Chinese bonsai style. Beside the hall and behind a closed door is the **Inner Palace**, where the king's many wives once lived. The king himself was the only male above the age of 12 allowed to enter the area, which was guarded by armed women.

The next building of interest is the **Dusit Maha Prasat** (Dusit Hall), built by King Rama I in 1789 to replace an earlier wooden structure. This is a splendid example of classical Thai architecture, with its four-tiered roof supporting an elegant nine-tiered spire. The balcony in the north wing contains a throne once used by the king for outdoor receptions. Deceased kings and queens lie in state here before their bodies are cremated on Sanam Luang.

To the left of the Dusit Hall stands the **Arporn Phimok Prasat** (Disrobing Pavilion). It was built to the height of the king's palanquin, so that he could alight from his elephant and don his ceremonial hat and gown before proceeding to the audience hall.

97

Pampering

Thai spas have an enticing allure that stems from their link to the country's unique culture and environment. To begin with, these spas draw on a vast and longstanding tradition of natural healing. Their treatments use indigenous herbs and formulas that have been used for centuries in native health and beauty practices. And when it comes to service, the country's masseurs and therapists are blessed with the natural warmth that Thai people are generally known for. This makes the Thai spa experience eminently gentle and relaxing, and adds that extra dimension of luxury.

Traditional Thai Massage

Traditional Thai massage, a holistic therapy with roots in ancient medicine, has been practised as a form of healing for centuries. Originating from ancient India, it arrived in Thailand with Buddhist missionary monks who were trained as healers. Along with the spread of the Buddhist faith, traditional massage became popular for relieving ailments like backache, headache and tension.

Thai massage technique is linked to the ancient Indian yoga philosophy, which is why some of the stretching actions of Thai massage resemble those of yoga. Thai massage uses pressure to release blocked energy in the body.

The masseur uses his or her thumbs, arms, elbows, knees and feet, and may climb all over your body and even 'walk' on your back. Expect to be twisted, stretched and flipped backwards. Do relax and trust that your masseur is doing the right thing. After a Thai massage, some people may find their bodies aching. This is because subconscious muscle tension causes energy blockages to be released during the massage, hence the resulting discomfort. A few more massage sessions usually relieve this type of ache.

Steams and Compresses

The use of heat therapies combined with herbal ingredients is a distinguishing trait of traditional Thai healing practices. One of the most popular is the Thai herbal steam or sauna. It uses indigenous herbs like turmeric, prai, lemon grass, camphor and kaffir lime, which is believed to boost overall health and even result in weight loss if done consistently over an extended period of time.

Another ancient Thai therapy is the use of warm herbal compresses made of medicinal herbs wrapped in a tight bundle, steamed for several hours, and then pressed against trouble areas of the body, such as tense shoulders or rheumatic joints.

Hotel Spas

Chi Spa
The Shangri-La, 89 Soi Wat Suan Plu; tel: 0 2236 7777; www.shangri-la.com; daily 10am–10pm; BTS: Saphan Taksin; map p.139 E1
Amid a hushed calm, enjoy spacious, luxurious treatment rooms and signature therapies that aim to restore the balance of your *chi* (energy flow).

COMO Shambhala Spa
The Metropolitan, 27 Thanon Sathorn Tai; tel: 0 2625 3357; www.metropolitan.como.bz; daily 8am–9.30pm; BTS: Sala Daeng or MRT: Lumphini; map p.141 C1
This chic spa offers holistic

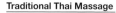
Wat Pho Thai Traditional Massage School (2 Thanon Sanam Chai; tel: 0 2221 2974; www.watpomassage.com; daily 10am–6pm) is the place to learn about traditional massage and meditation. The massage school, established in 1955, offers cheap hour-long massages, and also courses for those who want to learn the art.

Left: warm herbal compress treatment at the Devarana Spa.

11am–11pm; BTS: Phrom Phong; map p.18
Bangkok's most popular day spa has an excellent programme of traditional Thai massages and herbal compresses. Check its website for other branches located in renovated old houses around the Sukhumvit area.

Rasayana Retreat
57 Sukhumvit Soi 39; tel: 0 2662 4803–5; www.rasayanaretreat.com; daily 9am–9pm; BTS: Phrom Phong; map p.18
Come here for the detox programmes and Thailand's only raw-food restaurant offering organic meals.

Medical Spa

S Medical Spa
2/2 Phakdi Building, Thanon Withayu; tel: 0 2253 1010; www.smedspa.com; daily 10am–10pm; BTS: Phloen Chit; map p.141 D4
A chic spa with physicians and dermatologists on site. Besides its wide choice of treatments (including some specially designed for men) and health screenings, other facilities such as Eastern and Western steam rooms, hydrotherapy pools and jacuzzis are available.

Asian-inspired therapies, plus steam rooms, a hydro pool, outdoor lap pool and yoga studio.

Devarana Spa
Dusit Thani Hotel, 946 Thanon Rama IV; tel: 0 2636 3600; www.devaranaspa.com; daily 9am–10pm; BTS: Sala Daeng or MRT: Silom; map p.140 C2
An exquisite Thai-style spa that feels like an airy temple, this offers the usual range of therapies but is especially good for Thai massages and herbal compresses. The signature Devarana Spa Exclusive combines Thai, Ayurvedic and Shiatsu massage techniques and aromatherapy.

The Oriental Spa
The Oriental, 48 Oriental Avenue; tel: 0 2233 9630; www.mandarinoriental.com; daily 8am–10pm; BTS: Saphan Taksin; pier: Oriental; map p.139 E1
Ayurvedic therapies and signature treatments that meld Eastern and Western traditions in this spa designed like a Thai teak house.

The Peninsula Spa
The Peninsula, 333 Thanon Charoen Nakhon; tel: 0 2861

2888; www.peninsula.com; daily 9am–11pm; BTS: Saphan Taksin; map p.139 D1
Set in a colonial building, this spa has a varied menu of massages and body treatments. Splurge on one of its River Private Suites and enjoy perks like a jacuzzi and a view of the Chao Phraya River. Other amenities include a stylish Asian Tea Lounge and outdoor pools.

Independent Spas

Divana Spa
8 Sukhumvit Soi 35; tel: 0 2661 4818; www.divana-dvn.com; Mon–Fri 10am–11pm, Sat–Sun

Below: ingredients for traditional Thai herbal steam treatment.

Parks and Gardens

If you crave some contact with nature on your trip to Bangkok, it's best to make an excursion to one of the national parks outside Bangkok, a few hours away. That said, this city does offer a few public parks with well-manicured greenery and water features, perfect for a breather when you've had enough of shopping and dining, or before you head off to visit the next attraction. Some of them come alive during certain festivals, teeming with locals who gather to witness or participate in the celebrations or ceremonies.

Benjakitti Park

Thanon Sukhumvit; daily 5am–8pm; free; BTS: Phrom Phong; map p.18

Located near the Queen Sirikit National Convention Centre, south of Sukhumivit Soi 21 (Sok Asoke), this green space overlooks the artificial Lake Ratchada. Opened in 2004 as the first stage in the redevelopment of the adjacent Tobacco Monopoly grounds, this 'Water Zone' will be followed in the future by a large 'Forest Zone'. Enhanced with large fountains and cascading water displays, it is busiest in the early morning and evening when joggers and cyclists circle the lake on two designated paths.

Benjasiri Park

Thanon Sukhumvit; daily 5am–8pm; free; BTS: Phrom Phong; map p.18

Near Sukhumvit Soi 24 is the area's other green lung, Benjasiri Park. Opened in celebration of the present queen's 60th birthday, the small metropolitan garden is enlivened by a large pond, fountains and noteworthy sculptures by some of Thailand's most respected artists. There are also basketball courts, a skate park and a swimming pool with Thai pavilions.

Lumphini Park

192 Thanon Rama IV; daily 4.30am–9pm; free; BTS: Sala Daeng or MRT: Lumphini or Silom; map p.141 C2

Named after Buddha's birthplace in Nepal, Bangkok's premier outdoor retreat was given to the public in 1925 by King Vajiravudh, whose memorial statue stands in front of the main gates. It has lakes with pedal boats for hire, and a Chinese-style clock tower. Sunrise or sunset sees elderly practising tai chi, joggers, aerobic sessions, bodybuilders lifting weights at the open-air gym and youngsters playing the sport of *takraw* using a rattan ball. From November to February, the dry season, the Bangkok Symphony Orchestra and other music groups perform in the park.

Above: Sanam Luang.

Kite flying is popular from February to April.

Rommaninat Park

Thanon Maha Chai; daily 5am–9pm; free; MRT: Hualamphong; pier: Tha Chang; map p.135 C1

With its original watchtowers still standing, this lively park is a fun example of how punishment can be turned into recreation. The old prison was built in 1893 and, after over 100 years of service, was transformed into a public park to celebrate Queen Sirikit's birthday. This

Left: sitting by the lake in Lumphini Park.

restored in 1999, is one of two remaining defences of the old city wall.

Saranrom Park

Corner of Thanon Charoen Krung and Thanon Ratchini; daily 5am–8pm; free; pier: Rong Mo; map p.134 B1

Just behind Wat Ratchapra-dit, the tranquil Saranrom Park is the perfect place to relax after a day of palace and temple tours. It was originally a garden attached to Saranrom Palace, which was supposed to have been the retirement retreat for King Mongkut. However, he passed away before the palace was completed. This green space, dotted with bridges, ponds, a European-style fountain and a Chinese pagoda, was opened to the public in the 1960s. At its centre is a memorial erected by King Chulalongkorn for his wife Queen Sunanda, who drowned in a boating accident in 1880.

green spot has ponds, fountains and a large bronze sculpture of a conch shell.

Sanam Luang

North of Wat Phra Kaew and Grand Palace complex; free; pier: Prachan or Tha Chang; map p.134 B1–2

Royal cremations and impor-tant ceremonies are held at the large oval turf of Sanam Luang (Royal Field). The field is particularly lively on the King's and Queen's birthdays, the Songkran festival in April and the Ploughing Ceremony in May when the king welcomes the start of the rice-planting season and hopefully a bountiful harvest. During the early Rattanakosin period, rice was grown on the field; later, with tamarind trees providing shade, it became the recreation ground for Bangkok's wealthy.

These days, the often dusty field is used by vagrants and evening soothsayers foretelling destinies, and from February to April, a kite-flying competi-tion attracts contestants from Thailand and abroad.

Northeast of Sanam Luang, opposite the Royal Hotel, is an elaborate public drinking fountain in the shape of Mae Toranee, the earth goddess. Erected by King Chulalongkorn in the late 19th century, the ornate statue depicts the goddess wringing torrents of water out of her hair to wash away evil spirits trying to corrupt the meditating Buddha.

Santichai Prakan Park

Riverfront along Thanon Phra Athit; daily 5am–10pm; free; pier: Wat Sam Praya; map p.134 B3

The riverfront from Saphan Phra Pin Klao bridge along the length of Thanon Phra Athit to Santichai Prakan Park is one of the city's few easily accessible riverside paths. This lovely and vibrant bankside park fringes the whitewashed octagonal Phra Sumen Fort, and is said to have the only surviving *lamphu* trees, after which the area of Banglamphu is named, left in the neighbour-hood. The fort (not open to the public), built in 1873 and

Below: sculpture at Benjakitti Park.

Restaurants

Anyone who has been to Bangkok can vouch that the city is an incredibly vibrant food paradise. Bangkok is arguably the best destination to enjoy food from the kingdom's various regions, but fast emerging as an international culinary hotspot, it also offers far more than just Thai food. Traditional cuisines from all over the world as well as new-wave fusion styles are well represented. The city offers a slew of varied dining options at every corner, from humble stalls and casual eateries to fine-dining restaurants. It is certainly one foodie's heaven where one, even with a tight budget, will never go home hungry.

Rattanakosin

THAI

Coconut Palm
394/3-5 Thanon Maharat; mobile tel: 081 827 2394; daily 10am–7pm; $; pier: Tha Tien; map p.138 B4
Family-style restaurant serving far better meals than its Western-style fast-food interior suggests. The small range of soups and curries (red, green, *tom yam* and the coconut soup *tom kha gai*)

disappear by lunchtime. For dinner, try the excellent rice noodles.

Poh Restaurant
Tha Tien Pier; no phone; daily 6–10pm; $; pier: Tha Tien; map p.138 B4
The lovely setting at this wooden-shack, pierside café compensates for its ordinary menu. Sit upstairs for the best view across the river to Wat Arun. Serves squid, mussels and shrimp

with rice or noodles, a few curries and numerous fish dishes. Stays open well after the kitchen closes.

Sor Tor Lor
Royal Navy Club, Tha Chang; mobile tel: 081 257 5530; daily 11am–8pm; $; pier: Tha Chang; map p.134 A1
Part of the Royal Thai Navy Club but open to the public, this riverside operation is perched on a large wooden deck. Good for fish and seafood standards like spicy steamed snapper with Thai lime, curried crab and fried prawns with garlic.

Thonburi

THAI

Supatra River House
266 Soi Wat Rakhang, Thanon Arun Amarin; tel: 0 2411 0305; www.supatrariverhouse.net; daily 11am–2pm and 6–11pm. $$; pier: Wat Rakhang; map p.134 A1

Below: *nam prik ong*, a dipping sauce of minced pork, chillies and shrimp paste, often found in Thai restaurants.

Price per person for a three-course meal without drinks:
$ = under B300
$$ = B300–800
$$$ = B800–1.600
$$$$ = over B1,600

Left: Biscotti at the Four Seasons is one of Bangkok's best Italian restaurants.

Former family home of owners Patravadi Mechudhon (of Patravadi Theatre fame) and her sister. Decent Thai cuisine is served on the riverbank terrace or in one of the two Thai-style houses. On Friday and Saturday, traditional music and dance accompany your dinner. Take the express boat to Maharat pier and transfer to the opposite bank on Supatra's free shuttle boat.

The Old City and Dusit
INTERNATIONAL
Baan Phra Arthit Coffee & More
102/1 Thanon Phra Athit; tel: 0 2280 7878–9; Sun–Thur 10am–9.30pm, Fri–Sat 10am–11pm; $; pier: Phra Athit; map p.134 B3
Mochas and cappuccinos in a refined old house that used to house the Goethe Institut. Along with cheesecakes, meringues and other desserts, mains and snacks such as Chiang Mai sausage, lasagna and chicken curry are served. There's comfortable sofa seating to lounge on.

> Most Thai meals have dishes placed in the middle of the table to be shared by all; the larger the group, the more dishes you can try. Dish a heap of rice onto your plate together with small portions of various dishes at the side. It's polite to take just a little at a time.

ISRAELI
Chabad House
108/1 Soi Rambuttri; tel: 0 2282 6388; Sun–Thur noon–9pm, Fri noon–4.30pm; $; pier: Phra Athit; map p.134 B2
Run as a charitable business by the synagogue in the same building, this Israeli café offers nicer surroundings than most other Middle Eastern-style eateries in the neighbourhood. And all the food is kosher of course. Good falafel, salads, hummus and the usual tahini-based dips to accompany a wide choice of mains.

THAI
Mitr Go Yuan
186 Thanon Dinso; tel: 0 2224 1194; Mon–Sat 11am–10pm, Sun 4–10pm; $; pier: Phrachan; map p.134 C1
Traditional shophouse set-up that's busy at lunch and after 5pm with workers from the City Hall, who rave about its tom yum goong and spicy salads. This eatery is famous among locals, and occasionally attracts celebrities.
Nan Faa
164 Thanon Dinso; tel: 0 2224 1180; daily 8am–8pm; $; pier: Phrachan; map p.134 C1
Thai-Chinese café specialising in slow-roasted duck and goose basted with honey. Also has dim sum and traditional dishes like stewed pig's ears and pig's feet. If you can't get a seat here, go to **Tien Song**, two doors away, which serves similar food in air-conditioned surroundings.
Pen Thai Food
229 Soi Rambuttri; tel: 0 2282 2320; daily 7am–7.30pm; $; pier: Phra Athit; map p.134 B2
Khun Sitichai has had this spot since 1980, long before the first backpackers arrived. His menu has changed little. The spicy catfish curry, soups and deep-fried fish are still displayed outside in metal pots and trays in street-stall fashion. And at B20–40 per dish, the prices haven't changed much either.
Roti-Mataba
136 Thanon Phra Athit; tel: 0 2282 2119; Tue–Sun 7am–10pm; $; pier: Phra Athit; map p.134 B3
A whole army of women here make the Muslim-style breads – like flat unleavened roti and meat-stuffed mataba – by the hundreds in this busy shophouse. Dip the crisp roti into their delicious massaman and korma curries of fish, vegetables or meat.

Above: the classy setting at the Madison at the Four Seasons.

There are only a few tables, so be prepared to wait.

Thip Samai
313 Thanon Maha Chai; tel: 0 2221 6280; daily 5.30pm–3.30am; $; pier: Tha Chang; map p.135 C1
Located close to the Golden Mount, this is a very basic but legendary café that does several versions (and nothing else) of *paad thai*, the fried noodles with dried shrimps, roasted peanuts and bean sprouts that is often claimed as Thailand's national dish. If it's closed, try **Pad Thai Goong Pa** next door.

VEGETARIAN
May Kaidee
117/1 Thanon Tanao; tel: 0 2281 7137; www.maykaidee.com; daily 9am–11pm; $; pier: Phra Athit; map p.134 C2
Serving vegetarian food since 1988, May has a sound reputation for her meat-free Thai standards. Isaan-style (from northeast Thailand) vegetarian dishes with mushrooms, tofu and soya beans, *massaman* curry with

tofu, potatoes and peanuts, and the dessert of black sticky rice with coconut, banana and mango are popular selections. May also gives cooking lessons. To find this place, take the street next to Burger King and turn left. A second outlet is nearby at 33 Thanon Samsen.

Chinatown

CHINESE
Noodle N' More
513/514 Thanon Mong Muang; tel: 0 2613 8972; daily 11am–11pm; $; MRT: Hualamphong; map p.139 E3
This has a good corner location close to the Hualamphong Railway Station and a modern café interior. Upstairs seating by the window offers great street views. Serves a good range of Hong Kong-style noodle dishes, plus all-day dim sum.

Shangrila Yaowarat
306 Thanon Yaowarat; tel: 0 2224 5933; daily 10am–10pm; $$; MRT: Hualamphong; map p.139 D4

This busy Cantonese place serves casual café-style dim sum lunches, then brings out the tablecloths and napkins for dinner. The menu includes drunken chicken with jellyfish, smoked pigeon, and live seafood from the tanks on the ground floor. Or choose from the displays of roasted duck, steaming dim sum and freshly baked pastries.

INDIAN
Punjab Sweets and Restaurant
436/5 Thanon Chakraphet; tel: 0 2623 7606; daily 8am–9pm; $; MRT: Hualamphong; pier: Saphan Phut; map p.139 C4
Pahurat, Bangkok's Little India, sits at the western edge of Chinatown. Its alleyways are crowded with tiny Indian cafés, of which this is one of the best. Its meat- and dairy-free selections include southern Indian curries and *dosas* (rice-flour pancakes), and Punjabi sweets wrapped in edible silver foil.

THAI
Yok Yor
Yok Yor Marina, 885 Somdet Chao Phraya Soi 17; tel: 0 2863 0565–6; www.yokyor.co.th; daily 11am–midnight; $$; pier: Khlong San; map p.139 D2
Open-air and indoor seating at this restaurant bustling with locals and tourists. The Thai and seafood dishes are mostly decent, but the main attractions are the lovely riverside setting and the Thai cabaret show, which features comedy, singing and *katoey* (transvestite) acts.

> Dinner cruises along the Chao Phraya River couple a Thai dinner with sightseeing; contact Yok Yor *(see above)* or Manohra Cruises (tel: 0 2476 0022; www.manohracruises.com).

Above: *paad thai* is Thailand's favourite noodle dish.

Pathumwan and Pratunam

INTERNATIONAL
Madison
Four Seasons, 155 Thanon Ratchadamri; tel: 0 2251 6127; daily 6.30–10.30am, Mon–Sat 11.30am–2.30pm, Sun noon–3pm, daily 6–10.30pm; $$$; BTS: Ratchadamri; map p.141 C3
Fine dining on the likes of roasted foie gras and Belon oysters from Europe as well as US prime-grade beef and Tasmanian lamb. If you can't decide on dessert, go for the warm guanaja tart, pomelo soup and fresh marinated mango. The Tony Chi-designed interior features an open-style kitchen. A fabulous brunch blow-out on Sunday.

ITALIAN
Biscotti
Four Seasons, 155 Thanon Ratchadamri; tel: 0 2251 6127; daily noon–2.30pm and 6–10.30pm; $$$; BTS: Ratchadamri; map p.141 C3
A dining mecca styled with terracotta, marble and wood by Tony Chi. The large and busy open-kitchen sets the tone for its excellent contemporary Italian cuisine, while the open space is ideal for being seen. Packed with business people for lunch and socialites for dinner.

Calderazzo
59 Soi Lang Suan; tel: 0 2252 8108/9; daily 11am–2pm and 5.30–11pm; $$–$$$; BTS: Chit Lom; map p.141 C3
Clever lighting and lots of wood, stone, metal and glass create a warm and stylish atmosphere. Enjoy good homey southern Italian food such as grilled vegetables in hazelnut pesto, hand-rolled rag pasta with goat-cheese sauce, lamb loin in red wine, and heavenly profiteroles with ice cream and warm chocolate sauce.

Gianni's
51/5 Soi Tonson; tel: 0 2252 1619; daily noon–2.30pm and 6–11.30pm; $$–$$$; BTS: Chit Lom; map p.141 D4
Larger-than-life Gianni Favro is perhaps Bangkok's first non-Thai celebrity chef. His original Italian restaurant in Soi Tonson serves all the classics – vitello tonata, osso bucco, tiramisu – and has proven so enduringly popular that Gianni now has other branches around the city.

JAPANESE
Shin Daikoku
2/F, InterContinental Hotel, 973 Thanon Ploenchit; tel: 0 2656 0096/7; www.ichotelsgroup.com; daily 11.30am–2pm and 6–11pm; $$–$$$; BTS: Chit Lom; map p.141 C4
Dine on high-quality sushi and sashimi, Matsuzaka beef and superb *ishikarinabe* (salmon stew). Bamboo cabinets divide the restaurant proper from the teppanyaki room. A second outlet on Sukhumvit Soi 19.

SPANISH
Rioja
1025 Thanon Ploenchit; tel: 0 2251 5761–2; Mon–Fri 11am–2.30pm and 6–11pm, Sat–Sun 11am–11pm; $$; BTS: Chit Lom; map p.141 C4
Bangkok's only authentic Spanish restaurant offers fine Iberico ham, shrimp carpaccio on sour cream with salmon roe, Rioja-style oxtail stew, and an exceptional seafood paella. Of the two dining rooms, the cellar-like bodega, with its stone floor and dark woods, is more appealing.

THAI
Curries & More
63/3 Soi Ruam Rudi; tel: 0 2253 5405–7; daily 11am–11.30pm; $$; BTS: Ploen Chit; map p.141 D3

Below: order wine by the glass at the Four Seasons' Biscotti.

A branch of the famous Baan Khanitha (at 69 Thanon Sathorn Tai and 31/1 Sukhumvit Soi 23) serving tasty Thai food with the spices toned down to suit international palates. This is set in a charming townhouse with sculptures, paintings and ceramics. The *kaeng leuang* (yellow curry) is excellent. It also has some international dishes, such as pasta, pies, crepes and an excellent apple crumble.

Gai Tort Soi Polo

137/1–2 Soi Polo, Thanon Withayu; tel: 0 2252 2252; daily 7am–7pm; $; MRT: Lumphini; map p.141 D2

One of Bangkok's most famous fried-chicken shops. The delicious *gai* is marinated in soy sauce, tamarind and pepper, and served piping hot topped with fried garlic. Enjoy it with lip-smacking sauces and *somtam* (green papaya salad).

Khanom Chine Bangkok

G/F, Mahboonkrong, 444 Thanon Phaya Thai; tel: 0 2620 9403; daily 10.30am–10pm; $; BTS: Siam; map p.140 B4

This place serves the delicious street-food noodle dish called *khanom chine* amid brushed concrete walls, clever spotlighting and a wall of windows. Don't miss the traditional northern-style curry (or choose from several other versions) and the good *tom yum kai jeaw* (*tom yum* with omelette).

Lan Som Tam Nua

392/2 Siam Square Soi 5; tel: 0 2251 4880; daily 11.15am–9pm; $; BTS: Siam; map p.140 B4

Eat Thai food with a fork and spoon, using the fork to push food onto the spoon. Chopsticks are used only for Chinese and noodle dishes.

Above: young Thais dining out in a stylish eatery.

Modern, funky, bustling Isaan (northeastern Thailand) restaurant so popular there are cushions outside for people waiting to be seated. The action whirls around an open kitchen where staff make a great fiery mixed salad (*somtam mua*) with noodles and northeastern sausage, and other excellent Isaan dishes. Thai-only menu, so some finger pointing or gesticulating is necessary.

Mahboonkrong Food Centre

Mahboonkrong, 444 Thanon Phaya Thai; tel: 0 2217 9491; daily 10am–9pm; $; BTS: Siam; map p.140 B4

MBK's huge food court offers an excellent variety of affordably priced local dishes. Buy vouchers at the counter, choose from as many stalls as you like and sit down anywhere. Redeem unused vouchers for cash on your way out.

Bangrak and Silom

CHINESE
China House

The Oriental, 48 Oriental Avenue; tel: 0 2659 9000; www.mandarinoriental.com; daily 11.30am–2.30pm and 7–10.30pm; $$$; BTS: Saphan

Taksin; pier: Oriental; map p.139 E1

The beautiful 1930s Shanghainese art deco interior features red lanterns, carved wood and ebony pillars. Miniature black-and-white photos and Chinese calligraphy cover the walls; a brass samovar steams in the central tearoom. It's a wonderful setting for top-quality dishes like hot-and-sour soup filled with fresh herbs and sweet lobster meat.

FRENCH
D'Sens

Dusit Thani Hotel, 946 Thanon Rama IV; tel: 0 2236 9999; www.dusit.com; Mon–Fri 11.30am–2pm, Mon–Sat and public holidays 6–10pm; $$$$; BTS: Sala Daeng or MRT: Silom; map p.140 C2

This branch of the three Michelin-starred Le Jardin des Sens in Montpellier, France, is full of delicate and delicious surprises. Chef Philippe Keller works wonders in his kitchen with dishes like porcini mushrooms and duck-liver ravioli in a frothy truffle sabayon. Desserts are equally outstanding. Amazing city views from its expansive windows.

Le Bouchon

37/17 Patpong Soi 2; tel: 0 2234 9109; Mon–Sat noon–3pm and 6.30–11.30pm, Sun 6.30–11.30pm; $$–$$$; BTS: Sala Daeng; map p.140 B2

This atmospheric seven-table bistro is very French and slightly naughty, like a Marseille dockyard diner. Very popular with French expats for its simple homestyle cooking. Friendly banter at the small bar where diners wait for seats while sipping aperitifs.

La Boulange

2-2/1 Thanon Convent; tel: 0 2631 0355; daily 7am–8pm;

$$; BTS: Sala Daeng;
map p.140 B1
Enticing bakery and
patisserie with takeaway
outlets in supermarkets
around the city. This branch
serves freshly baked crois-
sants and brewed coffee to
the breakfast crowd, all-day
snacks such as *croque
monsieur*, pâtés and salads,
and daily specials like duck
confit and *coq au vin*.

Le Normandie
The Oriental, 48 Oriental
Avenue; tel: 0 2236 0400;
www.mandarinoriental.com;
Mon–Sat noon–2.30pm, daily
7–10.30pm; $$$$; BTS: Saphan
Taksin; pier: Oriental;
map p.139 E1
Formal French dining with
jacket and tie required for
men. Concoctions like
goose-liver dome with
Perigord truffles, and sole
fillets with Oscietra caviar
cream sauce verge on
brilliance. In the stately,
marmalade-coloured interior,
crystal chandeliers hang from
a quilted silk ceiling while the

floor-to-ceiling windows
overlook the Chao Phraya
River. Save this experience
for a special night out.

INDIAN
Tamil Nadu
Silom Soi 11; tel: 0 2235 6336;
daily 11.30am–9.30pm; $;
BTS: Chong Nonsi; map p.140 A1
A simple southern Indian
café serving the workers in
this area. The speciality is
masala dosa, a pancake
made of rice flour and *urad
dal*, stuffed with potato and
onion curry and served with
coconut chutney. You can
also order meat and
vegetable curries to comple-
ment the plain *dosa*.

INTERNATIONAL/FUSION
Cy'an
The Metropolitan, 27 Thanon
Sathorn Tai; tel: 0 2625 3333;
www.metropolitan.como.bz;
daily 6–10.30am, noon–2pm
and 6.30–10.30pm; $$$–$$$$;
BTS: Sala Daeng or
MRT: Lumphini; map p.141 C1
Serves inspired Asian-

Above: the bar at Cy'an.

Mediterranean seafood
amid the cutting-edge
minimalism of this hip hotel.
Spanish and Moroccan
flourishes bring sweet and
spicy flavours to seared tiger
prawns, and tortellini with
pine nuts, raisins and
parmesan. Or try the Wagyu
beef with anchovy and caper
butter and tender slow-grilled
vegetables. Some poolside
seating is available.

Eat Me
1/F, 1/6 Piphat Soi 2, off Thanon
Convent; tel: 0 2238 0931;
daily 3pm–1am; $$$;
BTS: Sala Daeng; map p.140 B1
Very popular restaurant with
art exhibitions often featuring
edgy young artists promoted
by the nearby H Gallery.
The menu features Modern
Australian dishes such as
charred scallops with mango,
herb salad, pickled onions
and citrus dressing. Low
lighting and a fragmented
layout lend a sense of
intimacy. On cool nights ask
for a table on the terrace.
Excellent wine list of mainly
Australian varietals.

Jester's
The Peninsula, 333 Thanon
Charoen Nakhon; tel: 0 2861
2888; www.peninsula.com;
daily 6–10.30pm; $$$; BTS:
Saphan Taksin; map p.139 D1

Below: dine on fine Chinese at the art deco-style China House.

Exciting East-West fusion of ingredients in dishes like crispy duck pancakes with mustard vinaigrette and grilled pork loin on chilli crab with fermented black-bean broth. Beautiful river view through a wall of glass, and the ultra-modern detailing in the décor goes perfectly with the cutting-edge Buddha Bar soundtracks.

Sirocco

63/F, Lebua at State Tower, 1055/111 Thanon Silom; tel: 0 2624 9555; www.the domebkk.com; daily 6pm–1am; $$$–$$$$; BTS: Saphan Taksin; map p.139 E1

This spectacular 200-m-high rooftop restaurant has magnificent views of the river. Greco-Roman architecture and a jazz band add to the sense of occasion. Excellent food well worth the money. In the same complex, there's the classy **Distil Bar**, the Italian eatery **Mezzaluna**, and the alfresco pan-Asian restaurant **Breeze**.

ITALIAN
Scoozi

174/3–4 Thanon Surawong; tel: 0 2267 0934; daily noon–2.30pm and 6–11pm; $$–$$$; BTS: Sala Daeng or MRT: Sam Yan; map p.140 A2

Set on two floors of a beautiful 120-year-old house, with private rooms and a bar area. Features southern Italian cuisine with an accent on imported seafood: snow crabs, lobster, oysters and mussels. Its stand-alone pizza bar in front of the house serves delicious thin-crust pizzas with innovative toppings.

Zanotti

G/F, Saladaeng Colonnade, 21/2 Soi Sala Daeng; tel: 0 2636 0002; www.zanotti-ristorante.com; daily 11.30am–2pm and 6–10.30pm; $$$; BTS: Sala Daeng; map p.140 C2

Chef-owner Gianmaria Zanotti has created a restaurant that people visit for the buzz as much as for the food.

The homey Italian fare from the Piedmont and Tuscany regions includes over 20 pasta dishes and quality seafood and steaks charcoal-grilled over orange wood from Chiangmai. Good selection of wines by the glass. The chic wine bar **Vino di Zanotti**, opposite, also serves a full menu and has live jazz.

JAPANESE
Aoi

132/10–11 Silom Soi 6; tel: 0 2235 2321–2; Mon–Fri 11.30am–2pm and 5.30–10.30pm, Sat–Sun 11am–3pm and 5–10.30pm; $$; BTS: Sala Daeng; map p.140 B2

Black-stone walkways invoke a cool calm in this unfussy restaurant serving well-prepared Japanese food. Downstairs is a sushi bar, and two floors of private and semi-private rooms are available for a surcharge.

KOREAN
Nam Kang

5/3–4 Silom Soi 3; tel: 0 2233 1480; daily 11am–10pm; $$; BTS: Sala Daeng; map p.140 B1

Nam Kang serves many *yangban* dishes usually associated with upper-class dining. The speciality is the herbal cure-all *samgyetang* (whole chicken stuffed with rice and ginseng). Also try the *gucholpan* (pancakes with shredded vegetables and meat).

THAI
The Blue Elephant

233 Thanon Sathorn Tai; tel: 0 2673 9353; www.blue elephant.com/bangkok; daily 11.30am–2.30pm and 6.30–10.30pm; $$–$$$; BTS: Surasak; map p.16

One of a few very upmarket Thai restaurants located outside hotels, this is part of

Below: sky-high dining at Sirocco offers views to die for.

Above: Jester's is renowned for its East-meets-West flavours.

a Belgian-owned international chain. The menu mixes Thai standards with a few fusion dishes like foie gras in tamarind sauce. The food is excellent, but the flavours are slightly toned down to suit Western palates. It is housed in a beautiful century-old restored building, formerly the Thai-Chinese Chamber of Commerce.

Café de Laos
16 Silom Soi 19; tel: 0 2635 2338/9; daily 11am–2pm and 5–10pm; $–$$; BTS: Surasak; map p.140 A1

This place occupies a handsome 100-year-old wooden house. Serves all the famous Isaan dishes like green papaya salad (*somtam*) and *laab* (spicy minced meat salad with ground roasted rice). Photos of old Laos on the walls add a nice touch.

Harmonique
22 Charoen Krung Soi 34; tel: 0 2237 8175; Mon–Sat 10am–10pm; $–$$; BTS: Saphan Taksin; map p.139 E1

Charming restaurant occupying several old Chinese shophouses with leafy courtyards and filled with antiques.

Because there's usually a large contingent of Western diners, the spices used in the Thai cooking are subdued. Still, the food is generally good, and it's a relaxing place to hang out at.

Kalpapruek
27 Thanon Pramuan; tel: 0 2236 4335; Mon–Sat 8am–6pm, Sun 8am–3pm; $; BTS: Surasak; map p.140 A1

The original restaurant of a rapidly expanding chain, this is one of the city's few surviving royal Thai kitchens. It features some of the Western influences first brought to Thai cooking through palace connections. On the street is a small, popular café-restaurant, and inside, a covered garden area and a bakery.

Krua Aroy Aroy
Thanon Pan; tel: 0 2635 2365; daily 10am–6pm; $; BTS: Surasak; map p.140 A1

Opposite the Maha Uma Devi Temple, this simple wooden-stool café features

> The more expensive restaurants add a service charge of 10 percent to the bill.

regional Thai dishes seldom found on the same menu. Curries include *nam ngeow* (pork broth with chicken's blood) and *nam ya ka ti* (minced fish in coconut milk). Noodle specials come deep-fried (*mee krob*) or cold (*khanom jeen*).

Le Lys
104 Narathiwat Soi 7; tel: 0 2287 1898; www.lelys. info; daily noon–10.30pm; $; map p.140 B1

The Thai–French owners avoid Thai clichés like *tom yum goong* and green curry in favour of dishes like tamarind sour soups (*tom som* with stuffed squid), spicy jungle curries and delicious baby clams in curry sauce. The homey interior resembles a French bistro, with checked cotton tablecloths, arched window frames and ballet posters on the walls.

Sukhumvit

AMERICAN
New York Steakhouse
JW Marriott, 4 Sukhumvit Soi 2; tel: 0 2656 7700; daily 6–11pm;

Below: Mezzaluna is a hot table in Bangkok.

Above: the Asian-themed Hazara offers a feast for the eyes as well.

$$$$; BTS: Nana or Phloen Chit; map p.141 E4

Top-notch restaurant with a relaxed atmosphere despite the formal trappings of club-like dark woods and high-backed leather chairs. The grain-fed Angus beef is sliced at the table from a silver trolley, and is imported chilled – which accounts for the high prices. There's a long martini list and refined wines.

FRENCH
Le Banyan
59 Sukhumvit Soi 8; tel: 0 2253 5556; Mon–Sat 6–10pm; $$$; BTS: Asok or MRT: Sukhumvit; map p.141 E3

Great little French restaurant with a formal but appealingly eccentric air. Chef Michel Binaux prepares many dishes tableside, including the specialities of pressed duck and pan-fried foie gras with apple and fresh morel mushrooms.

INDIAN
Akbar
1/4 Sukhumvit Soi 3; tel: 0 2253 3479; daily 10.30am–midnight; $; BTS: Nana; map p.141 E4

This serves North Indian fare such as tandoori chicken, vindaloo and korma curries, on two floors decorated like a curio shop with Arabic lanterns, Indian rugs, fairy lights and wooden parrots.

Hazara
29 Sukhumvit Soi 38; tel: 0 2713 6048–9; www.facebars.com; daily 6–10.30pm; $$; BTS: Thong Lo; map p.18

Tasty North Indian fare, such as peppery *khadai kheenga* (shrimps stir-fried with bell peppers), in a glorious setting embellished with Asian antiques and artefacts. The restaurant is housed in a traditional Thai complex that also comprises the trendy **Face Bar**, a Thai restaurant called **Lan Na Thai**, a patisserie and a spa.
SEE ALSO NIGHTLIFE, P.90

INTERNATIONAL
Bed Supperclub
26 Sukhumvit Soi 11; tel: 0 2651 3537; www.bedsupperclub.com; daily 7.30pm–1am; $$$; BTS: Nana; map p.141 E4

Extraordinary tubular construction with an all-white interior where diners lie on beds and cushions to eat the brilliant fusion cuisine. Choose from multi-choice three-course set menus. Also has mixed media shows including dance, theatre and video. Next door is the city's top club.
SEE ALSO NIGHTLIFE, P.92

Crepes & Co
18 Sukhumvit Soi 12; tel: 0 2251 2895; Mon–Sat 9am–midnight, Sun 8am–midnight; $$; BTS: Nana; map p.141 E3

Reliable creperie specialising in unusual fillings, with tagine stews and other Moroccan dishes, as well as Greek favourites like *kotopolou* (tomato and chicken casserole). The tasteful wooden interior with Berber-style tented ceiling and world music on the sound system lend an exotic atmosphere.

Greyhound
2/F, Emporium, 622 Thanon Sukhumvit, corner with Soi 24; tel: 0 2664 8663; www.grey hound.co.th; daily 11am–9.15pm; $$; BTS: Phrong Phong; map p.18

Trendy Thai café serving European-influenced dishes, such as the signature spaghetti with chilli and anchovies, in a minimalist interior. The menu is chalked up on blackboards, and there are glass-fronted displays of

Below: fusion food in chic surroundings at the Greyhound Café.

mouthwatering cakes. Outside seating on the balcony offers views of the Emporium mall. Other outlets around the city.

ITALIAN
Giusto
16 Sukhumvit Soi 23; tel: 0 2258 4321; daily 11.30am–2pm and 5.30–11pm; $$$; BTS: Asok or MRT: Sukhumvit; map p.18
Split into a bar area, private rooms and a glass-walled main dining space, this Italian restaurant has stylish fittings and a burgundy and black-and-white décor. Specialities include skewered fish, seafood and meats and foie gras terrine.

MIDDLE EASTERN
Nasir Al-Masri
4/6 Sukhumvit Soi 3/1; tel: 0 2253 5582; daily 10am–4am; $; BTS: Nana; map p.141 E4
Home-style specials, such as *fuul* (mashed beans in oil) and *molokhaya* (a spinach-like vegetable mixed with garlic) are served here. Outside, men smoke *shisha* pipes. This area is often called Soi Arab because of its many Middle Eastern operations.

THAI
Basil
Sheraton Grande Sukhumvit, 250 Thanon Sukhumvit; tel: 0 2649 8366; www.starwood.com/bangkok; daily noon–2.30pm and 6.30–10.30pm, Sun 11.30am–3pm (brunch); $$–$$$; BTS: Asok or MRT: Sukhumvit; map p.141 E3
This doesn't overcompromise local flavours for tourists. For something unusual, try the stir-fried wild boar with chilli paste, or papaya salad with bananas from the extensive menu of traditional staples.

Cabbages & Condoms
10 Sukhumvit Soi 12; tel: 0 2229 4610; daily 11am–11pm; $–$$; BTS: Asok; map p.141 E3
The owner is former senator Mechai 'Mr Condom' Viravaidhya, who has done much for AIDS awareness. This two-storey restaurant with a courtyard serves decent Thai standards. Free condoms as you leave.

Lemon Grass
5/1 Sukhumvit Soi 24; tel: 0 2258 8637; daily 11am–2pm and 6–11pm; $$; BTS: Phrom Phong; map p.18
This is a little faded now, but still has the attraction of a house and garden. The food

Above: Basil's crispy rice-flour pancakes stuffed with curried prawns.

is excellent, though spices are toned down; try the satay and minced chicken with ginger and cabbage leaves.

VEGETARIAN
Tamarind Café
Sukhumvit Soi 20; tel: 0 2663 7421; www.tamarind-cafe.com; Mon–Fri 11am–11pm, Sat–Sun 9am–11pm; $; BTS: Asok or MRT: Sukhumvit; map p.18
This stylish all-white branch of a Hanoi café holds photo exhibitions. European-Asian flavours in tapas-style starters such as falafel and Thai crispy mushrooms. Follow up with a vegetable gratin and coconut cream pie.

WESTERN
Offshore Fish and Chips
7/8 Sukhumvit Soi 23; tel: 0 2661 7830; daily 11am–2am; $; BTS: Asok or MRT: Sukhumvit; map p.18
Bangkok's only UK/Australian-style fish and chips. For better flavour pay the few baht extra for the cod, rather than the standard fish, and don't forget the mushy peas. There's also steak and kidney pie, mince and onion pie, and all the battered edibles you'd expect in Sydney or London.

Below: the sleek, futuristic Bed Supperclub.

Shopping

Bangkok is a retail destination for both spend-thrifts and penny-pinchers. You can sniff out an antique under the awnings of an outdoor market or pick up an Hermès handbag from a glitzy luxury mall. If you know where to look, just about anything is available, from traditional Thai pottery and handwoven silks to creative home furnishings and funky streetwear. While imported items are expensive, you will find locally and regionally produced products incredibly affordable. And with most shops, malls and markets *(see Markets, p.72)* open daily, you can easily shop till you drop, from morning till night.

Best Times to Shop

Every June–July and December–January, major department stores and malls take part in the **Thailand Grand Sales**, though many also offer a 5 percent tourist discount year round – simply show your passport at the point of purchase. Alternatively, you can claim the 7 percent VAT discount at the airport.

Bangkok also hosts seasonal sales offering unique items, such as the twice-yearly prison sale of wooden furniture made by Thai prisoners. Also worth attending are the annual export sales events such as Made in Thailand and Bangkok International Gifts & Houseware (BIG).

Traditional Products

Thailand is famous for the fine quality of its traditional handicrafts, and there is an extraordinary variety on offer. **Teakwood carvings** come in the form of practical items such as breadboards and salad bowls, as well as more decorative trivets and statues

Above: a woodcarving depicting a scene from the *Ramakien*.

of mythical gods, angels and elephants. **Bronze statues** of classical drama figures like the recumbent deer from the *Ramakien* make elegant decorations. Natural fibre woven into placemats, baskets and handbags also make great buys.

Thai craftsmen also excel at **lacquerware**, the art of overlaying wooden or bamboo items with glossy black lacquer, then painting scenes in gold leaf on this black 'canvas'. One of Thailand's lesser-known arts is **nielloware**, which involves applying an amalgam of black metal onto etched portions of silver or, to a

lesser extent, gold. Thai craftsmen are also supremely skilled at setting oyster shells aglow in black lacquer backgrounds to create scenes of enchanting beauty.

Thais have been crafting **pottery** for over 5,000 years with great skill. While original antiques are rarities, most ceramics are still thrown along the same shapes and designs of their age-old counterparts. Among the most well-known are Sangkhaloke ceramic plates from ancient Sukhothai with their distinctive twin-fish design. Celadon is a beautiful stoneware with a light jade-green or dark-brown glaze,

Left: bustling Mahboonkrong.

and platinum into delicate jewellery settings and are able to produce both traditional and modern designs.

Be careful when shopping for gems and jewellery; on streets and in some small shops, the stones may not be of the quality and weight advertised. Buy only from reputable shops endorsed by the Tourism Authority of Thailand and the Thai Gem and Jewellery Traders Association. These shops carry the Jewel Fest (www.jewelfest.com) logo and issue a certificate of authenticity that comes with a money-back guarantee.

Shopping Malls

Central World
Thanon Ratchadamri; tel: 0 2255 9400; BTS: Chit Lom; map p.140 C4
Bangkok's largest mall has a cineplex, restaurants and Zen and Isetan department stores.

Emporium
622 Thanon Sukhumvit, corner with Soi 24; tel: 0 2664 8000–9; BTS: Phrong Phong; map p.18
Mainly brand-name stores

Below: jewellery boxes embedded with coloured stones.

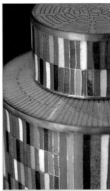

and is used to make dinnerware, lamps and statuary. *Bencharong* originated in China and was later developed by Thai artists. Its name describes its look: *bencha* is Sanskrit for 'five', and *rong* means 'colour'. The five colours of *bencharong* – red, blue, yellow, green and white – appear on delicate porcelain bowls, containers and decorative items. Popular blue-and-white porcelain, which also originated in China, has been produced extensively in Thailand for centuries.

Antiques

Thai and Burmese antiques are among the finest in Asia, but the real thing is rare nowadays. For the tenacious and well-informed though, treasures can still be unearthed. The centre of the city's antiques trade is River City, with an array of shops selling genuine antiques and look-a-like objets d'art. Note: the Fine Arts Department maintains strict control over the export of religious antiques; dealers are usually able to clear buyers' purchases by obtaining export permits and shipping them abroad.

Gems and Jewellery

Thailand mines its own rubies and sapphires from the east-coast city of Chantaburi, and also acts as a sale conduit for stones from Burma and Cambodia. Thailand is a major player in the international jewellery market, and Bangkok is home to the world's leading cutters of coloured gems. Rubies range from pale to deep red (including the famous 'pigeon's blood' red); sapphires come in blue, green and yellow, as well as in the form most associated with Thailand – the star sapphire. Thai jewellers can turn gold, white gold, silver

> Don't follow touts who offer to take you to a gem factory for 'special deals'. The gems are usually synthetic or of substandard quality, and there is no way you can get your money back.

Department stores are generally open daily 10.30am–9pm, though larger stones stay open as late as 10pm. Ordinary shops generally open at 8.30am or 9am and close between 6pm and 8pm, depending on location and type of business.

and electronics shops. The department store, also named Emporium, is one of the classiest in the city. There's a section on the 4th floor with a good selection of Thai handicrafts and jewellery, plus an excellent food hall.

Erawan Bangkok
494 Thanon Ploenchit; tel: 0 2250 777; www.erawan bangkok.com; BTS: Chit Lom; map p.141 C4
Behind the famous Erawan Shrine and connected to the Grand Hyatt Erawan, this boutique mall has chic shops and eateries and a wellness and beauty centre.

Gaysorn Plaza
999 Thanon Ploenchit; tel: 0 2656 1149; BTS: Chit Lom; map p.141 C4
This glitzy mall is good for high-fashion labels; its 3rd floor has elegant home décor shops.

H1
998 Sukhumvit Soi 55 (Soi Thonglor); tel: 0 2714 9578; BTS: Thong Lo; map p.18
A clutch of low-rise trendy shops, restaurants and bars on the road that is Bangkok's home to boutique malls.

Mahboonkrong (MBK)
444 Thanon Phaya Thai; tel: 0 2217 9119; BTS: Siam; map p.140 B4
One of Bangkok's most popular malls. In general, most goods and services are aimed at Thai youth or bar-gain-hunting tourists. Great for cheap leather luggage, jewellery and electronics.

Playground
818 Sukhumvit Soi 55 (Soi Thonglor); tel: 0 2714 7888; www.playgroundstore.co.th; BTS: Thong Lo; map p.18
This boutique mall combines art installations with home décor and fashion shops, trendy cafés, and a cooking school.

Siam Centre
989 Thanon Rama I; tel: 0 2658 1000; BTS: Siam; map p.140 B4
Several tailors and numerous clothing stores, a games arcade for kids and home décor stores. Restaurants and sports zone on the top floor.

Siam Discovery Centre
989 Thanon Rama I; tel: 0 2658 1000; BTS: Siam; map p.140 B4
Packed with imported brands. On the 5th floor is Kids World, a whole floor devoted to youngsters.

Siam Paragon
991/1 Thanon Rama I; tel: 0 2610 9000; www.siam paragon.co.th; BTS: Siam; map p.140 B4
Something for everyone at this enormous mall. All the famous international brands are represented, as are many local ones. The department store with the same name as the mall contains a vast array of clothing, electronics and housewares. Excellent eateries, gourmet market and the Siam Ocean World aquarium add to the mix.

Department Stores

Central Chidlom
1027 Thanon Ploenchit; tel: 0 2655 7777; BTS: Chit Lom; map p.141 D4
One of Bangkok's top department stores. The hip Loft food court offers a superb range of international food.

Isetan
Central World, Thanon Ratchadamri; tel: 0 2255 9898–9; BTS: Chit Lom; map p.140 C4
Japanese department store with high-quality goods at slightly above-average prices.

Robinson
Sukhumvit Soi 19; tel: 0 2252 5121; BTS: Asok or MRT: Sukhumvit; map p.18
The chain's most popular branches are on Thanon Silom, Thanon Sukhumvit and Thanon Ratchadaphisek. The quality of the goods are not as high as that of those in Central but they are cheaper.

Zen
Central World, Thanon Ratchadamri; tel: 0 2255 9667/9; BTS: Chit Lom; map p.140 C4

Below: MBK offers trendy goods popular with the younger set.

Left: Thai craftsmen are adept at fashioning lacquerware.

With a similar look and feel as Isetan, Zen has a wide range of international and local products.

Markets

One of the joys of shopping in Bangkok is its markets. Many of them, such as the **Suan Lum Night Bazaar**, **Thanon Sukhumvit night market** and the gigantic **Chatuchak Market**, are worth a browse for their sights and sounds, even if you are not buying.
SEE MARKETS, P.72

Antiques

O P Place
Soi 38 Thanon Charoen Krung; tel: 0 2266 0186; BTS: Saphan Taksin; pier: Oriental; map p.139 E1
This upmarket mall opposite The Oriental offers antiques as expensive as you can expect for the location.

River City
23 Trok Rongnamkaeng; tel: 0 2237 0077–8; MRT: Hualamphong; pier: Sri Phraya; map p.139 E2
The 2nd to 4th floors sell art and antiques. Auctions are held monthly in the Auction House. Be aware of pilfered artefacts from historical sites.

Electronics

Panthip Plaza
604/3 Thanon Phetchaburi; tel: 0 2251 9724–8; BTS: Ratchathewi; map p.136 C1
With 150 shops spread over five floors, this is Thailand's biggest marketplace for computer gear.

Gems and Jewellery

Ki-Ti's Jewellery
2/F, Playground, Sukhumvit Soi 55 (Soi Thonglor); tel: 0 1821 1275; www.kittijewelry.com; BTS: Thong Lo; map p.18
Khun Ittipol's stylish take on the ethnic look has given him a following. Another outlet, Ki-Ti's Gallery at Baan Silom, is on Silom Soi 19.

Uthai's Gems
28/7 Soi Ruam Rudi; tel: 0 2253 8582; BTS: Phloen Chit; map p.141 D3
Foreign residents like the personal touch and approach of this reputable jeweller.

Handicrafts/Homeware

Asian Motifs
3/F, Gaysorn Plaza, Thanon Ploenchit; tel: 0 2656 1093; BTS: Chit Lom; map p.141 C4
Unique and contemporary spins to traditional celadon, lacquerware and silks.

Narayana Phand
127 Thanon Ratchadamri; tel: 0 2252 4670; BTS: Chit Lom; map p.141 C4
Spread over several floors, this is a one-stop shop for all things Thai, from traditional musical instruments to ornamental headpieces.

Rasi Sayam
82 Sukhumvit Soi 33, tel: 0 2262 0729; BTS: Phrom Phong; map p.18
Sells fine traditional Thai handicrafts and objets d'art, with many one-of-a-kind pieces.

Cocoon
3/F, Gaysorn Plaza, Thanon Ploenchit; tel: 0 2656 1006; BTS: Chit Lom; map p.141 C4
Modern twists to traditional Thai and Asian fabrics and home décor items.

Propaganda
4/F, Siam Discovery Centre, Thanon Rama I; tel: 0 2658 0430; www.propagandaonline.com; BTS: Siam; map p.140 B4
Think of this as a Thai version of Alessi: Propaganda has quirky home décor items, from funky tableware and dog-shaped lamps to molar-shaped toothbrush holders. Its second outlet is located at Emporium mall.

Below: merchandise in a handicraft shop in Silom.

Sport

Thai men and women are sport enthusiasts, playing and watching both their traditional sports and those originating from the West. Other than mainstream sports such as football and tennis, the Thais are fanatic about *muay thai*, or Thai kickboxing, and *takraw*, in which two opposing teams face off in a highly acrobatic game of kicking a rattan ball. There are two principal places to view *muay thai* matches, at the Lumphini and Ratchadamnoen stadiums, while *takraw* is commonly practised in outdoor parks. Go-karting at RCA's indoor track is also a popular nighttime activity.

Venues

The principal sports venues in Bangkok are the **National Stadium**, on Thanon Rama I just west of Mahboonkrong shopping centre; the **Hua Mark Stadium**, east of the city next to Ramkhamhaeng University; and the **Thai-Japanese Sports Centre**, at Din Daeng near the northern entrance to the expressway.

Muay Thai

If you enjoy seeing a punch-out, the frenzied sport of *muay thai*, or Thai kickboxing, will keep you on the edge of your seat. *Muay thai* training is especially rigorous and tough, and requires high commitment. Employing not just fists but elbows, feet and knees, in fact almost any part of the body except the head, this highly ritualised sport is accompanied by high-pitched Thai music played by a *phipat* orchestra. Matches are divided into 10 bouts, each session consisting of five 3-minute rounds with a 2-minute rest between each round. Before the match begins, the fighters do a *ram*

muay, a stylised dance that also warms up and stretches the boxers' muscles. The cheers of the audience and the frantic betting at the sidelines almost steal the thunder from the action in the ring.

VENUES

Lumphini Boxing Stadium
Thanon Rama IV; tel: 0 2251 4303; MRT: Lumphini; map p.141 D1
Matches at 6pm on Tue, Fri and Sat. Tickets at B500, B800 and B1,500. Note: this stadium is scheduled to relocate in the near future, although a date has not been set.

Ratchadamnoen Boxing Stadium
1 Thanon Ratchadamnoen Nok; tel: 0 2281 4205; pier: Wisut Kasat; map p.135 D2
Matches at 6pm on Mon, Wed and Thur, and 5pm on Sun. Tickets at B500, B800 and B1,500.

COURSES

Jitti's Gym (International Muay Thai Training Gym)
12 Soi Chokchairuammit Yak 29,

Above: *takraw* is an energetic contact sport.

Vibhavadi Rangsit, Thanon Ratchadapisek, Din Daeng; tel: 0 2691 4238; www.jittigym.com
Muay Thai Institute
336/932 Phahon Yothin, 118 Thanon Vipravadi Prachatipat, Thayaburi Prathumthani, Rangsit; tel 0 2992 0096; www.muaythai-institute.net

Takraw

The game of *takraw* has close relatives in the Philippines, Malaysia and Indonesia, Laos and Burma. It employs all the limbs except the hands to propel a woven rattan ball (or a more modern

Left: *muay thai* is a must-see for Bangkok visitors.

tel: 0 2203 1205; www.karting stadium.com

One might think of indoor karting in a room full of petrol fumes, but in fact PTT Speedway's 600-m-long race circuit is a cool, clean and well-managed place. The karts are extremely fast and light, reaching a top speed of around 60 km/h. The stadium has a hi-tech computerised time clock, highlighting individual fastest laps and printing it out on a time sheet for you to take away.

Yoga

Absolute Yoga Bangkok
4/F, Amarin Plaza, Thanon Ploenchit; tel: 0 2252 4400; www.absoluteyogabangkok.com; BTS: Chit Lom; map p.141 C4
Part of a world trend for Bikram or hot yoga that is done in a heated room (as if in Bangkok one needs it). The contortionist postures will leave you dripping with sweat.
Prana Yoga
Sareerarom Spa, Sukhumvit Soi 55 (Soi Thonglor); tel: 0 2391 9919; www.pranabangkokyoga. com; BTS: Thong Lo; map p.18
One-off yoga classes available for B450. Both Iyengar and Power Vinyasa versions of yoga are taught here.

East of Chulalongkorn University along Thanon Henri Dunant is the members-only Royal Bangkok Sports Club (tel: 0 2255 1420 for race info). Dating from the early 1900s, horseracing quickly became the favourite recreational sport for the city's upper class. Today, the races attract large crowds of feverish gamblers, among them non-members who are allowed into the club only on alternate Sundays.

many points as it can, after which it is the opposing team's turn.

Tournaments are held at the **Thai-Japanese Sports Complex** (tel: 0 2465 5325 for dates and times; free). Competitions are also found in the northwestern corner of Bangkok's Sanam Luang during the February–April kite contests. Otherwise you'll usually find games being played in Lumphini Park.

Go-Karting

PTT Speedway Karting Stadium
2/F, RCA Plaza, Royal City Avenue, Thanon Rama IX;

plastic ball) over a net or into a hoop. In the net version, two three-player teams face each other across a head-high net, like that used in badminton. It is not unusual for a player to turn complete somersaults to spike balls across the net.

In the second type, six players form a wide circle around a basket-like net suspended high in the air. Using heads, feet, knees and elbows to keep the ball airborne, they score points by putting the ball into the net. A team has a set time period in which to score as

Below: go-karting is a popular sport in Bangkok.

Temples

As a philosophy, Buddhism has a profound influence in shaping the Thai character. The Buddhist concept of the impermanence of life and possessions, and that of the necessity to avoid extremes of emotion or behaviour, predetermine the way the Thai people react to events and give rise to the relaxed, carefree charm that is one of their most appealing characteristics. With Buddhism and its rituals and practices so central to the lives of most Thais, it is little wonder Bangkok has some of the most exquisite Buddhist temples and sacred Buddha images in the world.

Theravada Buddhism

Most Thai people follow Theravada Buddhism, which is also the main Buddhist form practised in countries like Laos, Cambodia, Burma and Sri Lanka. Over the centuries, the Thais have evolved a Buddhism of their own cast. Theravada Buddhism is a mixture of Buddhist, Hindu and animistic beliefs, and, as the oldest of all Buddhist faiths, it is the only one to trace its origins directly back to the teachings of the Gau-

Below: a monk with an alms bowl.

tama Buddha in the 6th century BC. The central doctrines are based on the temporary nature of life and the imperfections of all forms of beings.

Each Thai, whether lay person or monk, tries to achieve spiritual merit in the present life so that it will favourably influence the next life – thus permitting an existence that will be characterised by less suffering and will ultimately lead to nirvana, or enlightenment. Almost all the religious activities that a visitor will experience have to do with merit-making. A man who spends some part of his life as a monk will earn merit by living in accordance with the strict rules of monastic life. So, too, will a person who gives alms to monks on a daily basis, or who visits a temple to pray for a sick person.

The Buddha image in front of which the prayers are offered provides only a formal background for these activities. Neither the statue, nor the Buddha himself, is worshipped.

Mahayana Buddhism

Mahayana Buddhism is practised by those of Chinese descent. Visitors are likely to spot Mahayana temples in Bangkok's Chinatown. 'Mahayana' means 'Greater Vehicle'; the defining belief, according to this doctrine, is that those who have attained nirvana return to help others reach the same state. The various Buddhist sects and practices that predominate in China, Tibet, Taiwan, Japan, Korea and Vietnam are classified as Mahayana. Chinese Buddhism, at least that practised in Thailand, primarily consists of incense, lucky charms, and other folk practices. The visitor entering a *sanjao*, or inner shrine, of such a temple will have a chance to shake sticks out of a canister, from which a fortune can be told.

Temple Art and Architecture

A typical Thai *wat* (or temple) has two enclosing walls that divide it from the secular world. The monks' quarters are situated between the

Many of the Thais' non-Buddhist beliefs are Brahman in origin, and even today Brahman priests officiate at major ceremonies. The Thai wedding ceremony is almost entirely Brahman, as are many funeral rites. Royal ceremonies, such as the Ploughing Ceremony in May, are presided over by Brahman priests.

outer and inner walls. In larger temples the inner walls may be lined with Buddha images and serve as cloisters for meditation. This part of the temple is called *buddhavasa* or *phutthawat*. Inside the inner walls is the *bot* or *ubosot* (ordination hall) surrounded by eight stone tablets and set on consecrated ground. This is the most sacred part of the temple and only monks can enter it. The *bot* contains a Buddha image, but it is the *viharn* (sermon hall) that contains the principal Buddha images. Also in the inner courtyard are the bell-shaped *chedis* (relic chambers), which contain the relics of pious or distinguished people. *Salas* (pavilions) can be found all around the temple; the largest of these areas is the *sala kan prian* (study hall), used for afternoon prayers. Apart from Buddha images, various mythological figures, such as the *naga* (serpent), *erawan* (elephant) and *garuda* (half-eagle, half-man demigod) are found within the temple compound.

Ayutthaya Historical Park

Ayutthaya, 85km north of Bangkok; daily 8am–5pm; entrance charge; train from Hualamphong, bus from Northern Bus Terminal, or boat *(see box on p.75)*; map p.20
Grand ruins aside, this historical park is home to a number of impressive temples.
SEE MONUMENTS, P.74–7

Devasathan

Thanon Dinso; daily 9am–5pm, chapel Thur and Sun only 10am–4pm; free; pier: Tha Chang; map p.134 C1
The Devasathan is a row of three adjoining Brahman shrines built in 1784 at the same time as the Giant Swing. These house images of Shiva, Ganesha and Vishnu. Although the Thais are largely Buddhists, certain Brahman beliefs have been integrated into their faith.

Erawan Shrine

Corner of Thanon Ratchadamri and Thanon Ploenchit; daily 8am–10pm; free; BTS: Chit Lom; map p.141 C4
The Erawan shrine is dedicated to the four-headed Hindu god of creation, Brahma. Erected on the site of the former Erawan Hotel, which has been rebuilt as the present Grand Hyatt Erawan, the original spirit house was deemed ineffective after a spate of unfortunate events, including deaths, slowed the

Below: making offerings at the Erawan Shrine.

Above: Wat Arun at dusk.

hotel's construction. This plaster-gilded 1956 replacement halted the unlucky run, and ever since then it has been revered for its strong talismanic powers. In 2006 the shrine was hacked to pieces by a mentally ill man, who was subsequently lynched to death by an angry mob – such is the devotion that Thais accord to this shrine. It has since been restored.

Wat Arun

Thanon Arun Amarin; daily 8.30am–5.30pm; entrance charge; pier: Wat Arun; map p.138 A4

When King Taksin first moored at the Thonburi bank of the Chao Phraya River after arriving from the sacked capital of Ayutthaya, he supposedly found an old temple shrine and felt

Shorts are taboo for men and women who wish to enter some of the more highly revered temples. Women wearing sleeveless dresses and short skirts may also be barred from certain temples. Improperly dressed and unkempt visitors will be turned away from Wat Phra Kaew and the Grand Palace (though some clothing can be borrowed at the entrance).

compelled to build a fitting holding place for the sacred Emerald Buddha. Eventually it became known as Wat Arun, the Temple of Dawn.

After Taksin's demise, the new King Chakri (Rama I) moved the capital and the Emerald Buddha to Bangkok, but the temple held the interest of the first five kings. In the early 19th century King Rama II raised the central *prang* to 104m, making it the country's tallest religious structure.

Recycling piles of broken ceramic that was leftover ballast from Chinese merchant ships, Rama III introduced the colourful fragments of porcelain that cover most of the temple's exterior. When builders ran out of porcelain, the king asked his subjects to contribute broken crockery to complete the decoration.

The great *prang* represents the Hindu-Buddhist Mount Meru, home of the gods with its 33 heavens. The peak of the *prang* is topped by a thunderbolt, the weapon of the Hindu god

Indra. There are four smaller *prangs* standing at each corner of the temple with niches containing statues of Nayu, the god of wind, on horseback. Between the minor *prang* are four beautiful *mondops*, smaller towers placed at the key points. The niches at the foot of each stairway contain images of the Buddha in the four key events of his life: birth, meditation, preaching to his first five disciples, and at death. The entire complex is guarded by mythical giants called *yaksa*, similar to those that protect Wat Phra Kaew.

Wat Benjamabophit

Thanon Rama V; daily 8am–5.30pm; entrance charge; pier: Thewet; map p.135 E3

Wat Benjamabophit, the Marble Temple, is the last major temple built in central Bangkok and the best example of modern Thai religious architecture. Started by King Chulalongkorn in the early 20th century, the wat was designed by the king's half-brother Prince Naris together with Italian

Below: worshippers at a night service at Wat Benjamabophit.

architect Hercules Manfredi. Completed in 1911, the temple is a fusion of East and West elements to dramatic effect. The most obvious of these must be the walls of Carrara marble from Italy, the cruciform shape and the unique European-crafted stained-glass windows depicting Thai mythological scenes. The principal Buddha image in the *bot* is a replica of the famous Phra Buddha Chinarat of Phitsanulok, with the base containing the ashes of King Chulalongkorn.

Behind the *bot* is a gallery holding 53 original and copied significant Buddha images from all over Buddhist Asia. Early in the morning merit-makers gather in front of the temple's gates to donate food and offerings to the line of bowl-wielding monks – unlike elsewhere where monks walk the streets searching for alms.

Wat Bowonniwet

Thanon Bowonniwet; daily 8am–5pm; free; pier: Wat Sam Praya; map p.134 C2
This modest-looking monastery, built in 1826 during King Rama III's reign, has strong royal bonds. King Mongkut served as its abbot for a small portion of his 27 years as a monk. More recently the present King Bhumibol donned saffron robes here after his coronation in 1946.

Home to Thailand's second Buddhist university, the temple is known for its extraordinary murals painted by innovative monk-artist Khrua In Khong. Krua had never travelled outside Thailand, but had looked at Western art reproductions and understood the concept of perspective. Unlike the flat, two-dimensional

Above: Buddha images at Wat Mangkon Kamalawat.

paintings of classical Thai art, these recede into the distance and are characterised by muted colours. Also interesting are the subjects: antebellum southern American mansions, horseracing tracks and people dressed in the fashions of 19th-century America.

Wat Mangkon Kamalawat

Thanon Charoen Krung, near Soi Itsaranuphap; daily 8.30am–3.30pm; free; MRT: Hualamphong; map p.139 D4
Also known as Leng Noi Yee (Dragon Flower Temple), this is the most revered temple in Chinatown. Built in 1871, it is one of the most important centres for Mahayana Buddhism in all of Thailand. Elements of Taoism and Confucianism are also prevalent. The dragon-crowned roof overlooks a courtyard containing several structures that house altars and images of gilded Buddhas, the Four Heavenly Kings and other Taoist deities. It is a constant swirl of activity and incense smoke, and as with the rest of Chinatown, the temple is overrun at Chinese New Year.

Above: the *chedis* at Wat Pho sit on square bases.

Wat Pho

Thanon Thai Wang; daily 8am–6pm; entrance charge; pier: Rong Mo or Tha Tien; map p.138 B4
South of the Grand Palace and Wat Phra Kaew complex is Wat Pho, Bangkok's largest and oldest-surviving temple. The site retains a more casual ambience to the younger and more dominant Wat Phra Kaew. Apart from its historical significance, visitors come to Wat Pho to pay homage to the monumental Reclining Buddha, and to unwind at the **Wat Pho Thai Traditional Massage School**.

The temple dates back to the 16th century, although it did not achieve real importance until the establishment of Bangkok as the capital. It was a particular favourite of the first four Bangkok kings, all of whom added to its treasures. The four towering coloured *chedis* to the west of the *bot* are memorials to the past monarchs, and around the hall are 90-plus other *chedis*. The cloisters contain 394 bronze Buddha images, retrieved from ancient ruins in Sukhothai and Ayutthaya. The Reclining

121

Above: the Reclining Buddha at Wat Pho.

Buddha was added by King Rama III in 1832, who also converted the temple into the country's earliest place of public learning. The monarch instructed that the walls be inscribed with lessons on astrology, history, morality and archaeology. It is no wonder locals fondly call the temple the kingdom's first university.

The **Reclining Buddha**, 46m long and 15m high, is made from brick, plaster and gilded in gold. It depicts the resting Buddha passing into nirvana. The flat soles of the Buddha's feet are inlaid with mother-of-pearl, illustrating the 108 auspicious signs for recognising Buddha. Also numbering 108 are the metallic bowls that span the wall; a coin dropped in each supposedly brings goodwill to the devotee. With the building's pillars preventing full view, the head and feet are the best vantage points.

Girding the base of the main hall are superbly carved sandstone panels depicting scenes from the *Ramakien*. The striking doors are also devoted to *Ramakien* scenes, brilliantly rendered in some of the finest mother-of-pearl work found in Asia. The

ashes of King Rama I are interred in the pedestal base of the hall's principal Buddha image.
SEE ALSO PAMPERING, P.98

Wat Phra Kaew

Grand Palace complex, entrance along Thanon Na Phra Lan; daily 8.30am–3.30pm; free; pier: Tha Chang; map p.134 B1
Wat Phra Kaew, the Temple of the Emerald Buddha, serves as the royal chapel of the Grand Palace. The magnificent temple compound is modelled after palace chapels in the former capitals of Sukhothai and Ayutthaya, and contains many typical monastic structures, except living quarters

for monks, a feature found in most other Thai temples.

At the main entrance to the temple compound is the statue of Shivaka Kumar Baccha, said to be Buddha's private physician. Behind it is the temple's most important building housing the *bot* containing the Emerald Buddha statue. To get to it, begin walking in a clockwise direction. On the upper terrace on the left are the gleaming gold mosaic tiles encrusting the Sri Lankan-style circular **Phra Si Rattana Chedi**. Erected by King Mongkut, it is said to enshrine a piece of the Buddha's breastbone.

In the centre is **Phra Mondop** (Library of Buddhist Scriptures), surrounded by statues of sacred white elephants, symbols of royal power. The library was erected to hold the holy Buddhist scriptures called *Tripitaka*. It is a delicate building, studded with blue and green glass mosaic tiles, and topped by a multi-tiered roof fashioned like the crown of a Thai king.

Adjacent to it is the **Prasat Phra Thep Bidom** (Royal Pantheon). This contains life-sized statues of the Chakri kings and is open

Below: temple exteriors are often very ornate, such as that of the Bot of the Emerald Buddha at Wat Phra Kaew.

to the public only on Chakri Day, 6 April. Around the building stand gilded statues of mythological creatures, including the half-female, half-lion *aponsi*. Flanking the entrance of the Prasat Phra Thep Bidom are two towering gilded *chedis*.

Behind Phra Mondop is a large sandstone model of the famous Khmer temple of Angkor Wat in Cambodia. The model was built during King Mongkut's reign when Cambodia was a vassal Thai state. Just behind, along the northern edge of the compound, is the **Viharn Yot** (Prayer Hall), flanked by the **Ho Phra Nak** (Royal Mausoleum) on the left and **Ho Phra Montien Tham** (Auxillary Library) on the right.

The walls of the cloister enclosing the temple courtyard are painted with a picture book of 178 murals depicting scenes from the *Ramakien*.

THE EMERALD BUDDHA
Finally you will come to the Wat Phra Kaew's most sacred structure, the **Bot of the Emerald Buddha**. Remove your shoes before entering the hall. It is particularly busy on weekends and holidays when worshippers fill the main sanctuary, prostrating themselves on the marble floor before the temple's 11-m-tall golden altar.

At the top of the elaborate altar, in a glass case and protected by a nine-tiered umbrella, is the country's most celebrated image, the diminutive 75-cm-tall Emerald Buddha. Surprisingly, it is not made of emerald but carved from a solid block of green jade.

The Emerald Buddha was found in Chiang Rai in 1434, in a temple also known as

Above: the Emerald Buddha.

Wat Phra Kaew. The image, kept hidden in a *chedi* there for some reason, was revealed when the *chedi* was struck by lighting. Subsequently, the Lao army took brought it to Vientiane, Laos, in the mid 16th century where it remained until 1779 when it was seized by the Thais. When Bangkok was established as the new capital, King Rama I brought the statue with him in 1784. The statue is claimed to bestow good fortune on the kingdom that possesses it.
SEE ALSO PALACES, P.96; MUSEUMS AND GALLERIES, P.85

Wat Suthat

Corner of Thanon Ti Tong and Thanon Kanlayanamit; daily 8.30am–9pm; entrance charge; pier: Tha Chang; map p.134 C1
Wat Suthat is considered one of the country's six principal temples. Begun by King Rama I in 1807, it took three reigns to complete. The temple is noted for its enormous *bot*, said to be the tallest in Bangkok, and for its equally large *viharn*, both of them surrounded by cloisters of gilded Buddha images.

The 8-m-tall Phra Sri Sakyamuni Buddha is one of the largest surviving bronze images from Sukhothai, and was transported by boat to Bangkok from the northern kingdom. The base of the

The Emerald Buddha is graced with three costumes, which change with the seasons: a golden, diamond-studded tunic is used for the hot season; a gilded robe flecked with blue for the rainy season; and a robe of enamel-coated solid gold for the cool season. The change is done in a ritual ceremony presided over by the king.

image contains the ashes of King Ananda Mahidol, older brother of the present king. The wall murals date from the reign of King Rama III; the most intriguing are the depictions of sea monsters and foreign ships on the columns.

Accounts vary, but it is said that King Rama II himself carved the ornate teakwood doors of the *bot*. Incised to a depth of 5cm, the carvings follow the Ayutthayan tradition of floral motifs, with tangled jungle vegetation hiding small animals. The temple courtyard is virtually a museum of statuary, with stone figures of Chinese generals and scholars. They came as ballast in rice ships returning from deliveries to China and were donated to temples.

Below: detail from a wall mural at Wat Suthat.

Transport

Getting to Bangkok is easy. The new Suvarnabhumi Airport is served by over 80 international airlines, and the city is also connected by rail to Malaysia and Singapore. Bangkok is not only a key gateway between Asia and the West, but is also a major transport hub linked to the rest of Southeast Asia. While the City of Angels is infamous for its traffic snarls, getting around it is really not that difficult, especially if you make use of its efficient Skytrain and subway, as well as its river ferries. Taxis are cheap and provide a good way to get around during off-peak hours as well.

Getting There

BY AIR

Suvarnabhumi Airport

Bangkok's Suvarnabhumi (pronounced 'su-wa-na-poom') Airport (www.airport thai.co.th) is located about 30km east of Bangkok in Samut Prakan province. It takes about 45–60 minutes to get to the airport from the city by taxi, depending on traffic conditions. The airport handles all international flights to Bangkok as well as many domestic connections.

Suvarnabhumi has one main passenger terminal with seven concourses, capable of handling 76 flights per hour with ease, according to the Airport Authority of Thailand (AOT). In practice however, the airport has been mired in controversy since its hurried opening, and complaints have been rife – everything from inadequate toilet facilities and cracked runways to a congested arrival hall and long walks from one gate to another. Most of these kinks should have been ironed out by the time you read this.

Above: the sleek Suvarnabhumi Airport.

The airport has a good range of facilities, including foreign exchange outlets, ATMs, a Tourism Authority of Thailand (TAT) office, medical centre, Internet facilities, fitness centre and a wide array of shops and restaurants.

For more details check the airport website or call any of the following:

Airport Call Centre
Tel: 0 2132 1888
Departures:
Tel: 0 2132 9324–7
Arrivals
Tel: 0 2132 9328–9

In line with the practice of major airports the world over, the airport tax for international flights out of Suvarnabhumi is now incorporated into the price of your air ticket.

Don Muang Airport

The old Don Muang Airport (tel: 0 2535 1111; www.airport thai.co.th) reopened in March 2007 following the teething problems that Suvarnabhumi was experiencing. At the time of press, a small number of THAI Airways domestic flights and all domestic flights operated by Nok Air and Orient Thai use Don Muang Airport.

Don Muang is about 30km north of the city centre. It

Left: waiting for motorcycle taxi passengers.

centre takes 45–60 minutes, depending on traffic conditions (the worst period is 4–9pm). Emerging in the Arrival Hall, you may be harangued by touts both inside and outside the barriers. Never volunteer your name or destination to these people. If you already have a reservation at a hotel, a representative will have your name written on a sign, or at least a sign bearing the name of your hotel. If you haven't made prior arrangements, use one of the following modes to get to the city.

If making a flight connection between Suvarnabhumi and Don Muang airports, be sure to allow for sufficient time as taxi travel time between the two airports could be up to 1½ hours.

takes about 40–45 minutes, depending on traffic, to get to or from the airport by taxi.

BY RAIL
The **State Railway of Thailand** (www.railway.co.th) operates trains that are clean, cheap and reliable. There are two entry points by rail into Thailand, both from Malaysia to the south. The more popular is the daily train that leaves Butterworth near Penang at 2.10pm for Hat Yai (south Thailand) and arrives in Bangkok's Hualamphong Station at 10.05am the next morning. Trains leave Hualamphong daily at 2.45pm for Malaysia.

BY ROAD
Malaysia provides the main road access into Thailand, with crossings near Betong and Sungai Kolok. From

Laos, it is possible to cross from Vientiane into Nong Khai in northeast Thailand by using the Friendship Bridge across the Mekong River. From Cambodia, the most commonly used border crossing is from Poipet, which connects to Aranyaprathet, east of Bangkok. One other option is overland from Kompong Cham in Cambodia, crossing over to Hat Lek in Thailand.

Getting Around
FROM THE AIRPORT
The journey from Suvarna-bhumi Airport to the city

By Taxi
Operating 24 hours daily, all taxis officially serving the airport are air-conditioned and metered. When you exit from the Arrival Hall, take the lift or travellator one level down to where the taxi desk is. Join the queue and tell the person at the desk where you want to go to. A receipt will be issued, with the licence plate number of the taxi and your destination in Thai written on it. Make sure the driver turns on the meter. At the end of your trip, pay what is on the meter plus a B50 airport surcharge. If the

Below: ask your taxi driver to turn on the meter for city trips.

Above: Bangkok's Skytrain system is efficient and affordable.

driver uses the expressway to speed up the journey, he will ask for your approval first. If you agree, you have to pay the toll fees of B60 (B20 for the first toll booth and B40 for the second). Depending on traffic, an average fare from the airport to the city centre is around B300 (excluding toll fees and airport surcharge).

By Limousine
Airports of Thailand Limousines (AOT) (tel: 0 2134 2323–6) operates a variety of vehicles that can take you to the city centre for between B800 and B1,000, which is overpriced given that the taxi fare is about a third of the price. Luxury cars like a top-end 7-series BMW cost B1,900. Rates for a transfer to Pattaya start around B2,600, depending on the vehicle used.

By Airport Bus
The Airport Bus passes the main hotels in downtown Bangkok. You must first get on the free airport shuttle to the Public Transportation Centre, which is separate from the main terminal building. Buses depart every 15 minutes from 5.30am to 12.30am, and the cost is B150 per person.

Airport Bus Routes:
AE-1 – to Silom via Pratunam, Thanon Phetchaburi, Thanon Ratchadamri, Thanon Silom and Thanon Surawong
AE-2 – to Banglamphu via Thanon Phetchaburi, Thanon Lan Luang and Thanon Khao San
AE-3 – to Sukhumvit (Nana) via Bangna, Thanon Phrakhanong, Ekkamai, Asok, Thanon Ratchadamri, Thanon Phetchaburi and Thanon Sukhumvit
AE-4 – to Hualamphong Railway Station via Victory Monument, Thanon Ploenchit, Thanon Rama, Thanon Phaya Thai and Thanon Rama IV

By Rail
Construction of the overhead 28-km **Suvarnabhumi Airport City Rail Link** connecting the airport to the city has started. This is expected to cut travel time to 15 minutes. Slated for completion in 2008 (or later), this high-speed electric train service will connect the airport with eight stations: Ladkrabung, Bantubchang, Huamak, Ramkamhaeng, Makkasan/Asok, Phayathai and Ratchaprarop. This service will be integrated with the BTS and MRT, allowing passengers to switch lines.

Getting Around

BY BTS (SKYTRAIN)
The Bangkok Transit System's (BTS) elevated train service, also known as the Skytrain, is the perfect way to beat the city's traffic-congestions.

It consists of two lines: **Sukhumvit Line** from Mo Chit station in the north to On Nut in the southeast; **Silom Line** from National Stadium near Siam Square, south to Saphan Taksin station near the Sathorn pier. Both lines intersect at Siam station.

Trains operate from 6am to midnight (3 minutes peak; 5 minutes off-peak). Single-trip fares vary according to distance, starting at B10 and rising to B40. Self-service ticket machines are found at all station concourses. It is useful to buy the 1-Day Pass (B120) with unlimited rides or the 30-Day Adult Pass, which comes in two types: B440 for 20 rides and B600 for 30 rides.

BTS Tourist Information Centres are found on the concourse levels of Siam, Nana, and Saphan Taksin stations (daily 8am–8pm).
BTS Tourist Information Centre
Tel: 0 2617 7340; hotline: 0 2617 6000; www.bts.co.th

BY MRT (METRO OR SUBWAY)
Bangkok's underground MRT line has 18 stations, stretching 20km between Bang Sue in the northern suburbs of Bangkok and the city's main railway station, Hualamphong, at the edge of Chinatown.

Accessibility for the disabled and aged on the Skytrain is a problem as there aren't enough escalators or lifts.

Three of its stations – Silom, Sukhumvit and Chatuchak Park – are interchanges, and passengers can transfer to the BTS network at these points.

Operating from 6am to midnight, the air-conditioned trains are frequent with never more than a few minutes' wait (2–4 minutes peak, 4–6 minutes off-peak). Fares start at B14, increasing B2 every station, with a maximum fare of B36.

Unlike the BTS, coin-sized plastic tokens are used instead of cards, with self-service ticket machines at all stations. Also available at station counters are passes with unlimited rides: the 1-Day Pass (B150), 3-Day Pass (B300) and the stored-value Adult Card (B200, includes a B50 deposit).

Customer Relations Centre
Tel: 0 2624 5200;
www.mrta.co.th or
www.bangkokmetro.co.th

BY TAXI

Taxis are in Bangkok are metered, air-conditioned, inexpensive, and comfortably seat 3 to 4 persons. They can be hailed anywhere along the streets; otherwise, head to a taxi stand outside hotels or shopping centres. Metered taxis are recognisable by the sign on their roofs. An illuminated red light above the dashboard indicating whether it's available for hire or not.

The flagfall is B35; after the first 2km, the meter goes up by B4–5.50 every kilometre, depending on distance travelled. If stuck in traffic, a small per-minute surcharge kicks in. If your journey crosses town, ask the driver to take the expressway. The network of elevated two-lane roads can cut the journey time by half. The toll fare of B20–50 is given to the driver at the payment booth, not at the end of the trip.

Before starting any journey, check whether the meter has been reset and turned on; many drivers conveniently 'forget' to do so and charge a lump sum at the end of the journey. On seeing a foreign face, some drivers may quote a flat fee instead of using the meter. Unless you're desperate, don't use these. Fares, however, can be negotiated for longer distances outside Bangkok: for instance, to Pattaya (B1,200), Koh Samet (B1,500) or Hua Hin (B1,500–2,000).

Drivers don't speak much English, but all know the locations of major hotels. It is a good idea to have a destination written down in Thai.

The following taxi companies will take bookings for a B20 surcharge:
Siam Taxi
Tel: 1661
Julie Taxi
Mobile tel: 081 846 2014;
www.julietaxi.com

Julie's taxis are slightly more expensive than metered ones, but its drivers are polite and speak some English. It also has a range of car and minivan options.

BY TUK-TUK

Tuk-tuks are the brightly coloured three-wheeled taxis, whose name comes from the incessant noise their two-stroke engines make. They have been increasingly losing favour – the heat, pollution and noise have become too overwhelming for most passengers. Few *tuk-tuk* drivers speak English, so make sure your destination is written down in Thai. Unless you bargain hard, *tuk-tuk* fares are rarely lower than metered taxi fares.

Expect to pay B30–50 for short journeys of a few

Below: only in Thailand: don't miss a *tuk-tuk* ride.

Some *tuk-tuk* or taxi drivers may offer to take you anywhere for 10 baht (or for free). No matter where you want to go, the destination will always be a gem shop along the way. You will be pressured to buy flawed gems at high prices. If you succumb to any of Bangkok's numerous gem scams, don't expect to get a refund after you've handed over your money or credit card. The police are almost no help whatsoever in such cases.

around 15 minutes [...] nd B50–100 for [...] journeys. A B100 ride should get you a half-hour ride across most parts of downtown. Be sure to negotiate the fare beforehand.

BY MOTORCYCLE TAXI

Motorcycle taxi stands (with young men in fluorescent orange vests) are found at the mouth of most *sois* and beside any busy intersection or building entrance.

Hire only a driver who provides a passenger helmet. Fares must be negotiated beforehand, and they are rarely lower than taxi fares for the same distance travelled. Hold on tight and keep your knees tucked in. If the driver is going too fast, ask him to slow down in Thai: *cha-cha*.

A short distance, like the length of a street, will cost B10–20, with longer rides at B50–100. During rush hour (8–10am and 4–6pm), prices are higher. A B80–100 ride should get you a half-hour trip across most parts of downtown.

BY BUS

Bus transport in Bangkok is very cheap but arduous. With little English signage and few conductors or drivers speaking English, taking the right bus is an exercise in frustration. Municipal and private operators all come under the charge of the **Bangkok Mass Transit Authority** (tel: 0 2246 0973; www.bmta.co.th). Public buses come in four varieties: microbus, Euro II bus, air-conditioned and non-air-conditioned 'ordinary'.

BY BOAT
Chao Phraya River Express Boat

The Chao Phraya River Express Boat (tel: 0 2623 6001) travels from the Nonthaburi pier in the north and ends at the Wat Rachasingkhon pier near Krungthep Bridge in the south. Boats run every 15 minutes from 6am to 6.40pm, and stop at different piers according to the coloured flag on the top of the boat. Yellow-flag boats are the fastest and do not stop at many piers, while the orange-flag and no-flag boats stop at most of the marked river piers. Tickets cost B6–15 and are purchased from the conductor on board or at some pier counters.

Chao Phraya Tourist Boat

The Chao Phraya Tourist Boat (www.chaophrayaboat.co.th) operates daily from 9.30am to 3.30pm and a trip costs B75. After 3.30pm, you can use the ticket on the regular express boats. A useful commentary is provided on board, along with a small guidebook and a bottle of water. The route begins at the Sathorn pier and travels upriver to the Phra Athit pier, stopping at 10 major piers along the way. Boats leave every 30 minutes and you can get off at any pier and pick up another boat later on this hop-on-and-off service.

Cross-River Ferry

These ferries are used for getting from one side of the river to the other. They can be boarded at the jetties that also service the Chao Phraya River Express Boats. Costing B2 per journey, cross-river ferries operate from 5am to 10pm or later.

Longtail Boat Taxi

These ply the narrow inner canals, carrying passengers from the centre of town to the outlying districts. Many of the piers are located near traffic bridges. Be sure to tell the conductor your destination as boats do not stop otherwise. Tickets cost B5–10, depending on distance, with services operating roughly every 10 minutes until 6–7pm. While there are routes serving Thonburi's canals and Bangkok's outskirts, tourists will probably only use the main downtown artery of Khlong Saen Saep, which starts from the Saphan Phanfah pier near Wat Saket, into the heart of downtown and beyond to Bang Kapi. It's useful if going to Jim Thompson's House, Siam Centre and the Thanon Ploenchit malls to Thanon Withayu and all the way to Thonglor and Ekkamai.

Below: standing room only on this ferry.

Above: BTS track in the Silom and Sathorn area.

Private Longtail Boat

If you wish to explore the canals of Thonburi or Nonthaburi, private longtail boats can be hired from most of the river's main piers. A 90-minute to two-hour tour will take you into the quieter canal communities. Ask which route the boat will take and what will be seen along the way. Ask to pull up and get out if anything interests you. Negotiate rates beforehand; an hour-long trip will cost B400–500, rising to B900 for two hours. The price is for the entire boat, which seats up to 16 people, not per person.

Trips Out of Bangkok

BY ROAD

Thailand has a good road system with road signs are in both Thai and English. An international driver's licence is required.

Unfortunately, driving on a narrow but busy road can be a terrifying experience. The right of way is often determined by size. It is not unusual for a bus to overtake a truck despite that the oncoming lane is filled with vehicles. A safer option is to hire a car or a van with a driver for trips outside of Bangkok. A small car can be hired for around B1,500 (including insurance) a day.

Avis
2/12 Thanon Withayu;
tel: 0 2255 5300–4; and
Bangkok International Airport
Building 2; tel: 0 2535 4031–2
Hertz
Soi 71, Thanon Sukhumvit;
tel: 0 2711 0574–8
Krungthai Car Rental
233–235 Thanon Asok-Din
Daeng; tel: 0 2291 8888;
www.krungthai.co.th

BY AIR

Thai Airways International (THAI), Bangkok Airways and some low-cost airlines fly to the main tourism centres.
Air Asia
Bangkok International Airport;
tel: 0 2215 9999;
www.airasia.com
Bangkok Airways
99 Thanon Vibhavadi Rangsit;
tel: 0 2265 5555;
www.bangkokair.com
Nok Air
Bangkok International Airport;
tel: 1318; www.nokair.com
One-Two-Go Airlines
18 Thanon New Ratchadapisek;
tel: 0 2229 4260;
www.fly12go.com
Orient Thai Airlines
18 Thanon New Ratchadapisek;
tel: 0 2229 4260;
www.orient-thai.com
PB Air
16th Floor, ubc II Building, 591
Thanon Sukhumvit, Soi 33; tel: 0
2261 0220; www.pbair.com

You can get to several places outside the city, like Pattaya and Hua Hin, simply by flagging down a taxi along a Bangkok street or booking one beforehand. Be sure to negotiate a flat rate before boarding; don't use the meter.

Phuket Air
Lumphini Tower, 1168 Thanon
Rama IV; tel: 0 2679 8999;
www.phuketairlines.com
Thai Airways International
89 Thanon Vibhavadi Rangsit;
tel: 0 2628 2000; www.thai
airways.com

BY BUS

Air-conditioned buses service many destinations in Thailand. VIP coaches with extra leg room are the best for overnight journeys. All buses are operated by the Transport Company Ltd (www.transport. co.th). Terminals are as follows:
Eastern (Ekkamai) Bus Terminal
Thanon Sukhumvit, opposite
Soi 63; tel: 0 2391 8097
Northern and North-eastern Bus Terminal
Thanon Khampaengphet 2;
Northern: tel: 0 2936 2852–66
ext. 311; Northeastern:
tel: 0 2936 2852–66 ext. 611
Southern Bus Terminal
Thanon Boromrat Chonnani,
Thonburi; tel: 0 2435 5605

BY TRAIN
State Railway of Thailand
(tel: 1690; www.railway.co.th) operates three routes – north, northeast and south – from the Hualamphong Railway Station (tel: 0 2225 0300). Express and rapid services on the main lines offer first-class air-conditioned or second-class fan-cooled carriages with sleeping cabins or berths. Some trains depart from Bangkok Noi Station (tel: 0 2411 3102) in Thonburi.

Walks and Views

If you prefer to see the city on foot – and can take to the heat and humidity well enough, the good news is that Bangkok is a rather walkable destination as many sights are huddled close to one another. If the weather gets too overwhelming, take cover on a shaded longtail boat and thread through Bangkok's ubiquitous canals to explore their bustling riverside communities. Or, if time permits, embark on an overnight excursion to cool off in one of its nearby national parks, located in the hills with refreshing waterfalls and hiking trails. Remember to bring along water and wear good walking shoes.

Erawan National Park

200km northwest of Bangkok; daily 6am–6pm; entrance charge; train from Bangkok Noi station or bus from Southern Bus Terminal to Kanchanaburi, then bus from Kanchanburi Bus Terminal; map p.20

The spectacular seven-tiered **Erawan Waterfall** is found in the Erawan National Park, best visited during and just after the rainy season from May to November when the water is at full flow.

The route to the waterfall starts from the national park office. The climb up to level five of the waterfall is manageable; getting up to the slippery sixth and seventh levels is not recommended unless you are fit and have

> There are some 140 gazetted national parks in Thailand, a number of which are easily accessed from Bangkok, like Erawan, Sai Yok, Kaeng Krachan and Khao Sam Roi Yot. For more information on Thai national parks, look up www.dnp.go.th or www.trekthailand.net.

enough guts. You can cool off in the inviting natural pools (don't forget your swimsuit) at the bases of the tiers. The thundering cascade from the highest level is said to take on the shape of the mythological three-headed elephant Erawan, hence its name.

There are several hiking trails in the park, which covers some 550sq km and comprises mainly deciduous forests with limestone hills rising up to 1,000m. One of the more popular hiking trails is the 90-minute Khanmak-Mookling trail; the 1,400-m-long circular trail starts from the national park office. Also taking 90 minutes is the Wangbadan Cave trail, which leads you through bamboo and evergreen forests along a 1,350-m-long route.

Khao Yai National Park

Khorat province, 200km north of Bangkok; daily 6am–6pm; entrance charge; train from Hualamphong or bus from Northern Bus Terminal to Pak Chong, then *songthaew* (pick-up truck); map p.20

Above: the cool and misty Khao Yai National Park.

Khao Yai is one of Thailand's oldest and most popular nature reserves. The second largest at 2,168sq km, it cuts across four different provinces.

Most of Khao Yai is located 400m above sea level, making it a pleasant escape from the hot, humid lowlands of central Thailand. Most people visit during the dry season from November to February; be sure to bring warm clothing during this period as temperatures can plummet to as low as 10°C at night. The rainy season is

Left: Erawan Waterfall in the Erawan National Park.

A popular end to a day at Khao Yai National Park is a walk to Khoa Luk Chang Bat Cave at dusk to watch thousands of bats fly out of the cave to feed.

Thonburi Canal Cruise

Thonburi; map p.8

For a more leisurely cruise, it may be better to hire your own private longtail boat. Boat operators (found at major piers like Tha Thien and Tha Chang) are notorious for overcharging tourists, so bargain hard and set a price before embarking; B400–500 an hour (per boat) is a rough guide. Discuss beforehand where you want to visit and how much time you want to spend at each place.

The boat will travel upstream and enter **Khlong Bangkok Noi**. A little after turning into the wide *khlong* (canal), and just before reaching a bridge, ask the driver to stop at the **Museum of Royal Barges**, located on your right, to view its collection of gilded barges put on sail only on special royal occasions.

Continue up the canal to **Khlong Chak Phra**, then go left. Among the palm trees are many beautiful old

one of the best times for animal spotting, but remember to cover up bare legs and arms as leeches are common.

Often clad in mist, Khao Yai's highest peaks lie in the east along a landform known as the Khorat Plateau, with the 1,350-m-high Khao Laem (Shadow Mountain) and 1,020-m-high Khao Khiew (Green Mountain). Evergreen and deciduous trees, palms and bamboo blanket the park, and unlike much of Thailand, patches of indigenous rainforest can still be seen here. Monkeys, gibbons and langurs are commonly spotted, as are bears, boars and deer. Khao Yai is also home to large mammals such as leopards, elephants and tigers, but they are rarely seen. In addition, over 300 species of migrant birds, including hornbills, have been identified.

More than 50km of marked trails criss-cross the park, most of them originally forged and are still used by elephants. In several clearings, there are observation towers where you can watch animals feed.

Other attractions in the park include the 20-m-high **Heaw Suwat** waterfall, east of the park headquarters, and the larger three-level **Heaw Narok** waterfall, rising to a height of 150m and located further south.

Near the entrance to the park are numerous lodges and bungalows, including the luxury **Kirimaya**, a boutique resort styled like an African safari with plush tented villas (1/3 Moo 6 Thanon Thanarat, Moo-Si; tel: 0 4442 6099; www.kirimaya.com).

Below: longtail boats on the Chao Phraya River.

Above: climbing up to the top of the Golden Mount.

Above: *baat*, or alms bowls, are crafted by artisans in Ban Baat.

houses. The cruise takes you past boats, laden with charcoal and fresh produce, on their way to the market, people living under bridges, old temples, beautiful heliconia and lilies, orchid nurseries and the people of Thonburi. In other words, you slice through a cross-section of Thai life.

Khlong Chak Phra changes its name to **Khlong Bang Kounsri** and then to **Khlong Bangkok Yai**. If sated, continue along Bangkok Yai, re-enter the Chao Phraya River and finish at one of the piers.

To extend your cruise, turn right from Bangkok Yai into **Khlong Ban Dan**. Next is **Wat Sai**, followed by the jungled area of **Suan Phak**. Turn left into **Khlong Bang Mod**, then **Khlong Dao Khanong**, re-entering the river below Krung Thep Bridge. Head upstream and end at one of the piers.

Golden Mount and Surroundings

Begin at Thanon Boriphat, Old City; map p.135 D1

Take an early-morning taxi ride to the **Golden Mount** (Phu Khao Thong) to take in a panoramic view of the city. For many years this was the highest point in the city. This was started by King Rama III as a huge *chedi*, but the city's soft earth made it impossible to build and the hilly site became overgrown with trees and shrubbery. King Mongkut then added a more modest *chedi* to the abandoned hill, and later King Chulalongkorn completed work on the 78-m-high plot.

Climb up to the summit via a stairway that curves around the side of the hill. Go through frangipani boughs, pausing to look at the inscriptions on crypts containing ashes of deceased donors, to reach **Wat Saket** (daily 8am–5pm; free), the temple at the hill's base. Built during the Ayutthayan period, Wat Saket was the city's charnel house during the cholera epidemics in the 19th century, with bodies laid out on its pavements for vultures to eat. Be sure to visit the main hall, which is adorned with fine murals usually ignored by tourists.

The 318 steps end at a room containing a Buddha image. Enjoy the view through the open windows or climb one more flight of steps to the upper terrace dominated by the gilded *chedi* that gives the hill its name. Back at the bottom, go through the gate and turn right into a narrow lane that leads to Thanon Boriphat, where you will turn left. At the next junction, cross Thanon Bamrung Muang and turn left into a small street named Soi Ban Baht.

MONK'S BOWL VILLAGE

Walk to the first junction and then turn right down an unpaved road, into what appears to be a junkyard. Then begin listening for the sound of tapping hammers. You are now in the village of **Ban Baat**, known as Monk's Bowl Village, the only remaining craft village of the many that once existed within the city. The small community here consists of traditional alms-bowl makers.

Retrace your steps to Thanon Boriphat, turn right and walk to the junction.

> The alm bowl or *baat* was traditionally handcrafted from eight pieces of metal, representing the eight spokes in the wheel of Dharma. The bowl makers at Monk's Bowl Village have been hammering out these metal receptacles since the late 18th century. Finished in enamel paint, the bowls sell for about B500.

Turn left and cross the canal. Turn right into Thanon Maha Chai and walk to the city wall. At the second entryway, turn right. Along the way you will have passed two temples on the left. The first, **Wat Thep Thidaram**, is of minor interest. The second is Wat Ratchanatda, which you will visit a little later. The first thing that will strike you are dozens of beautiful bird cages containing singing doves. Some are valued at more than B100,000, especially if they have won contests with huge prizes for cooing the prettiest song. Leave via the same doorway you entered.

WAT RATCHANATDA

Cross the street towards a pyramidal pink building that sits behind **Wat Ratchanatda**. This is **Loha Prasat**, called the Metal Temple after the metal spires that rise from it and modelled after an ancient Indian monastery. The building is usually closed.

Walk towards Wat Ratchanatda (daily 9am–5pm; free) and see the interior walls of its *viharn*, covered with lovely murals depicting heaven and hell. If the doors are closed, ask a monk if you can peep inside.

Above: an expansive view spreads beneath Phra Nakhon Khiri.

In front of the wat is a busy **amulet market**. Strictly speaking, the amulets on sale here have more to do with animism and magic than with Buddhism. Nonetheless, the images, mostly of the Buddha, are strung on gold necklaces and worn by many Thais. The amulets can supposedly fend off bullets, create fortunes or induce potency and fertility.

Phra Nakhon Khiri Historical Park

Phetchaburi, 125km south of Bangkok; Mon–Fri 8am–5.30pm, Sat–Sun 8am–6pm; entrance charge; train from Hualamphong or bus from Southern Bus Terminal; map p.20

Phetchaburi is one of Thailand's oldest towns and has been an important trade and cultural centre since the 11th century. Lying on the Phetchaburi River, the town came under the influence of the Mons, Khmers and Thais at various times, and has over 30 temples that reflect the different cultures and architectural styles of its past invaders.

It is famed for its historical park, Phra Nakhon Khiri (Hill of the Holy City), just west of the town. The 92-m-high hill, locally known as Khao Wang, is studded with temples and the remains of the early 19th-century palace that was built as a retreat by King Mongkut.

A cable tram ascends the northern flank of the hill, but you must hire a minibus to get to and from the station. A steep path lined with fragrant frangipani trees leads past the elephant stables to the main halls, which combine European and Chinese architectural styles; two of these have been turned into a museum housing furniture and collectibles that belonged to King Mongkut.

There is also a neoclassical observatory, built by King Mongkut who was was a keen astronomer, as well as a large white *chedi* and **Wat Maha Samanaram** (daily 8am–4pm; free).

Many of these buildings offer vantage for fabulous panoramas of the vicinity, especially at sunset.

Left: the pointed metal spires of the Loha Prasat.

133

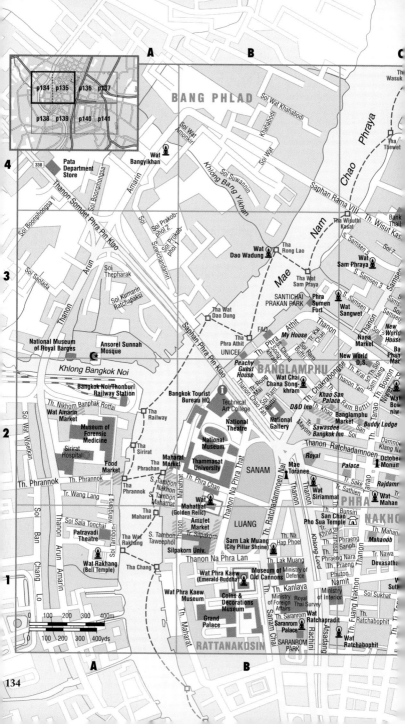

A **B** **C**

p134 p135 p136 p137
p138 p139 p140 p141

BANG PHLAD

Soi Wat Khahabodi

Chao Phraya

Tha Tiewet

Soi Wat Anonkul

4

Pata Department Store

Wat Bangyikhan

Amarin

Thanon Somdet Phra Pin Klao

Soi Boonphongsa 1

Soi Boonphongsa

Saphan Rama VIII

Tha Wisuthi Kasal

Th. Wisut Kas.

Bank Thail

Khlong Bang Yikhan

Soi Suwannin

Soi Wat

Khahabodi

Soi 7

Soi

Arun

Thanon

Soi Saolada

Soi Prokobphol 2

Soi Prokobphol

Soi Suwichandamri

Nam

Mae

Wat Dao Wadung

Tha Rong Lao

Wat Sam Phraya

S. Samsen 3

Soi

Sams

3

Soi Thepharak

Soi Kumarin Ratchapaksi

Tha Wat Sam Praya

S. Samsen T

New World House

SANTICHAI PRAKAN PARK

Phra Sumen Fort

Wat Sangwet

Thanon

Samsen

National Museum of Royal Barges

Ansorel Sunnah Mosque

Saphan Phra Pin Klao

Tha Wat Dao Dung

Tha Phra Athit

FAO

Th. Athit

Th. Phra Athit

Nana Market

New World D.S.

Ba Phan Mar

Khlong Bangkok Noi

UNICEF

Th. Song Khram

Th. Rong Mai

Th. Kai Chae

Th. Fem

Th. Buffin

BANGLAMPHU

Thanon Tani

Wat Bow niw

Bangkok Noi/Thonburi Railway Station

Th. Nikhom Banphak Rotfai

Tha Railway

Bangkok Tourist Bureau HQ

Peachy Guest House

Technical Art College

Wat Chai Chana Song-khram

Th. Chakrabongs

Khao San Road

Ram Buttri

Th. Krai Si

Sam Sen

Th. Bowon

Meyer

2

Wat Amarin Market

Museum of Forensic Medicine

Siriraj Hospital

Tha Sirirat

Tha Phrachan

Maharat Market

National Theatre

National Museum

National Gallery

D&D Inn

Banglamphu Market

Buddy Lodge

Th. Khao San

Soi

Th. Tanao

Th. Mayon

Sawasdee Bangkok Inn

Damno

Klang N

Food Market

Th. Phrannok

Th. Phrannok

Tr. Wang Lang

Tha Phrachan

S. Tambon Nakhon Tambon Mahathat

Th. Phra Chan

SANAM

Thammasat University

Wat Mahathat (Golden Relic)

Thanon Ratchadamnoen

Royal

Mae Toranee

Palace

October Monun

Rajdamr

Wat Siriammat

PHRA

Patravadi Theatre

Tha Maharat

Tha Wat Rakhang

S. Tambon Taweephol

Amulet Market

Silpakorn Univ.

Thanon Na Phra Lan

LUANG

Sarn Lak Muang (City Pillar Shrine)

Th. Na Hap Phoel

Wat Mahan

NAKHO

Wat Rakhang (Bell Temple)

Tha Chang

Soi Sala Tonchai

Soi Tambon

Tr. Silpakorn

S. Tambon

Thanon Na Phra Lan

Wat Phra Kaew (Emerald Buddha)

Coins & Decorations Museum

Museum of Old Cannons

Wat Lak Muang

San Chao Pho Sua Temple

Th. Khunlong

Bunsiri

Th. Phraeng Sanph.

Tr. Phraeng Nara

Th. Praeng

Th. Mahan.

Th. Nawa

Mahanob

Devasatha

1

Soi Ban Chang

Arun Amarin

Grand Palace

Th. Maharat

RATTANAKOSIN

Wat Phra Kaew Museum

Th. Kanlaya

Ministry of Foreign Affairs

Ministry of Defence

Th. Saranrom

Saranrom Palace

SARANROM PARK

Sanam Chai

Ratchini

Royal Thai Survey

Ministry of Interior

Phuton Namit

Wat Ratchapradit

Wat Ratchabophit

Soi Sukha

Fuang Nakhon

Th. Ratchabophit

Atsadang

0 100 200 300 400m
0 100 200 300 400yds

A **B**

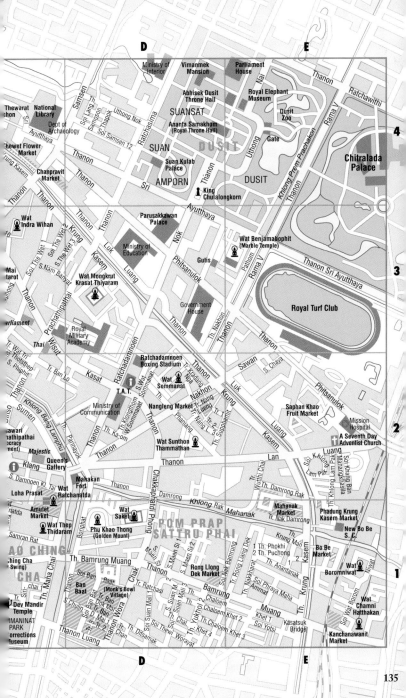

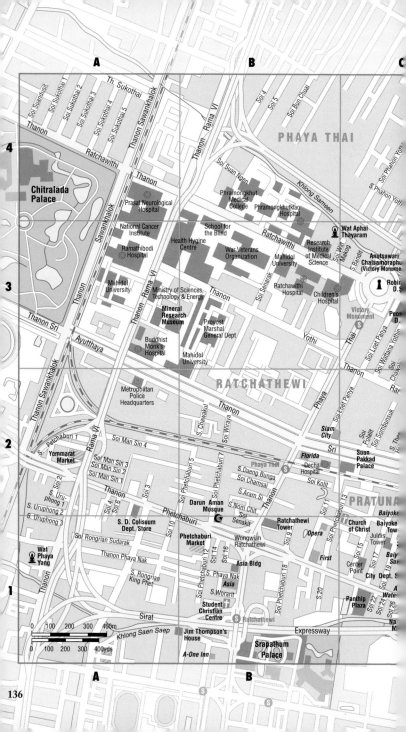

D   **E**

31

4

Yothin

inental

Ⓢ Sanam Pao

TV Channel 5

Thanon Sa Nam Phao

Phahon Yothin 2

Veterans
General
Hospital

Thanon Wiphawadirangsit

Soi Din Daeng

Thanon Mit Maitri 2

Thanon Mit Maitri 3

S. Phien Lae Phuen

Din Daeng
Sports Complex &
Auditorium

HUAY KHWANG

Soi Sanisuk

Soi Phra Nang

Soi Atthawimon

Soi Bun Chu Si

Soi Bun Chu

Soi Amnoanaumit

Soi Ruamit

Thanon Mit Maitri 1

S. Rongrian Chamnong

Uthawon
Market

hawithi

Thanon

Asoke Din Daeng

Thanon Prachasongkhro

Soi Rongrian Ratprasong

chum

t Pinisan

Thanon

Asoke

Din

Daeng

Ratchanukun
Hospital

Phayathai
Market

Soi Sutthiphon

Century
Park

Soi Wat
Taphan

Soi Saeng

Soi Uthai Thip

Soi Uthai Thip

Soi Phrasan Saraban

Thanon Din Daeng 1

Soi Sutthiphon 1

Soi Thabsuwan 1

atchaprarop

Soi Attanamoratha

Soi Bun Prarop

Si Din
Daeng
Market

Soi Tukkhipa

Soi Pracha Santi

Soi Sutthiphon 2

Soi Mahawong Nua

Soi Khwanphatana 1

thaya 1

Soi Ratchaprarop

Bangkok
Doll Factory
& Museum

Soi Moradok

Soi Thimakon

Fatima
Church

Soi Mae Phra Fatima

S. Hemawong

S. Thabsuwan

S. Chumchuen

S. Maha-
wong Tai

Khwan
Patthana
Market

utthaya 1

Makkasan
Market

S Ratchadaphan

S Ratchadanhan

Wongwian
Makkasan

Makkasan Railway
Plant

Khlong Samsen

Bung Makkasan

2

Soi
hipan

Dept

a

ent

unam
rket

Chalerm

Soi Watthanawong

Makkasan
Market

Mahanakhon

Makkasan
Railway Station

Thanon

Nikhom

Makkasan

Railway
Hospital

Soi Watthanasin

Bangkok
Palace

Metro
Department
Store

Soi Phetchaburi 35

31

Expressway

Chalermlap
Market

Soi Hasadin

Soi 25

Soi 27

S 29

Soi Chaurat

Soi 33

New

Phetchaburi

Soi 39

Soi 41

1

Thanon

Soi 30

Soi 32

Soi Chitlom

Phetchaburi
Hospital

Swissotel
Nai Lert Park

Thanon

Soi 37

Khlong Saen Saep

Soi Nana Nua

Soi 36

TAT

D   **E**

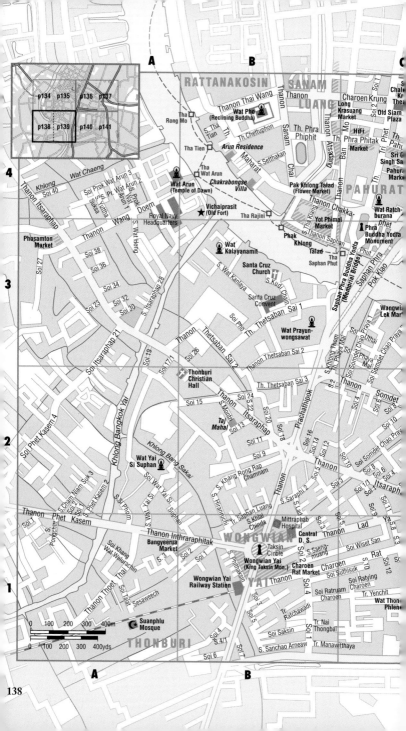

RATTANAKOSIN

SANAM LUANG

A

B

C

Thanon Thai Wang
Wat Pho (Reclining Buddha)
Tha Rong Mo
S. Tha Tien
Th Chettuphon
Th. Phra Phiphit
Th. Phra Phitak
Charoen Krung
Long Krasuang Market
Old Siam Plaza
HiFi Market
Sri G. Singh Sa
Pahura Marke

Tha Tien
Arun Residence
Mahar
Tha Wat Arun
Wat Arun (Temple of Dawn)
Chakrabongse Villa
S. Setthakan
Cha

Wat Chaeng
Khlong Soi 40
Thanon Itsaraphap
Vichaiprasit (Old Fort)
Tha Rajini
Pak Khlong Talad (Flower Market)

Thanon Chakka
PAHURAT
Wat Ratchaburana

Soi Prok Wat Arun 3
S. Prok. Pt. Wat Arun 2
Vuttha Suksa
S. Wat Arun 1
Wat Arun 2
S. Pt. Wat Arun
S. Prok

Phosamton Market
Thanon Wang Doem
Royal Navy Headquarters

Wat Kalayanamit
Yot Phimai Market
Thanon Saphan
Saphan Phra Buddha Yodfa
Phra Buddha Yodfa Monument

Soi 27
Soi 38
Soi 36
Soi 34
Soi 23
Soi 32
Soi 30
S. Itsaraphap 28

Santa Cruz Church
Santa Cruz Convent
S. Wat Kanlaya
S. Kudi Chan
Phak Khlong Talad
Tha Saphan Phut
Saphan Phut (Memorial Bridge)
Saphan Phra Pok Klao

Thanon Thetsaban Sai 1
Wat Prayun-wongsawat
Soi Pho
Wangwi Lek Mar

Thanon Itsaraphap
Soi Itsaraphap 21
Soi Itsaraphap 19
Thanon Thetsaban Sai 2
Thanon Soi 26
Soi 17/1
Khlong Thom
Th. Phya Mai
Soi Somdet Chao Utha
Soi Somdet Phaya
Somdet Chao Praya
Th Phya Mai

Khlong Bangkok Yai

Thonburi Christian Hall
Th. Thetsaban Sai 3
Prachathipok
Thanon
Somdet
Soi 10
Soi 8
Soi 11
Soi 1/1
Soi 12
Soi 14
Soi 16

Soi 15
Soi 24
Soi 22
Thanon Itsaraphap
Soi 20
Soi 18
Soi 13
S. Monti
Taj Mahal
Soi 11
Soi 9
Soi 7
Soi 5
Soi 3
Itsaraph
Soi 8
Soi 6
Soi Somdet Chao Pray

Khlong Bang Sakai
Wat Yai Si Suphan
S. Kharg Rong Rap Chamnam
S. Saraghi 2

Soi Phet Kasem 4
Khlong Bangkok Yai
S. Wat Yai Si. Suphan
S. Wat Yai S. Suphan 2
S. S. Phrom
S. Hiramchi
Tr. Saphan Luang
S. Khlai Chinda
S. Saraghi 2
Soi 3
Mittraphab Hospital
Central D. S.
Thanon Lad
Soi 9
Soi 15
Soi 5
S. Ya

Thanon Phet Kasem
Soi 1
S. Chan Niam Suk 3
S. Chan Niam Suk 2
Pongchit
Thanon Inthraraphitak
Bangyeerua Market
Soi 2
Soi 1
S. Phitanakin

WONGWIAN
Taksin Circle
Wongwian Yai (King Taksin Mon.)
S. Saeng-muang
Charoen Rat Market
Thanon Rat
Charoen
Soi Wiset San

Soi Khang Wat Weurachin
Wongwian Yai Railway Station
YAI
Thanon
Soi 4
Soi Suthisuk
Charoen
Soi Ratying Charoen
Wat Thon Phlen

Thanon Thoet Thai
Soi Talat
Sesaweech
Suanphlu Mosque
S. 4/1
Soi 6
Soi 4
Soi 7
Tr. Ratchawadi
Tr. Nai Thongbal
Soi Saksin
S. Sanchao Arneaw
Tr. Manawitthaya
Tr. Yenchit

THONBURI

0 100 200 300 400m
0 100 200 300 400yds

A

B

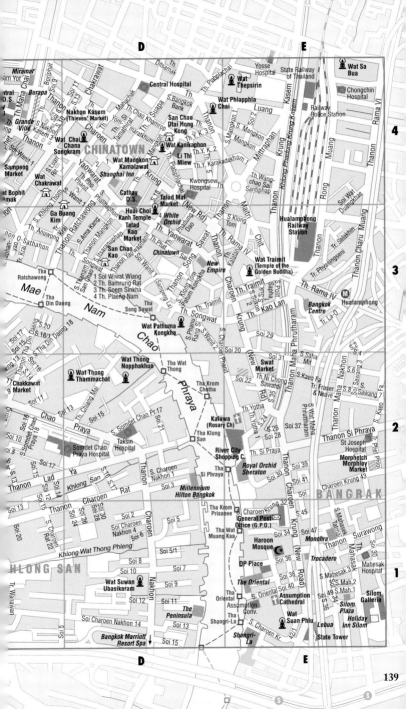

D **E**

Miramar
am Yot
Central
D.S.
Burapa Thanon
Grande S.Nakhon
Ville Kasem 3
Nakhon Kasem (Thieves' Market)
Ditsanak
Yosse Hospital
State Railway of Thailand
Wat Sa Bua
Central Hospital
Th. Platunachai
Wat Thepsirin
Chongchin Hospital
Th. Ditsanak
S.Bangkok Bank
Wat Phlapphla Chai
Railway Police Station

Sampeng Market
Wat Chakrawat
at Bophit muk
CHINATOWN
Wat Chai Chana Songkram
Charoen Thanon
San Chao Dtai Hong Kong
Wat Kanikaphon
Li Thi Miew
Kwongsew Hospital
Hualamphong Railway Station

Ga Buang Kim
Huai Choi Kanh Temple
Talad Kao Market
San Chao Kao
Talad Mai Market (New Rd)
White Orchid
Chinatown
New Empire
Wat Traimit (Temple of the Golden Buddha)
Bangkok Centre
Hualamphong

1 Soi Wiwat Wiang
2 Th. Bamrung Rat
3 Th. Soem Sinkha
4 Th. Plaeng Nam
Tha Ratchawong
Mae
Tha Din Daeng
Nam
Tha Song Sawat
Wat Pathuma Kongkha
Chao

Wat Thong Nopphakhun
Wat Thong Thammachat
Chakkawat Market
Phraya
Tha Wat Thong
Swat Market
Tha Krom Chetha

Chao
Praya
Somdet Chao Praya Hospital
Taksin Hospital
Kalawa (Rosary Ch)
Tha Klong San
River City Shopping C.
Royal Orchid Sheraton
St Joseph Hospital
Morphetch Morphloy Market
BANGRAK

Thanon Lad Ya
Khlong San Rat
Millennium Hilton Bangkok
Tha Krom Prisanee
Charoen Krung 32
General Post Office (G.P.O.)
Monohra
Trocadero

HLONG SAN
Wat Suwan Ubasikaram
Khlong Wat Thong Phleng
Tha Wat Muang Kaa
Haroon Mosque
OP Place
The Oriental
Assumption Cathedral
Wat Suan Phlu
Silom Plaza
Holiday Inn Silom
Mahesak Hospital

Bangkok Marriott Resort Spa
The Peninsula
Tha Oriental Assumption Conv.
Shangri-La
Lebua
State Tower
Silom Galleria

D **E**

139

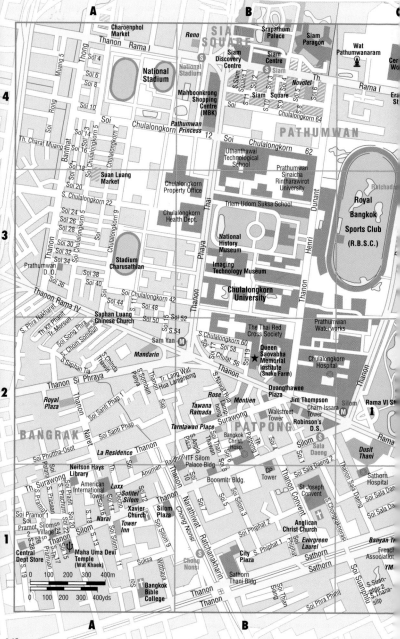

A map page showing a section of Bangkok including areas of Pathumwan, Bangrak, and Patpong.

Grid reference labels (top): A B C

Grid reference labels (left side): 4 3 2 1

Major labels on the map:

- Charoenphol Market
- Thanon Rama I
- Reno
- SIAM SQUARE
- Srapathum Palace
- Siam Paragon
- Wat Pathumwanaram
- National Stadium
- Siam Discovery Centre
- Siam Centre
- National Stadium (S)
- Siam (S)
- Novotel
- Mahboonkrong Shopping Centre (MBK)
- S. Siam Square
- Siam Square
- Th.
- Chulalongkorn 64
- Pathumwan Princess
- Soi 12
- Soi Chulalongkorn 62
- PATHUMWAN
- Th. Charat Muang
- Uthenthawai Technological School
- Prathumwan Sinaicta Rintharawirot University
- Suan Luang Market
- Chulalongkorn Property Office
- Triem Udom Suksa School
- Ratchadam
- Royal Bangkok Sports Club (R.B.S.C.)
- Chulalongkorn Health Dept.
- National History Museum
- Stadium Charusathian
- Imaging Technology Museum
- Prathumwan D.O.
- Prathumwan
- Thanon Rama IV
- Soi Chulalongkorn 42
- Chulalongkorn University
- Prathumwan Waterworks
- Saphan Luang Chinese Church
- Sam Yan (M)
- The Thai Red Cross Society
- Mandarin
- Queen Saovabha Memorial Institute (Snake Farm)
- Chulalongkorn Hospital
- Thanon Si Phraya
- Royal Plaza
- Rose
- Montien
- Duangthawee Plaza
- Jim Thompson
- Charn Issara Tower
- Silom (M)
- Rama VI St.
- Tawana Ramada
- SURAWONG
- PATPONG
- Wallstreet Tower
- Robinson's D.S.
- BANGRAK
- Tarntawan Place
- Bangkok Christ. Hosp.
- Sala Daeng (S)
- Dusit Thani
- La Residence
- ITF Silom Palace Bldg
- Silom
- Neilson Hays Library
- American International Tower
- Luxx
- Sofitel Silom
- Xavier Church
- Silom Plaza
- Boonmitr Bldg.
- CP Tower
- St Joseph Convent
- Sathorn Hospital
- Narai
- Tower Inn
- Anglican Christ Church
- Evergreen Laurel
- Banyan Tr
- Central Dept Store
- Silom Village
- Maha Uma Devi Temple (Wat Khaek)
- Suksa
- City Plaza
- Chong Nonsi
- Sathorn
- Banyan Tr
- French Association
- YM
- Bangkok Bible College
- Sathorn Thani Bldg
- Thanon
- Soi Suanplu
- Suan-plu 2 Thana-slip

Scale bars:
0 100 200 300 400m
0 100 200 300 400yds

Selective Index for Street Atlas

PLACES OF INTEREST

Index

Insight Smart Guide: Bangkok
Compiled by: Amy Van
Environment text by: Sarah Rooney
Edited by: Low Jat Leng
Proofread and indexed by: Jocelyn Lau
Layout by: Derrick Lim
Maps: Neal Jordan-Caws, James
Macdonald
Picture Manager: Steven Lawrence
Series Editor: Jason Mitchell
Photography by: Marcus Wilson Smith/Apa;
except 100 Tonson Gallery 80b; AFP/Getty
Images 44b, 47b, 57tl; Anantara Hua Hin
67b; Anthony Blake Photo Library/photoli-
brary 105t; Apa Archives 55bl, 68/69t;
ArkReligion.com/Alamy 70b; Atleenta 66r;
Bangkok Marriott Resort & Spa 58b; Banyan
Tree Bangkok 62t; Bed Supperclub 19b,
88b; Bettmann/Corbis 56br; Bjorn
Svensson/Alamy 40/41t; Calypso Cabaret
88/89t, 93; Conrad Bangkok 61b, 92l;
CPA Media/CPA 54br, 55tl, 56bl; Darby
Sawchuk/Alamy 41b; David Henley/CPA
46/47t, 54bl&tr, 74/75t, 130/131t;
Devarana Spa 98/99t; Dream BKK 65t, 90t;
epa/Corbis 57tr; Four Seasons Bangkok 61t,
102/103t, 104t, 105b; Francis Dorai/Apa
5tc, 9b, 11b, 16, 42, 83l&r, 131b; Gerald
Cubitt 15t; Getty Images 55br; Hard Rock
Hotel Pattaya 67t; Hazara 110t; InterContinental Bangkok 60; istockphoto 43t, 70/71t;
Jason Lang/Apa 4b, 5bn, 6, 8, 13t&b, 17t,
19t, 21t, 22b, 24, 26/27t, 27b, 30/31t, 30b,
33t, 44/45t, 54cr, 72/73t, 72b, 73b, 74b,
77, 79b, 82t, 86/87t, 87b, 97r, 100/101t,

101b, 102b, 107t, 112/113t, 113b, 114,
124/125t, 126, 127, 128, 132r, 133b; Jock
Montgomery 2/3t, 2b, 3b, 9t, 25t, 81b, 99b,
120b, 129, 130b; Joe Louis Theatre 35b;
John W. Ishii/Apa 26b, 29b, 49b; Jon Arnold
Images/Alamy 133t; Kevin R. Morris/Corbis
38b; Landmark Hotel 65b; Lebua 90b, 108,
109b; Ling Shuo/Xinhua Press/Corbis 57cr;
Luca Invernizzi Tettoni 5tr, 50, 56tl, 78t, 84,
86b, 95b, 97l, 120t, 123t; Luca Invernizzi
Tettoni/Corbis 54tl; Luke Duggleby/onasia
110b; Marcus Gortz 111b; The Metropolitan
62r, 91t; Michael Freeman 5tl, 5bc, 22/23t,
80/81t, 82b; Mike Dobel/Alamy 117b;
Narong Sangnak/epa/Corbis 52/53t; Neilson
Hays Library 85; Oliver Hargreave/CPA 25t;
The Oriental 37t, 48/49t, 51, 63b, 107b;
Patravadi Theatre 36; The Peninsula
Bangkok 59b, 109t; Pompe Ingolf/hemis.fr
88b; Rembrandt Hotel 92r; Reuters/Corbis
116b; Royal Household/Pool/Corbis 56tr;
Rungroj Yongrit/epa/Corbis 57br; The
Shangri-La 58/59t; Sheraton Grande
Sukhumvit 66l, 111t; Simon Bowen/Alamy
23b; Sofitel Silom 63t; Steven John Pettifor
46b; The Sukhothai 64; Sukree Sukplang/
Reuters/Corbis 57bl; Travis Rowan/Alamy
100b; Udo Weitz/epa/Corbis 52b; Vinai
Dithajohn/onasia 14; WoodyStock/Alamy
124b; Yvan Cohen/onasia 91b, 106

First Edition 2008

© 2008 Apa Publications GmbH & Co.
Verlag KG Singapore Branch, Singapore.
Printed in Singapore by Insight Print
Services (Pte) Ltd

Worldwide distribution enquiries:

Apa Publications GmbH & Co. Verlag KG
(Singapore Branch) 38 Joo Koon Road,
Singapore 628990; tel: (65) 6865 1600;
fax: (65) 6861 6438

Distributed in the UK and Ireland by:
GeoCenter International Ltd
Meridian House, Churchill Way West,
Basingstoke, Hampshire RG21 6YR; tel:
(44 1256) 817 987; fax: (44 1256) 817 988

Distributed in the United States by:
Langenscheidt Publishers, Inc.
36–36 33rd Street 4th Floor, Long Island
City, New York 11106; tel: (1 718) 784
0055; fax: (1 718) 784 0640l

Contacting the Editors
We would appreciate it if readers would
alert us to errors or outdated information
by writing to:
Apa Publications, PO Box 7910, London SE1
1WE, UK; fax: (44 20) 7403 0290;
e-mail: insight@apaguide.co.uk